Purchasing and Supply Chain Management:
Strategies and Realities

Michael Quayle
University of Glamorgan, UK

IDEA GROUP PUBLISHING
Hershey • London • Melbourne • Singapore

Acquisitions Editor:	Michelle Potter
Development Editor:	Kristin Roth
Senior Managing Editor:	Amanda Appicello
Managing Editor:	Jennifer Neidig
Copy Editor:	Becky Shore
Typesetter:	Sharon Berger
Cover Design:	Lisa Tosheff
Printed at:	Integrated Book Technology

Published in the United States of America by
    Idea Group Publishing (an imprint of Idea Group Inc.)
    701 E. Chocolate Avenue
    Hershey PA 17033
    Tel: 717-533-8845
    Fax: 717-533-8661
    E-mail: cust@idea-group.com
    Web site: http://www.idea-group.com

and in the United Kingdom by
    Idea Group Publishing (an imprint of Idea Group Inc.)
    3 Henrietta Street
    Covent Garden
    London WC2E 8LU
    Tel: 44 20 7240 0856
    Fax: 44 20 7379 0609
    Web site: http://www.eurospanonline.com

Copyright © 2006 by Idea Group Inc. All rights reserved. No part of this book may be reproduced, stored or distributed in any form or by any means, electronic or mechanical, including photocopying, without written permission from the publisher.

Product or company names used in this book are for identification purposes only. Inclusion of the names of the products or companies does not indicate a claim of ownership by IGI of the trademark or registered trademark.

    Library of Congress Cataloging-in-Publication Data

Purchasing and supply chain management : strategies and realities / Michael Quayle, editor.-- 1st ed.
   p. cm.
  Summary: "This book shows readers how to develop supply chain strategy and implementation and use it gain an advantage in the 21st century competitive marketplace"--Provided by publisher.
  Includes bibliographical references and index.
    ISBN 1-59140-899-7 (hardcover) -- ISBN 1-59140-900-4 (softcover) -- ISBN 1-59140-901-2 (ebook)
  1. Business logistics--Management. 2. Strategic planning. I. Quayle, Michael, 1947-
  HD38.5.P87 2006
  658.7--dc22
                        2005023882

British Cataloguing in Publication Data
A Cataloguing in Publication record for this book is available from the British Library.

All work contributed to this book is new, previously-unpublished material. The views expressed in this book are those of the authors, but not necessarily of the publisher.

Purchasing and Supply Chain Management:
Strategies and Realities

Table of Contents

Foreword viii

Preface ix

Chapter I.
**Developments in Purchasing and Supply Chain Management
and Logistics** 1
*Procurement, Purchasing, Outsourcing, Supply Management and
Supply Chain Management* 1
The Sustainable Supply Chain 9
Resource-Based View and Competitive Advantage 10
Business Issues in the 21st Century 13
Supply Chains into the Future 14
Supply Chain Education 16
Professional Competence: Food for Thought 19

Chapter II.
Strategic Purchasing Management 21
Corporate Planning 21
Purchasing Planning and Purchasing Strategies 27
Corporate and Environmental Factors 29
Strategic Planning 29
Market Strategic Flexibility 30
Objectives and Responsibilities 30

    SWOT and Gap Analysis 32
    Functions Involved in Corporate Planning 33
    Functional Contribution to Corporate Strategy 34
    Monitoring Performance 35
    Purchasing Needs and Corporate Strategies 36
    Purchasing Strategies 38
    Flexible Strategies 41
    International Trade: Implications for Purchasing
        Management 44
    Ethical Purchasing 47
    Procurement Agencies 48
    Food for Thought 49

Chapter III.
Purchasing Policy 50
    Policy Issues 50
    Selecting Overall Policy 53
    Structure of Purchasing Organisation 53
    Structure of the Purchasing Function in Simple Organisations 54
    Division of Work amongst Buying Groups 57
    The Position of Purchasing Management in the Organisation 59
    Structure of the Purchasing Function in Complex Organisation 60
    A Multilevel Structure for Purchasing Management 63
    Other Methods of Achieving Coordination 65
    The Selection of an Appropriate Structure for Particular
        Circumstances 66
    Multinational Supplies Structures 67
    Public Sector 68
    Benchmarking 69
    Materials Management 71
    Exemplar Case Study: Procurement Business Strategy 73

Chapter IV.
Quality Management and Customer Service 89
    Defining Quality 89
    Design and Conformance 92
    The Costs of Quality 93
    Efficient Consumer Response 99
    Total Quality Management 100
    Food for Thought 103

Chapter V.
Supply Chain Management 104
The Role of Supply Chain Management 104
The Supply Chain Mix 107
The Scope of the Supply Chain 109
The Value Chain and Interlock Strategy 113

Chapter VI.
Managing the Supply Chain Function 120
Staffing the Department 121
Operating Manuals 124
Qualities of Supply Chain Personnel 125
Recruiting Personnel 126
Managing the Department 130
Implications for Supply Chain Management 133
Management and Implementation of Change 133
Supply Chain and Change 135

Chapter VII.
Operating Environments 138
Integrated Logistic Support 138
ILS Management Structure 143
Level of Repair Analysis 148
Logistics Information Systems 150
Logistics and Other Organisational Functions 155

Chapter VIII.
Provisioning and Inventory Control 161
Provisioning 161
The Use of Computers 171
The Objectives of an Inventory Control System 174
Method of Inventory Control 180
Cost of Inventory Investment 185
Inventory Control and Accounting Methods 187
Pricing Issues 189
Price Analysis 195
Inventory in the Final Accounts 196
Identification and Coding of Materials 198
Development of the Coding System 205

The Stores Vocabulary 210
Inventory Reduction 217
Review of Other Concepts 221
Materials Requirements Planning 224
Manufacturing Resource Planning 226

Chapter IX.
Stores Management **228**
Stores Management Objectives 228
The Siting of Stores Buildings and Stockyards 230
Construction of the Buildings and Stockyards 231
Stockyards 233
Internal Layout 233
Detailed Planning of Layouts 234
Types of Stores 235
Special Storage Facilities 240
Planning Storage Equipment 242
Handling Equipment 245
Types of Handling Equipment 248
Security 255
Safety and Safe Methods of Working 256
Case Studies 260

Chapter X.
Transport **264**
Introduction 265
Fleet Management 266
Vehicle Scheduling 269
Maintenance and Security 273
Facilities for Maintenance 273
Quality Control 274
Security 275
Containers, Unitisation and Palletisation 276
Mechanical Aids to Loading and Off-Loading 280
Loading and Unloading Equipment Available on Vehicles 282
Road Vehicle Design and Road Planning 282
Road Haulage 287
Operating Costs of Own Fleet 291
Rail Freight 295

Air Freight 297
Food for Thought 300
Case Study 301

Chapter XI
Physical Distribution 303
Distribution 303
Distribution Planning 304
Logistics and Delivery Planning 307
Budgetary Control in Distribution 312
Food for Thought 315
Case Study 317
United Parcel Service 318
Modelling Systems 318
Radio Frequency Identification 319

Chapter XII.
E-Business 320
A Definition of Electronic Data Interchange 320
Why Use EDI? 323
Viewpoint 340

References and Bibliography 342

About the Author 355

Index 356

Foreword

For too long the emphasis on logistics in academia has focused on the economics of time and place and the physical movement of materials and finished goods. How refreshing to see a new book by Michael Quayle, which looks at logistics and the supply chain in the widest sense. This book looks at current thinking and development of the supply chain concept through purchasing and purchasing policies. Management issues surrounding quality, and value chain and controls within the supply chain follow. This is not a theoretical treatise but rather a look at various operating environments that will change emphasis within supply chain. It looks at the balance between service levels and profitability. This logically leads to issues such as inventory control and the alternative to holding stock and all the implications surrounding warehousing. Stores management is covered in considerable detail, giving current thinking on all aspects of storage of goods.

Next, Michael considers transport, including the issues surrounding exports and imports. This is, in itself, a valuable reference to current practice. He next covers physical distribution and concepts of channel formation, and this is a comprehensive treatment of current thinking. Finally, he addresses e-business and the capture of information as a resource to be managed. I found this to be a stunning book that will reach a wide audience, because - every supply chain, logistics, production, purchasing, and service manager must have it as an office reference book.

Sir Roger S. Jones, OBE

Preface

This first edition of *Purchasing and Supply Chain Management: Strategies and Realities* has been produced in response to market demand. I have developed and reinforced the concept of purchasing and supply chain management as a dynamic and managerial process, and have added material that reflects the current more general view of purchasing and supply chain management as a strategic function. The terrorist attacks of September 11, 2001, in the United States of America, subsequent impacts, and other worldwide tragic events resulting from the war on terror have created a need to revisit how we achieve effective purchasing and supply chain management. Post 9/11 has had no effect? On September 11, 2001, terrorists left their mark of murder and took the lives of many citizens. With the passing of months and years, it is the natural human desire to resume a quiet life and to put that day behind us, as if waking from a dark dream. The hope that danger has passed is comforting, is understanding, and is false. The attacks that followed on Bali, Jakarta, Casablanca, Bombay, Mombassa, Najaf, Jerusalem, Riyadh, Baghdad, and Istanbul, for example (and indeed London in July 2005), were not dreams. They are part of the global campaign by terrorist networks to intimidate and demoralize all who oppose them (Bush, 2003).

Ask those trans-Atlantic and trans-America passengers and airlines who have had flights cancelled because of terrorist concerns. Ask customers, purchasers, and suppliers worldwide who have seen shipping costs and timescales increase as enhanced security measures are embodied. The threat matrix is a clear and present danger. Similarly, on a humanitarian scale, integration of purchasing and supply chain management and a sharing of resources can be a crucial element in international disaster relief. Indeed, integrative practices are an important area in the effectiveness of purchasing and supply chain management. In general, however, the 21st century events such as the Iranian earthquake and the Asian tsunami disaster suggest the world still has much to learn in terms of integrating resources in order to achieve supply chain effectiveness. Consequently, I have attempted to reflect the emergence of purchasing and supply chain management and e-business as a 21st century activity recognised as "key" to corporate social responsibility and sustainability in both the public and private sectors. The text will be useful to a broad range of students and practitioners, and the practical style will be popular. Thanks are due to colleagues and friends who have contributed their ideas and advice and to the business concerns and copyright holders of included material. Specific acknowledgments and references are, of course, given in the book where appropriate. I am particularly grateful to my colleagues Bryan Jones and Neil Fuller for their support and agreement to use their material. The book is organised into 12 chapters:

- Chapter I: *Developments in Purchasing and Supply Chain Management and Logistics*, discusses procurement, purchasing, outsourcing, supply management and supply chain management; buying links in the supply chain; resource-based view; business issues affecting organisations; supply chains into the future; supply chain education; professional competence; and business issues in the 21st century.

- Chapter II: *Strategic Purchasing Management*, discusses corporate planning, purchasing planning and strategies, corporate and environmental factors, SWOT (Strengths, Weaknesses, Opportunities, Threats) gap analysis, flexibility, buying decisions, buying practice, ethical purchasing, procurement agencies, purchasing needs and corporate strategies, single vs. multiple sourcing, and factors affecting purchasing strategy.

- Chapter III: *Purchasing Policy*, discusses structure; definition and purpose, centralisation and decentralisation in complex organisations, purchasing consortia, policy issues, the public sector, benchmarking, and exemplar purchasing strategy.

- Chapter IV: *Quality Management and Customer Service*, discusses definitions, costs of failure, ISO9000, ISO14000, total quality management, the TQM diamond, quality & service as competitive variables, partnering, efficient consumer response.

- Chapter V: *Supply Chain Management*, discusses definitions and concepts, the value chain, the bullwhip effect, logistics management and corporate profit, global sourcing, public sector and military variations, logistics in small organisations, interlock strategy, and bottlenecks.

- Chapter VI: *Managing the Supply Chain Function*, discusses directing the function, staff, resources, job description, motivation, professional and supervisory management, management and implementation of change, impact of change on people and jobs, effect on performance, scope for more creative work and decision making, and the supply chain and change.

- Chapter VII: *Operating Environments*, discusses logistic action planning; manufacturing, public services, and utilities; the armed forces; construction, retailing, and distribution; integrated logistics support; logistics information systems; case study; coordination of physical control; and contribution to overall profitability and service capability.

- Chapter VIII: *Provisioning and Inventory Control*, discusses stores links in the chain, the need to hold stock, provisioning, pareto analysis, use of computers, coding and inventory systems, related effects on standardisation and variety reduction, accounting methods, stores vocabulary, price analysis, economic order quantity, inventory reduction and control, liaison with sales and production, application of JIT (Just in Time) concepts, and MRP (Multiple Resource Planning) and MRPII, and point of sale (POS).

- Chapter IX: *Stores Management*, discusses warehouse, storehouses, stockyards, depots; location and distribution networks. Premises: determination of handling requirements in relation to products (e.g., perishables, fluids, gases); design and layout; movement patterns and volume throughput; cost factors; and environmental factors. Operational requirements: automation, security, hazardous stocks, preservation, packaging, housekeeping, accounting; personnel: development of teams; health and safety; and training. Equipment: degrees of automation, applications of robotics; static and mobile equipment; surplus, scrap and obsolescent stocks; and treatment and disposal.

- Chapter X: *Transport*, discusses modes; alternative methods of transportation; performance variables; road, rail, air and sea transport: optimisation; roll on/roll off arrangements; and import/export documentation and procedures. Management considerations: procurement of transport services; purchase, lease and hire options; licensing; traffic regulation; transport laws; scheduling and planning and utilisation, containerisation; and control and monitoring of costs.

- Chapter XI: *Physical Distribution*, discusses despatch and delivery; resource planning, distribution channels; management; distribution audits; budgetary control; coordination; and military logistics.

- Chapter XII: *E-Business*, discusses electronic data interchange, information as a resource to be managed, evaluation of e-commerce systems, what the literature says, e-business strategies, opportunities for coherent procurement, tantric purchasing, hype versus reality, and case study.

As you can see, this book is about decision making and actions that determine whether an organisation excels, survives, or dies. This process is called "purchasing and supply chain management." The job of purchasing and supply chain managers is to make the best use of an organisation's resources in a changing environment. This book focuses on top-level decisions, but you should not have a problem with the relevance of the subject matter for your short-term career interests. Several reasons can be given for why the knowledge you can gain in the study of purchasing and supply chain management is practical and useful for your career: You are likely to perform better in your function, regardless of your level in the organisation, if you know the direction in which the organisation is going. As the manager of a subunit, you would like to know how what you do fits into the broader picture. If you know how your function contributes, you should be able to do a better job of helping the organisation reach its objectives. If your unit is successful, and higher level managers realise how you contributed to this success, it will reflect positively on you. Furthermore, lower level units often interpret strategies and policies set at higher levels. If you understand why those were established, you can implement them more effectively. Finally, if you understand how your job relates to others in the organisation, you will be in a better position to effectively work with peers when cooperation is called for and compete for resources when the time comes.

In your study of purchasing and supply chain management process you will begin to identify factors that may lead to significant changes in the organisation. Some of these strategic changes could be positive or negative to you personally. For instance, a major divestiture could eliminate your unit, or a new market thrust or product development could make your unit more critical for organisational performance. If you understand what factors may be pushing the organisation in certain directions and how your job fits in, you might decide to change or keep your job. Foresight about critical organisation changes can be a real asset to your career. If you are aware of the strategies, values, and objectives of higher level managers, you are in a better position to assess the likelihood of acceptance of proposals you might make. As you consider offering your suggestions, tying the reasons to your assessment of the interest of higher level managers is likely to enhance their acceptance and your visibility.

Thus, I believe that an understanding of how and why supply chain decisions are made can be helpful to you in terms of securing resources beneficial to your subunit, improving your job performance, and enhancing your career development. This book's purpose is to help you make sense of the supply chain management process while you are a first-line manager or a middle manager. It is also designed to help prepare you to become a successful top manager. Its goal is to show you that if you understand the business policy and purchasing and supply chain management process before you get to the top, you will be a more effective manager. The book is also designed to fulfill a teaching function at postgraduate, professional and undergraduate level in schools of business management and administration. The material is designed to help you integrate the functional tools you have learned. These include the analytical tools of purchasing and supply chain, such as physical distribution, logistics and purchasing management. All these provide help in analysing business problems. Remember that purchasing and supply chain management is about people, not just about processes. This book and the materials in it provide you with an opportunity to learn when to use which tools and how to deal with trade-offs when you cannot maximise the results or preferences of all the functional areas simultaneously. More important — enjoy it!

Chapter I

Developments in Purchasing and Supply Chain Management and Logistics

The purpose of this chapter is to provide an overview of the differences between procurement, purchasing, outsourcing, supply, and, sustainable supply chain management. An overview of the global marketplace and the emerging business issues of the 21st century will also be provided, along with some guidance on effective education programmes. Supply chain management a crucial element of competitive advantage (see, e.g., Figure 1).

Understanding what supply chain management is and what it means is vital.

Procurement, Purchasing, Outsourcing, Supply Management and Supply Chain Management

Supply chain management is not merely a fashionable set of words for supply, purchasing, and procurement! Understanding the differences is crucial to the development of a world-class culture.

Figure 1. Competitive advantage (UK competitiveness moving forward to the Next Stage DTI Economics paper no. 3; Porter & Ketels, 2003)

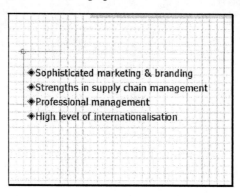

Procurement

Compton and Jessop (1995, p.26) defined procurement as "the obtaining by various means (e.g., loan, transfer, hire purchase) of supplies and services with or without consideration." Van Weele and Rozemeijer (1996, p.22) defined procurement as including "all activities required in order to obtain the product from the supplier and get it to the place where it is actually used. It encompasses the purchasing function, store, traffic and transportation, incoming inspection, and quality control and assurance. Some firms also include salvage and management of environmental issues (as they are related to materials) in procurement." Another definition might be that procurement is purchasing, contracting, and logistics, wherein logistics is taken to be inventory control, warehousing, transport, quality assurance, and control. The distinction between purchasing and contracting is that contracting is usually the purchasing activity associated with major works.

Often the term *procurement* is used, especially where government purchasing is involved. The specific activities of purchasing are, as described by Dobler (1990, p.100), "participation in the development of requirements and their specifications; managing value analysis activities; conducting supply market research; managing supplier negotiations; conducting traditional buying activities; administering purchase contracts; managing supplier quality; buying inbound transportation."

Purchasing

Dooley (1995) argued that purchasing and supply management has emerged as an important strategic area of management decision making. Porter (1987) referred to the "value chain" as fundamental to the performance of an organisation. In this value chain, inbound and outbound logistics and management of the manufacturing operations are prominent. Deming (1988) dealt with "supply chain" concepts as crucial to the successful introduction of TQM (Total Quality Management). Other references to this growing significance of the functions of purchasing and supply include Crosby (1979), Schonberger (1986), Womack et al. (1991), and Lamming (1993). Purchasing has two main purposes: to purchase for resale and to purchase for consumption or for conversion (Dobler, 1990). Merchants and speculators purchase for resale, and their task is knowing the final market for commodities so that, almost regardless of the cost of purchase, the on-sale can be made at a profit. Purchasing for consumption or for conversion requires a far more difficult decision. First, it is often a long-term decision (e.g., the decision to use gas as a source of energy). Second, although there are many different purchasing decisions, they are not repeated so often that a mistake can have long-term damaging effects, such as the decision to use a particular make of alternator in the assembly of a motor-vehicle engine (Dooley, 1995).

The clear definition of *purchasing* is given by Elliott-Shircore and Steele (1985), who stated that *purchasing* is the process by which a company (or other organisation) contracts with third parties to obtain goods and services required to fulfil its business objectives in the most timely and cost-effective manner. The terms *purchasing* and *procurement* are often used interchangeably; however, there might be a distinction in that purchasing is more concerned with establishing and managing a commercial relationship, whereas procurement is also concerned with the more physical material or service delivery control aspects after the contract has been let or the order placed. Van Weele and Rozemeijer (1996) suggested a possible model for future purchasing organisations to make simultaneous improvements in increasing both functional expertise and horizontal synergy and in improving focus and flexibility at the business unit level could be the hard-core/soft-core organisation. In this organisation, a small, centralised hard core of corporate purchasing professionals is surrounded by a rather fluid soft core of business specialists. The hard core is responsible for the purchasing process; the strategy; the professional development; and the recruitment, training, and development of the people involved in the purchasing process. Van Weele and Rozemeijer also use the term *the virtual purchasing organisation* to describe their vision of what is now required. I see absolutely no reason why, for example, a group of small- and medium-sized enterprises could not develop a "core" purchasing activity. Indeed, much has been written about what is now required of suppliers. Myer (1989) was an early proponent of supplier change and argued that if suppliers hope to regain a measure of control over their destiny, they must assert themselves and take responsibility for managing their customers. In doing this, suppliers face challenges in two realms: reallocating resources in the company and redesigning programs to better serve outside customers. This should be small- and medium-sized enterprise philosophy. Purchasers, suppliers, and customers are inevitably involved in sourcing strategies and decisions — the genesis of obtaining goods and/or services in both the public and private sectors. Clearly, these groups need to work together to secure competitive advantage and/or world class status.

Outsourcing

Hendry (1995) suggested that one of the strongest and most sustained trends within business over the last 10 years has been the trend towards outsourcing. With increased fervour and conviction, corporations have sought to reduce costs by contracting out services and activities traditionally provided in house. The rationale of this movement is simple and compelling. If contracting out something is cheaper than doing it yourself, then outsource. That way you not only save money through greater efficiency but also gain effectiveness by focusing more clearly on those things you can do better in house. The benefits are obvious. Hendry argued that — supported by political ideology, management fashion, and short-term responses to recessionary pressures — the benefits of outsourcing have become so obvious that they have hidden the very real associated costs. It is the purchasing and supply function that "generically" carries out the role of outsourcer.

Supply Management

The term *supply management* is often referred to as "material management." Materials management is described by Dobler (1990, p.105) as "procurement activities; inventory management; receiving activities; stores and warehousing; in-plant materials handling; production planning scheduling and control; traffic and transportation; surplus and salvage." Cavinato (2001, p.40) recognised this and suggested that supply management is "the identification, acquisition, access, positioning, and management of resources the organisation needs or potentially needs in the attainment of its strategic objectives." Although these descriptions are useful, it is important to realise that the practice of purchasing and supply management is changing rapidly (Kauffman, 2002).

Supply Chain Management

Supply chain management appears in current dialogue as relatively new terminology, but definitions of what it encompasses are, at best, vague. New (1997) suggested that the development of an idea of the supply chain owes much to the emergence from the 1950s onwards of systems theory and the associated notion of holism (Cavinato, 1992). This may be summarised by the observation that the behaviour of a complex system cannot be understood completely by the segregated analysis of its constituent parts (Boulding, 1956). However, New (1994) suggested the use of this idea in regard to supply chains is neither consistent nor straightforward. New also argued that the supply chain metaphor is used in many ways, but three meanings dominate discussion: "supply chain" from the perspective of an individual firm; "supply chain" related to a particular product or item (such as the supply chain for beef, or cocaine, or oil); and "supply chain" used as a handy synonym for purchasing, distribution, and materials management (New, 1997). Supply chain management can mean any one of these things, but one aspect is certain: Purchasing and/or outsourcing activity is being undertaken (CIPS, 1997). Macbeth, Ferguson, Neil, and Baxter (1989) and Ellram (1990) suggested that supply chain management is an integrative philosophy used to manage the total flow through a distribution channel from the supplier to the ultimate user. Another definition is the management of a chain or of operations and centres through which supplies move from the source of supply to the final customer or point of use (Compton & Jessop, 1995). In essence, the supply chain starts with the extraction of raw material (or origination of raw concepts for services), and each link in the chain processes the material or the concept in some way or supports this processing. The supply chain thus extends from the raw material extraction or raw concept origination through many processes to the ultimate sale of the final product, whether goods or services, to the consumer.

Some environmental thinkers have suggested that the supply chain should also cover the disposal of the waste associated with the consumed product. The recognition of the supply chain as a key and vital area both in the public and private sectors has focused attention on its effectiveness. In a number of organisations, a cost-effective supply chain is a matter of survival, as purchased goods and services account for up to 80% of sales revenue, whilst in the public sector there is an ever-increasing demand for savings in the procurement process. The globalisation of some sources makes it essential that the professional practice is improved and regarded as a key element in the preparation of company or organisation strategies. The linchpin in connecting functional strategies to business strategies — whose intention is to provide competitive advantage and competitive scope — is that of the product strategies. Figure 2

Figure 2. Interrelated strategies framework

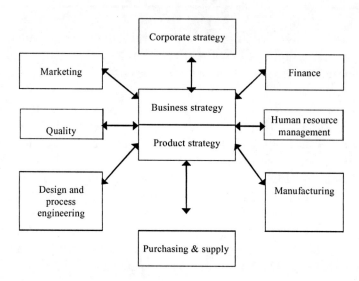

Figure 3. Supply chain strategy framework

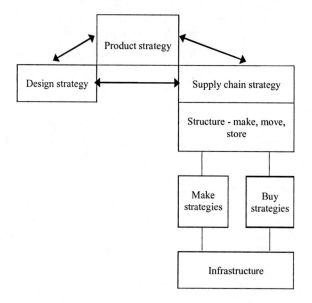

illustrates, as an exemplar, these connections in relation to the basic functions of a manufacturing firm (Saunders, 1994).

It is possible to break out of the conventional functional differentiation between purchasing (used generically!) and manufacturing and to consider a more integrated perspective, which links both together in a framework for supply chain strategy. This is illustrated in Figure 3 (Saunders, 1994). The phrase *supply chain* is inadequate to capture the full complexities of the interconnections between different organisations. The idea of a network with various nodes might be a more appropriate analogy and description. It is perhaps an evolutionary rather than a revolutionary process (Larson & Halldorsann, 2002). Perhaps the most popular convention, however, is the term *supply chain* (Lummus & Vokurka, 1999).

Product strategies establish the basic task for the supply chain, which, therefore, encompasses both internal and external activities. Product strategies include the determination of priorities, with regard to product objectives, needed to meet customer requirements and to beat the offerings of competitors. Differentiated strategies, with regard to quality, cost, time, and product innovation, impose different requirements on the supply chain. They should play an important part in the design and development of both the structural and infrastructure features of the supply chain (Ketchen & Guinipero, 2004). The primary function of the supply chain might be to provide goods and/or services required by customers and to provide appropriate form, time, place, and quantity utilities in the package offered. However, the chain also acts as a medium for the exchange of information and the communication of orders or instructions. As well as providing for the flow of products, the supply chain provides a channel for the flow of money from customers, which is the normal reward for the supplier. There is a fourth object of exchange, and this incorporates social values that are involved in the interpersonal relationship between suppliers and customers (Saunders, 1994). There are clear buying links in the supply chain, and this is shown in Figure 4.

Figure 4. Buying links in the supply chain

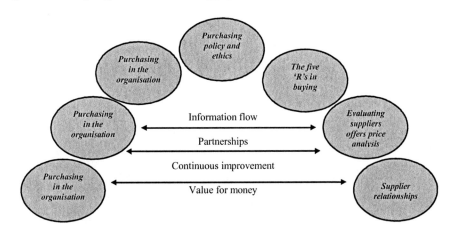

The structure of the supply chain is undergoing rapid transformation. Consumer pressures for lower prices and higher quality of services are forcing retailers, manufacturers, and distributors to achieve greater cost efficiencies and improve lead times, making supply chain efficiency a key factor in gaining competitive advantage. As a result, both retailers and manufacturers are increasingly looking across the supply chain, beyond their traditional logistics boundaries, to form partnerships with the aim of creating a seamless flow of goods and information from the raw materials supplier to the end consumer (Bibby, 2003).

The message here, I feel, is that there is a supply chain of events to be managed—the art, perhaps, is recognising that there is one and recognising where it can be influenced, in one form or another. The incentive for purchasers is that they need to develop a consistent approach to supplier performance and development; they should obtain an improvement in supplier performance, and, hence, their own. Indeed, purchasers may learn something about their own performance in terms of relationships with both suppliers and customers. Arguably, companies and organisations learn best from each other; therefore, supply chains and other networks are crucial; this is illustrated in Figure 5.

Supply chain management is the management of all activities in order to satisfy the ultimate consumer. It covers almost all business activity, including marketing, manufacturing, purchasing, logistics, and, more generally, such activities as finance and personnel. Supply chain management is arguably the holistic approach, and the holistic approach is what we need to take to create a world-class culture. The supply chain needs to be sustainable, but what is the sustainable supply chain?

Figure 5. Supply chain solution

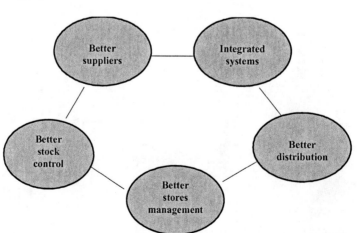

The Sustainable Supply Chain

What is sustainable development and a sustainable supply chain, and, indeed, why bother? It is no secret that development has often been at the expense of the environment, both at home and abroad. We are feeling the effects internationally, as global warming affects our weather patterns, and locally, as once-common species of plants and animals become rare. Development has had social costs, too. Once-lively towns and villages are in decline, and whole communities find themselves excluded from the benefits of economic growth. Sustainable development is about striking a better, more creative balance between economic development, environmental protection, and social change; about finding ways of meeting our needs without jeopardising the ability of our children to meet theirs. Development that is more balanced should be more enduring and offer a better chance of long-term prosperity. Broadly sustainable supply chains should follow the cycle shown in Figure 6.

Figure 6. The sustainable procurement and supply chain cycle

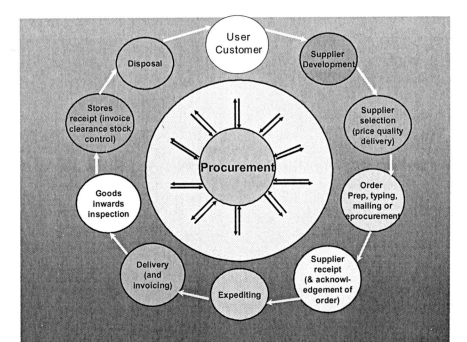

Resource-Based View and Competitive Advantage

For internal resources and capabilities (RCs) to be a source of sustainable competitive advantage, Barney (1991) and Sunil (2002) identified four key characteristics: The RCs must be valuable, rare, inimitable, and not substitutable. They are considered valuable if they enable the organisation to carry out its value chain activity with greater effectiveness. However, for the resources and capabilities to be a source of competitive advantage, they should be valuable and rare, and, inimitable. In addition, they should not be easily substitutable with another set of different resources and capabilities. In summary, the resource-based view focuses on internal RCs as the key source of sustainable competitive advantage and superior performance in the market place. Customers — the key players in a business — are conspicuous by their absence from the framework (Sunil, 2002). It is assumed that internal RCs can be created by taking into consideration the needs of the external market, or that RCs can be converted easily into products and services that are valued by the market.

There are however, multiple perspectives — global and local issues of an organisation's sustainability, together with societal and ecological systems in which they operate. It is also linked to corporate social responsibility. Some research in Wales, United Kingdom, shows that 92% of organisations claim to act ethically, 71% said that green policy is important, 79% thought that caring for the Welsh environment is important, and 80% disagreed that the bottom line is more important than acting ethically (Quayle, 2002a). This is all very impressive; *however,* some inconsistencies arise. Forty-one percent do not devote resources to social responsibilities or community-based initiatives. Only 37% audit their impact on stakeholders. Only 53% would buy renewable energy, but 75% thought the Welsh Assembly Government should provide (financial) assistance to develop environmental sustainability.

The research suggests a need to examine fundamental concepts of an inclusive stakeholder society in Wales. Perhaps the need for a Welsh supply chain, which is truly sustainable, would also change and enthuse stakeholder attitudes, and, indeed, offer that better chance of long-term prosperity I referred to previously. But what *is* this supply chain, and why does it matter? Remember, it covers almost all business activity, including marketing, manufacturing (or service provision), purchasing, logistics, and is arguably the holistic approach — it is this holistic approach that needs to be taken to create a world-class culture and, indeed, sustain economic development. The message is that there is a supply chain of events to be managed; the art is recognising that and ensuring that the supply chain is effectively managed.

Figure 7. Enterprise management (Note: Adapted from Sayers, 2002, Capturing Value presentation; UNCTAD/ITC Geneva)

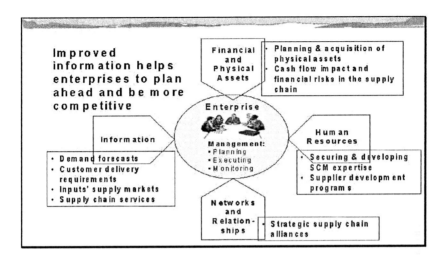

The holistic approach has a financial benefit. Typical improvements are 30% cost savings, lead-time reductions of circa 10%, price reductions of between 5% and 30%, on time delivery improvements from 75% to 98%. A government strategy to target existing supply chains and make provisions for new supply chains is essential for economic development. Supply chain is a growth area in terms of business operations, academic study, research output, consultancy and political awareness. Within the United Kingdom and Europe, there is a particular need to support and contribute to the economic success of the public and private sectors and to the SMEs (small and medium size enterprises) through applied supply chain management, applied research and the development of flexible education, training and development opportunities.

There is also a need to understand the forces of globalisation that are impacting employers internationally, nationally, and regionally. The supply chain starts with the extraction or raw material (or origination of raw concepts for services) and each link in the chain processes the material or the concept in some way or supports this processing. Arguably, it should also cover the disposal of waste associated with the consumed product. The recognition of the supply chain as a key and vital area both in the public and private sectors would focus attention on its effectiveness.

In a number of organisations, a cost effective sustainable supply chain is a matter of survival as purchased goods and services account for up to 80% of (sales) revenue, whereas in the public sector there are ever-increasing demands for savings in the procurement process. The globalisation of some sources of supply and a need to ensure local economic development make it essential that professional practice is improved and regarded as a key element in the preparation of company or organisational strategies. In short, procurement and supply chain principles need to be robust, supplier management is key, good management information and information technology systems are essential, and the need for world-class supply chain professionals is axiomatic. Strategy is usually formulated to gain competitive advantage at some point in the value chain. Supply chain development is a resource management function, and the management of resources is intrinsically strategic. The need for strategic and sustainable supply chains is naturally endorsed by those within the function, but it is seldom espoused with any real sincerity by others; thus, an opportunity for competitive advantage is being missed. Governments must therefore facilitate the provision to practitioners of quantitative data as well as conceptual food for thought. This data must be in the form of practical tools and techniques, contained within a framework of concepts and principles.

As a subject, within the discipline, interorganisational relationships overlap sustainable supply chain strategy but have interesting linkages with technology issues — technology management, innovation, information systems, and e-business. The overall aim of a sustainable supply chain is for all stakeholders to work together with large purchasers (public and private) and with SMEs to contribute to local economic development by encouraging regional procurement and providing everyone in the supply chain with an opportunity for competitive advantage. Generally, this agenda would also support the government's pursuit of enterprise management, as is illustrated in Figure 7. The enterprise operates in a national and international environment. It is from this environment the enterprise obtains its resource needs to manage its "business." These resources are information, human resources, financial and physical assets, and networks and relationships. The sustainable supply chain is crucial to the success of the enterprise. There are some blinding flashes of the obvious (BFO).

The non-EC (European Community) procurement legislation of public sector procurement spent could be used to facilitate the creation and development of sustainable supply chains. Purchasers will need help to source regionally, SMEs will need help to break into supply chains, and purchasers and SMEs will need to bury their prejudices. The various business and support agencies must work together and be coherent in their approach. Overall, strategy makers should focus on delivery performance and the supply chain structure in equal measures to market access and export promotion. Indeed, sustainable supply chains are about people, expertise, and performance — not just process — and finally, there is a need to recognise the reality of relationships within the sustainable supply chain. It is a risk and a revenue-sharing relationship that has to take into account the business issues of the 21st century.

Business Issues in the 21st Century

Rugman (2001) suggested that we operate in a mythical global marketplace. He argued that globalisation per se is misunderstood — it does not, and has never, existed in terms of a single world market. Rugman suggested that in reality there are simply three blocks: North America, the European Union, and Japan. Consequently, multinational companies operate within a block and access others. Thus, they have regional and not global strategies. Overall, this suggests that businesses need to think locally and act regionally. Indeed, businesses should forget about the global marketplace. Nevertheless, business issues emerge (see also, e.g., Kotabe & Murphy, 2004; Tan, Lymans, & Wisner, 2002). Business issues can be categorised into the drive for competitiveness, critical factors that emerge from that drive, and power relationships. Arguably, all those issues affect one of the biggest strategic opportunities in business history, namely, e-commerce. The drive for competitiveness is influenced, for example, by instability of the U.S. economy, perpetual local wars in Eastern Europe and the Middle East, the pace of technological change, fluctuating oil and fuel prices, and globalisation per se. Allied to this instability is the desire for product/service improvements, cost reduction, and the efforts by major purchasers to push risk as far down the supply chain as they can. Critical factors emerge from the drive for competitiveness. These include the need for a strategic approach to business, utilising new technologies, meeting the logistics demands of the 21st century, and ensuring the workforce updates its skills in a timely manner. Anecdotal evidence suggests that partnerships and trust now take a back seat to the old style adversarial relationships, and all this occurs as organisations (often encouraged by national governments) implement or consider implementing sophisticated supply chain management, which potentially provides opportunities for coherent procurement, improves buyer–supplier relationships, and eliminates time-zone obstacles (Fawcett & Magnan, 2002).

The issues of highest importance in many organisations tend to be leadership, strategy, marketing and waste reduction are perhaps a narrow vision of business survival. It may, of course, reflect the consultant's approach. The issues of medium importance, such as supply chain management and supplier development, are not unexpected, although financial management and time to market may be of higher importance. The issues of lowest importance to the businesses, particularly small- and medium-sized enterprises, are surprising. New technology, e-commerce, benchmarking, and purchasing tend to be low priority, but surely they are issues seen as ways to improve competitive advantage. Are customers not pursuing these issues? More important, the issues of lowest importance to businesses have to do with innovation. Why should this be? The answer may lie in the perception of customers' requirements. The small organisation's perception of their customers' requirements is interesting. The higher priorities of quality, price, production reliability, service reliability, and capability to support are the traditional buyer's results-orientated demands. The low priorities of e-commerce, R&D (Research & Development), new technology, purchasing and value engineering should be of concern to customers particularly those who have long-term relationships with smaller suppliers. It could be that customers have transmitted the wrong message. The customers may have focused simply on products and not the process. Whilst suppliers aim to satisfy customer needs, it may be that the customer has not quite worked out its need! Customer dominance is perhaps an important factor in terms of small business growth and competitiveness. If customer dominance is high, then the business strategy may focus on cost and efficiency. Business needs to shift to collaboration and innovation. *Innovation* is an overused term; the word means to introduce something new, to make changes. Innovation may therefore be used in the context of introducing e-commerce or supply chain professionalism, certainly in small businesses and probably in customers per se. Similarly, there may be an element of both suppliers and purchasers (customers) needing to manage themselves. Purchasers may need to consider whether they are simply managing suppliers and not really managing the interface or future logistics.

Supply Chains into the Future

Supply chain management is changing at a rapid and accelerating rate for two sets of reasons. The first set is the pressure for change arising from managerial and technical development from within the system itself. These include:

- The increased speed and intelligence of computing systems for the control of information flows. This has given rise to what is called "time compression." High-speed computing and data transmission can transmit and react to user demand almost instantaneously over any distance. Distributed data terminals coupled with real-time data processing makes planning and control more flexible and more accurate. When this occurs, "intelligence" can replace "investment"; for example, a computer system that can effectively plan inventory needs will reduce the necessity for holding contingency inventory levels. "Just-in-Time" also depends on fast data handling systems so that assets deployment outcomes can be improved.

- The availability of flexible computer facilities enables supply chain companies to engage in "dynamic simulation" of problems. There are many variables in the majority of logistics problems. Real-time interactive computer systems enable logistics undertakings to explore a variety of inventory level, transport mode warehouse location, and other problems. This increases the accuracy of logistics decisions.
- Finally, the realisation of the systems nature of the supply chain and of the potential importance of "trade offs" within the total system. These trade offs require an awareness of total cost measurement and sophisticated management accounting.

However, all these pressures for change will only take root with a sophisticated management process and, in particular, a willingness to manage across functional barriers in the organisation to meet particular organisational goals. This is sometimes described as a "missions" approach. The key to the introduction of this managerial culture in organisation lies in a strategic management informed on supply chain issues.

The second set of pressures for change comes from the wider economy. Again, these include five factors:

- Trends in the economy suggest a future uncertainty in the growth of consumer markets. This will require manufacturing and retail organisations to deal with markets that may vary in size at fairly short notice. The basis of effective business and logistics strategies in this context must be effective flexible options to enable organisations to compete in this tough global marketplace.
- Market structures are also changing, such as the expanding EC and East European Market, a slowing rate of exports to the United States, and fast-growing global and high-technology markets. There is increasing fragmentation and specialisation in markets and a growth in specialised retailing. This puts pressure on the marketing and, in turn, on the supply chain functions.
- Life cycles for products are also becoming shorter, with more selective and critical customers. As a result, systems are necessary to promote shorter product lead times and faster and more flexible distribution provisions.
- In the production function, there is a movement from mass production towards flexible manufacturing systems (FMS). These systems enable a company to switch production quickly from one product to another. In the marketing function, a variety of changes in distribution channels (e.g., the growth in large, out of town supermarkets) has led to a concentration of

buying power and an emphasis on improved distribution service levels, especially Just-in-Time delivery. Producers and retailers are sharing information systems to promote Just-in-Time delivery. This philosophy continues to evolve; the principle of lean production was first promoted by the Massachusetts Institute of Technology. World-class factories of the future will be lean producers characterised by teams of multiskilled workers, lower batch volumes, greater product variety, a total quality ethic, production flexibility, and a very high responsiveness to customer needs. This principle obviously extended itself into the supply chain and created the concept of lean supply to support the whole process, which demands a continual review of the organisation, management, suppliers, and the flow of information at every stage.

- Competitive pressures in markets are also growing. In static markets, competition becomes more aggressive. The growth in international marketing has made such aggression more acute. This, in turn, places pressure on systems to support production and marketing initiatives. It is especially true because so much competition, in both consumer and industrial goods, is now fought on dimensions of customer service. The need for effective supply chain education becomes axiomatic.

Supply Chain Education

Supply chain management has been an important feature of industrial and economic life for years, but it is only in the recent past that it has been recognised as a major function in its own right. Distribution activities make extensive use of the human and natural resources that affect a national economy. Recent studies have attempted to estimate the impact of distribution on economic life. One such study indicated that about 30% of the working population is associated with work related to physical distribution. Another study estimated that up to 40% of gross domestic product was spent on distribution and logistics activities. A further study has indicated that, using a fairly broad definition of *distribution*, the associated costs were approximately 17% of sales revenue. It is now accepted by both the academic and the business world that there is a need to adopt a more formal and global view of the many different supply chain and distribution-related functions. The appreciation of the scope and importance of distribution, especially with respect to new technology, has led to a more scientific approach being adopted toward the subject and to the recognition of the importance of managing the new technology and the changes that it can bring about. This approach is aimed at the individual subsystems, but especially at the overall concepts of the distribution and logistics function.

One of the major features of the supply chain in recent years has been the speed with which the industry has advanced. Technology has developed, demanding a good knowledge of both physical and information technology, and the jobs span a much greater area of responsibility, requiring a good overall logistics perspective together with the traditional demands for management and communication skills. Supply chain management is therefore now recognised as being a vital part of the business and economy of a country. In recent years, industry has set out to develop a distinct professionalism to reflect this new-found importance. In doing this, the industry has recognised the need for established career structures and good education and training programmes.

There has been a number of initiatives to provide education and training opportunities for those seeking to develop their career in distribution and logistics. These opportunities include:

- correspondence and various distance learning courses,
- professional vocational qualifications,
- diploma and first-degree courses,
- national diplomas in distribution,
- higher degrees, most notably master's and doctoral degrees, and
- "tailor-made" company/organisation programmes.

How does the busy supply chain manager keep up to date with new ideas in a rapidly changing environment? How can he or she learn about new techniques and how to apply them? How can he or she do this while also obtaining a recognised educational qualification? One way is to embark on an advanced course of study that provides relevant education and training without significant periods away from the workplace. It is for this purpose that the executive master's degrees, which have programmes in supply chain, have been set up.

The programmes are designed to cater to supply chain managers and executives, enabling them to continue in a full-time job while participating in postgraduate education. For young graduates who are just beginning their careers, the course provides an opportunity to receive a solid grounding in all major aspects concerning the supply chain. For more mature staff, who have already spent some years in industry or commerce, the course allows them to consolidate their existing knowledge, update themselves in the latest concepts and techniques in a more formal environment, and broaden their experience.

This initiative is aimed at enabling organisations to pursue an active management-training programme in supply chain management that also provides an internationally recognised postgraduate qualification. There are opportunities for organisations to attract and keep high-quality staff by using the executive masters and doctorate degrees to enhance their own management-training course.

Organisations will also be attracted by the work-based content of the programme. In the second year, the major input to the course is an organisation-based thesis, which will be of immediate relevance. The courses are based on the core elements of supply chain, covering strategy, distribution system design, the planning and management of transport and warehousing operations, and the design of appropriate operational systems. Emphasis is given to the impact of information technology and the development and use of distribution information systems and planning tools.

Relevant analytical and management techniques and methods are covered, such as modelling techniques, statistics, operational research, management accounting, materials and inventory management, human resource management, and the interface between law and business activity. Time is also given to developing personal effectiveness and communication skills. A selection of options and electives are available to allow participants to study particular aspects in greater depth, or to broaden their scope they selecting new topics. The following is a list of typical areas of specialisation:

- Distribution strategy and planning
- Distribution and transport management
- Warehousing and materials handling systems
- Distribution information systems
- Information technology and logistics
- Logistics system design
- Leadership
- Materials management
- Advanced warehouse design
- Supply chain management

Many of these topics are also pursued through doctoral dissertations, which have the added value of contributing to our collective knowledge. The course programmes have been structured to fit within a full-time working environment. Attendance in the first year consists of long weekends, single days, and a summer school. Of necessity, the teaching programme is intense and requires a full and active commitment. A certain amount of reading and support work will be undertaken on a home-study basis and through e-learning. Year two, which is concentrated on an organisation-based thesis, requires some work days as well as sessions with a tutor held at the individual's workplace for the planning, discussion, and review of the individual project.

What sort of manager and from what type of organisation typically participates in a course of this nature? Some useful facts are summarised, based on those who are currently undertaking the course:

- Ages range from 23 to 48 years, with the average age 34 years.
- Qualifications vary from those with some type of diploma (plus many years of relevant management experience) to those with a first-class degree.
- Positions vary from distribution analyst to distribution director, and include a number of different job titles — distribution development manager, European or global logistics manager, distribution consultant, general manager–quality control, distribution information systems manager, distribution services director, supply chain manager, or director supply chain.
- Difference industrial sectors and interest are well represented; there are manufacturers, retailers and third party companies. Industries represented include brewing, clothing, pharmaceuticals, leisure, telecommunications, and food.

This section has demonstrated the importance of supply chain education and competence and its overdue recognition in the academic world.

Professional Competence: Food for Thought

It is a sad fact that the level of understanding in the field of supply chain management is often low or not well balanced across the whole purchasing, production control spectrum. It is more worrying that we do not have a complete common yardstick by which to recognise the limited numbers of professional practitioners (see, for example, Gubi et al., 2003). Is it important? Of course it is. Without effective supply management, a business that markets products or services and that is supported by excellent manufacturing or R&D facilities and purchasing skills cannot survive. We are well aware of the impact supply chain management has on business performance and cost control. How can we expect professional performance if we do not measure capability and provide the help to obtain it?

We have internationally recognised professional and technical standards to declare the ability and potential of accountants, engineers, metallurgists and even our shop-floor workers. Until now, supply chain management staff have been handicapped, only half equipped, as it were. Admittedly the purchasing side of their professional responsibilities has been well supported by the long-established and readily accessible specialist programmes, taught in so many locations.

Supply chain management is not a profession, and it should not seek to become one. However, supply chain managers should certainly be professional — clearly, a relevant observation for 21st century businesses. The need has long existed for education of similar standing, a well-structured, modern syllabus, accompanied by recognised levels of accreditation of successful students. Unfortunately, most practitioners are trained by "sitting with Nellie" or by reading the manuals provided with the new computer system. It does not help having the best tools if the understanding is weak. Indeed, it can be positively dangerous. In the next chapter, I seek to develop that understanding with a focus on strategic purchasing management.

Chapter II

Strategic Purchasing Management

Purchasing is at the heart of any supply chain. Purchasing needs to be strategic to facilitate an effective supply chain. Within this chapter, I will explore corporate planning, purchasing planning and strategies, corporate and environmental factors and how to go about the strategy and planning process. I will also explore buying decisions, ethical purchasing, and procurement agencies.

Corporate Planning

Consider a business enterprise, and ask yourself the following questions:

- What are its objectives?
- How does it operate?
- What resources are required?
- How are the resources managed?
- What influences bear upon the success or failure of the enterprise?

In so doing, you are embarking on the first steps of corporate planning. All are important questions, and it is general management's responsibility to consider these matters in terms of long-range planning. Objectives must be agreed upon and the provision and management of financial, technical, and human resources set in motion.

In considering the responsibilities of general management, the planning objectives, and the controlling resources, we are considering the business strategy of the company or governing body — in other words, the *corporate plan*, which comprises the following:

- Objectives — survival, profitability, and social responsibilities
- Products and markets
- Finance
- Material resources
- Human resources
- Technical facilities
- Management and administration

Within the corporate plan, therefore, lies the important area of *purchasing resources*.

Corporate planning may be described as the careful systematic making of strategic decisions. Corporate planning is concerned with developing a long-term view of future developments and designing a plan so that the organisation can achieve its chosen objectives. During the last decade, many of the bigger companies in the United Kingdom had recognised the need to apply a formal approach to this need. It means that companies need to prepare "scenarios," or forecasts of future developments in the environment in which they wish to operate in order to examine whether decisions made in the present will result in a successful outcome in the future. Changes are taking place at a more rapid rate, but often the effects of decisions made now may still be influential more than 10 years later. Companies, therefore, have been developing more sophisticated techniques to analyse the risks involved in such decisions.

Consider, for example, the problem of deciding whether an oil company should invest in a new refinery, which might cost well over £100 million and which might have a life of 15 years or more. Such a company needs to know whether a market can be assured for the extra volume of its refined products, and it needs to know whether those products can be produced profitably. In addition, however, it is necessary to study the availability of crude oil and other supplies needed in the operation. Corporate planning, therefore, is a process concerned with determining the long-term objectives of the organisation, deciding what market opportunities exist and determining a product policy to satisfy them. Any plan, however, needs to be firmly based upon a study of supply markets and a plan to ensure that the required resources can be made available at the right price to support such a product policy. In short, an essential element in the corporate plan is a plan for purchasing. In the past, many companies have omitted this element, but problems of supply shortages and rising prices have made top management aware of the need to take into account long-term developments in supply markets.

The Need for Corporate Planning

The environments in which companies have to operate have become increasingly dynamic, and they have had to learn to live with and adapt to the changes that are taking place. Some examples of changes that have to be coped with are changes in products, in manufacturing processes, in communication techniques, in data processing techniques, as well as changes in both supply and sales markets. Companies have recognised the need to investigate these changes and to draw up plans in order to adapt to them and to survive. More sophisticated techniques have been developed to analyse the uncertainties and to assess the risks involved in the decisions that have to be made. A further impetus to the need to plan arises from the fact that companies have to invest large sums of money in new plant and equipment and they have to look carefully to see whether such schemes will offer sufficient benefits to justify the expenditure. In order to do so it may be necessary to look far ahead. The corporate plan establishes the basic objectives for the company as a whole and gives guidance to the actions of the various specialist departments, such as marketing, production and purchasing. It is also designed to coordinate the work of these departments to ensure that they all work together in order that the overall objectives of the company can be successfully achieved.

The Nature of Corporate Planning

One very important aspect of planning that has not yet been mentioned is the dimension of time. The consideration of this factor can lead to different perspectives and different types of plans. Everyone is, no doubt, familiar with the type of plan called a "budget," which is likely to cover, at most, a time span of 12 months. This is essentially a short-term planning device, and plans such as this cover only a short period of time; you may see these short-term plans referred to as "operational" or "tactical" plans. However, many companies have recognised the need to look much further ahead (investment in new plant and equipment may have significant implications for long periods of time in the future — often 10 years or more). In recent years, especially, there has been growing support for the need to develop long-term plans for companies, covering at least 5 years into the future. These plans may be referred to as "strategic" or "long-range plans."

It is important likewise to develop strategic plans for the specialist functions. From the purchasing point of view, it needs to be stated that many companies have been slow to develop such a strategic perspective of the purchasing specialism. It has to be admitted, too, that many purchasing personnel have been slow to see the need for and to develop the vision required to construct a strategic plan for purchasing. Many companies adopt only two planning horizons — operational and strategic — and some companies view the problems as being concerned with three planning horizons:

- Up to 1 year — operational, day to day
- One to 2 years — short-term, tactical
- Three to 10 years or more — long term, strategic

Having identified the time characteristics of corporate planning, it is essential to consider the basic approach to the preparation of corporate plans. It should be noted that this chapter will emphasise the longer term, strategic type of plan.

Typical studies need to be carried out:

- General economic conditions
- Product development
- New product developments
- Production facilities
- Key suppliers/competitors
- Process developments
- Activities and plans
- Transport facilities
- Merger and changes to market
- Industrial relations
- Structure
- Personnel development
- Government legislation

- Financial resources
- International factors (e.g., exchange rates, tariffs)
- Industrial relations

The objectives of these studies are to:

- develop a clear picture of existing markets and future opportunities and threats that are beginning to emerge, and to
- carefully analyse the resources that the company at present possesses. Once this work has been completed, it is possible to proceed with the development of the plan. Some companies employ specialist corporate planners, but others rely on departments to develop the plan.

The Contents of a Corporate Plan

The contents of a corporate plan will vary according to the nature of each company (e.g., taking into account whether the company is in manufacturing or distribution). The complexity of the company may also vary depending on whether the company operates on more than one site and whether it is involved in more than one product area. Corporate plans may need to be drawn up for separate divisions or subsidiary companies. The overall objective of the plan will be to set overall profit objectives and to show how these are to be achieved. In outline, this involves identifying the market opportunities that are to be pursued and showing how the resources of the company are to be utilised and developed to satisfy the target markets. In arriving at the details of the plan, the following aspects will need to be considered:

Marketing
- Products to be offered — types, range, degree of flexibility
- Project volumes
- Distribution policies and methods
- Promotion strategies

Production
- Product developments
- Process developments
- Manufacturing facilities and location

- Manufacturing strategy
    (e.g., "make for stock"
    or "make-to-customer order"
    or "mixed strategies")
- Quality and reliability

Purchasing and supply
- Make or buy strategies
- Research and development of new materials and suppliers
- Price cost analysis studies
- Inventory requirements
- Sourcing strategies
- Supply chain management

Finance
- Development of a financial plan
- Investment plans
- Financial requirements

Organisation
- Structure
- Personnel development
- Company development with regard to mergers and takeovers
- Growth strategies — horizontal and/or vertical integration or diversification into related or unrelated fields

It is important that the plan shows a coherent competitive strategy on which the detailed plans for each function can be based. It is also important to allow a certain amount of flexibility because of the uncertainties of predicting the precise nature of future operating conditions. Risks need to be carefully assessed and contingency plans drawn up where they might be needed.

Planning has long been regarded as an essential function of management; this applies to the highest level manager in the organisation as well as to managers within specialist departments of the company. Planning is simply deciding what to do, how to do it, when to do it, and who to do it. It involves, therefore, the setting of objectives or goals to be achieved and the plans or methods to be used in their attainment. If companies fail to pay sufficient attention to planning, they cannot hope to have a clear sense of purpose or to exercise any control over their destinies. This applies both in the public and the private sectors.

Purchasing Planning and Purchasing Strategies

This chapter has concentrated on the general aspects of corporate planning, and it has stressed the need to integrate functional or departmental plans with the overall corporate plan. Purchasing aspects must be taken into account if the corporate plan is to be realistic and effective. A strategic perspective of this specialist function should therefore be developed. Unless the appropriate material resources are made available at the right time and the right price, no corporate plan will succeed. However, there is some basic buying information and decisions to be made (see Figure 8). However, companies and writers have been slow to appreciate the strategic role that purchasing plays. Indeed many purchasing personnel themselves have not fully appreciated this aspect. Thus, many have regarded purchasing as being only concerned with short-term, operational problems. However, the need for a strategic perspective has now been more widely recognised and it will be the purpose of this chapter to support this change of view.

- Make or buy?
- How many suppliers do we have?
- What is the total value of our spend p.a.?
- Who are our top 10 suppliers by value?
- What are the top 10 products by spend?
- What are the critical low value items?

Several factors in recent years have given strength to the development of the strategic perspective of purchasing. Among these are the following:

- Rising prices and the need to control inflation
- The need to control investment in inventory more effectively
- Recognition of the importance of purchasing costs to profitability, especially in "purchasing intensive" companies where material costs as a percentage of total costs are very high
- Shortages of materials
- Growing scarcity of some key materials

Figure 8. Basic buying information and decisions

- Make or buy
- How many suppliers do we have?
- What is the total value of our spend per annum?
- Who are our top 10 suppliers by value?
- What are the top 10 products by spend?
- What are the critical low value items?

Although purchasing will form part of the short-term plan as represented by the annual budget, it is still important to develop the long-term view. The long-term strategic plan for purchasing provides a framework within which operational decisions can be made. Recognition of longer term implications of today's decision should prevent the long-term supply position of the company from being put in jeopardy. In this chapter, it will be useful to identify the basic stages involved in the development of a strategic plan for purchasing.

Stages in the Development of a Corporate Plan for Purchasing

- Collect information and monitor factors in supply markets and the external environment of the organisation. It will be necessary to investigate, for example, what new materials are being developed, what changes in supply and demand can be expected, and what price trends can be expected.

- Collect information and data concerning demand for materials and equipment within the company.

- Develop a long-term plan that establishes objectives and strategies to be adopted and that also covers short-term tactics and goals.

- Design an organisation and devise procedures and policies to implement the plan.

- Construct a manpower plan so that the required human resources are available to put the plans into operations.

- Monitor the performance of the department and of the staff to check that results are in accordance with the plans. It may become necessary to modify actions in order to get back on course to achieve the objectives of the plan.

It was mentioned previously in this chapter that "planning" is a key element in the task of the manager. In the above framework the other key functions of management can also be identified, namely, organising, staffing, and controlling. This chapter will also be concerned with these other functions, but it is the planning function that gives a sense of direction and purpose to the activities of people in the department. Strategic purchasing management is a significant strategic tool to improve competitive success (Tan et al., 2002). Purchasing needs a paradigm shift beyond simple buying to a strategic business operation.

Corporate and Environmental Factors

If we consider, for example, purchasing strategies, we are faced long term with the problems of:

- inflation,
- physical shortages,
- energy crises, and
- supply chain integration.

The general need, therefore, is for flexibility by alternative plans, and so continuous control and reassessment is essential as a major factor of flexible strategic planning, with alternative objectives positively introduced to meet change circumstances rather than passive acceptance.

A strategic long-term plan with no provision for change may lead to costly and disastrous emergency action. In-built flexibility by shorter-term progressive reassessment of the long-term plan gives meaning to the term. Good examples of the need for flexibility are sustainability and corporate social responsibility. These topics offer purchasers a chance to make a real difference to their organisations and local communities — if they use their relationships effectively.

Strategic Planning

The need for a considered approach to flexibility, as an important factor in long-term planning is evident when we consider the two-fold influences of internal and external flexibility that may affect the performance of any business.

Internal Flexibility

Internal flexibility comprises the pressure placed on finance to meet unanticipated contingencies and can be referred to as the liquidity strength of the company, measured by the relationship or ratio of equity to debts and asset position - current to fixed.

External Flexibility

External flexibility deals with markets, research (sales and supply), and the supply chain.

Market Strategic Flexibility

Market strategic flexibility can be described in terms of sales spread among customers (the avoidance of overdependence on a single customer or a few large areas), the diversification of products, the diversification of markets (domestic and overseas), and technological research into opportunity areas.

Objectives and Responsibilities

It is as well to define the areas covered by what appear to be similar aims - those of objectives and those of responsibilities. Although objectives and responsibilities are important corporate considerations, in modern management thought they comprise different approaches but contain interacting factors, which constitute aims and purposes inherent in company management processes and consist of planning economic development and available resources on a long-term basis.

Responsibilities

Responsibilities constitute social or moral considerations; for example:

- conservation of the environment,
- avoidance of pollution,

- employment security,
- social welfare, and
- philanthropic contribution to the general community.

Although classed as noneconomic objectives, these responsibilities can affect the strategic planning of a company. Good environmental conditions, internal and external employment security, and social welfare can contribute to productivity. Philanthropy, although appearing to use resources otherwise available for development, often appears in the later stages of company growth, as a reflection of stability and the primary satisfaction of economic objectives.

Social Accountability

Business, essentially focused on profitability and economic viability, is giving increasing attention to its role in social accountability. Enterprise has responsibilities to the customer that demand a social awareness of the need to consider the quality of life through the product, including safety, but there are also responsibilities towards the many small suppliers who depend on larger organisations for their continuing existence.

Socioeconomic Factors

The problem of pollution has exercised the minds of past generations and is today a matter of prime importance with governmental checks and controls. Most companies are conscious of their responsibilities in this area and have, in many cases, taken the opportunity to derive economic advantage from waste-polluting materials by converting them to saleable by-products, thus avoiding environmental problems, ensuring economic returns, and strengthening the company's position, both economically and in the community.

Social Welfare

There is an accepted awareness in modern industry of the responsibility of business enterprise to the welfare of employees — the result of enlightened management, governmental control and the trades unions. All relevant and current legislation needs to be taken into account.

Business and the Community

The contribution of business enterprises to the community at large, mainly in terms of philanthropy by established and successful concerns in the form of charitable and artistic trusts, has been mentioned previously. There is the further contribution made by the business managers themselves, in given time and energy to support company participation. In most cases the extramural activities spring from the company's awareness of responsibility to the public environment, but there is often a trade-off by-product of enhanced company image and increased trade.

The Effectiveness of Social Considerations

Whilst it first appears that, in long-term planning, there are restrictive influences involved in financial outlay in matters of social accountability and philanthropy, the question of trade-offs in terms of public image and trade potential must be given full consideration. Job satisfaction, participation, profit sharing, the question of machines and manpower, technical advancement, and employment security are social matters of grave importance for employment and competitive strength.

SWOT and Gap Analysis

SWOT is quite simply Strength, Weaknesses, Opportunities, and Threats. It is an analysis of any supply chain that will show quite clearly if any SWOT elements exist within it. A typical approach to SWOT is shown in the Figure 9.

Strategic planning involves the collection of relevant data, the identification of alternatives, the selection of the most attractive of these and the enactment of

Figure 9. SWOT Analysis

Strengths	Weaknesses
Opportunities	Threats

Figure 10. Gap analysis (Note: From "How Competitive Forces Shape Strategy," by M. E. Porter, 1979, Harvard Business Review, March/April, pp. 137-145)

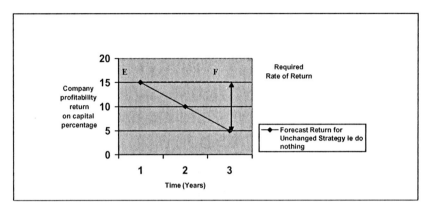

those selected. SWOT is necessary to recognise problems and opportunities. Gap analysis is a simple technique that is also useful in this connection.

Gap analysis shows graphically what the company or organisation is trying to achieve and what outcomes would be likely if its current strategy continued to operate. It shows the gap between what is desired and what is likely to happen. Gap analysis is best undertaken at corporate level. Purchasing has a significant impact on business results and needs to be involved at the planning stage. Often the purchasing function can make significant contributions towards closing the gap. Such contributions may be an examination of supply sources, prudent made or buy decisions, value engineering, and acquisition. A typical example of gap analysis is shown in Figure 10.

Functions Involved in Corporate Planning

It must not be assumed that a corporate plan emerges as the product solely of a high-level "think tank." If you consider the main areas of the company audit (finance, technology, administration, and production) and the external activities of marketing and purchasing involved in growth, you will readily see that these are considering functional areas of company management. Corporate planning therefore rests on functional support, in the main factual. Corporate policies emerge as decisions to operate in those areas that are considered best for successful achievement of objectives. For example, the following alternatives may present themselves:

- Market penetration by development of the existing market (i.e., effort concentrated upon obtaining a larger share of the existing market at the expense of competitors)
- Limiting product utility to a particular section of the market (e.g., industrial or domestic)
- Diversification into new products and new markets

Functional Contribution to Corporate Strategy

Consider the corporate audit in the light of functional activities and their particular contribution to corporate management.

- **Marketing**. Marketing is intimately concerned with growth and profitability. Demand regulates turnover, which must be supported by adequate and suitable administration of the following:
- **Manufacture**. The corporate audit will look to the adequacy of production facilities and the need to expand both operationally, and in the use of advanced technology and equipment to produce in economic quantities in time to satisfy the market.
- **Logistics**. Logistics are linked with both marketing and manufacturing operations in the movement and storage of goods at all stages to meet projected sales programmes.
- **Technology**. Technology involves the research and development of products to satisfy functionally and visually the need for economic production and to promote sales. Product reviews to support the company image for reliability and innovation.
- **Finance**. Costs administration and cash management are important in promoting attractive product prices, combating inflation, and conserving cash resources.
- **Purchasing**. Effective purchasing management is vitally necessary to ensure the free flow of materials at economic prices and in suitable quantities to meet production schedules and sales programmes.

- **Staffing**. Assessment of staffing levels are necessary to meet operational and administrative growth, that is, recruitment and training. Management development and the need for functional managers trained to think in corporate terms. However, supplier trust, commitment, and dependence can help in reducing buyer decision making and uncertainty in purchasing (Goa et al., 2005).

Monitoring Performance

Master Plan and Functional Plan

The two-way provision of support data for the functional level and long-term plan of the corporate strategy becomes evident in the master and functional budgets.

Appraisal of resources, their potentialities and limitations, in deciding upon objectives leads to:

- Corporate plans
- Estimates of financial implications
- Master budget

long-term with emphasis on profitability and return on investment (ROI). From the master budget stems the capital allocation of departmental budgets appropriate to support programmes functionally achievable to bring success to the corporate strategy and the fulfillment of the company objectives. At both levels, corporate and functional, the monitoring of performance is of prime importance. Whilst many of the departmental budgets are short-term, involving the "tactics" of annual programmes and day-to-day decisions, the longer term aspect of management by objectives ensures that the corporate plan is fully supported. For example:

- *Personnel* contributes to the staffing survey and is budgeted accordingly.
- *Finance* projects and monitors progressive return on investment.
- *Research and development* combat the possibility of shortages of supplies and demand change by seeking material substitutes and improved designs.
- *Purchasing* seeks new supply sources, new materials, promotes standardisation and rationalisation, with emphasis on cost reductions and economic materials management.

- *Manufacturing* is concerned with techniques and equipment to ensure production support and meet the problem of economy with flexibility.

Purchasing Needs and Corporate Strategies

The demand for goods and services to be satisfied by the purchasing department is derived from the demand in the company's market. Corporate plans must take into account marketing strategies on the output side. Production plans to support such strategies will also be drawn up; from these it is possible to determine input requirements. There is a need, therefore, to develop an understanding of the implications for purchasing arising from production and marketing strategies.

Marketing Strategies and the Demand for Inputs

During the last 2 decades, the importance of marketing to a company has been recognised, both as a general business philosophy and as a specialist function. It embodies the recognition that the success of an organisation depends on satisfying a market demand for particular goods and services. It follows that a company should identify market opportunities and then develop a corporate plan based upon an appraisal of those future market needs. "Produce what you can sell" rather than "sell what you can produce." Within the marketing function, the activities of market research, advertising, and promotion have been added to the selling task. Market research plays an important part in gathering intelligence about the nature of demand and the potential of particular product designs. On the basis of this information a number of different strategies can be considered, designed particularly to meet a corporate objective of growth, which many companies regard as the best way to achieve profitability in the long run.

Marketing Strategies to Achieve Growth

If growth is set as an objective, marketing plans can be drawn up to achieve this based upon four possible alternative strategies:

- **Market penetration**. The aim of market penetration is to increase the use of the company's existing products or service in the present markets. This increased demand may arise by increasing customers' rate of usage, attracting customers from competitors, and attracting nonusers.

- **Market development.** Market development is concerned with marketing present products in new markets, which may be opened up by expanding on regional, national, or international bases. Alternatively, an existing product range can be sold to a new segment of the market.
- **Product development.** The product development strategy involves the development of new or modified products designed to satisfy existing markets in which the firm operates. It may involve a broadening of the product range as well.
- **Diversification.** This final approach covers the addition of both new products and new markets to the firm's operations.
- **Implications for purchasing.** We can now analyse the effects of these alternative strategies on the demand for materials, which are the ingredients of these products. Market penetration and market development strategies lead to an increase in sales of a company's existing product range. Therefore, there will be an increase in the volume of materials of existing specifications to meet this expansion.

Product development and diversification strategies involve the development of new and modified products and, therefore, will change the specifications of the material inputs. New and modified inputs will be required, and research and development work will be needed to prepare new designs. Diversification, especially, may require the application of different technologies and purchasing may become involved in new supply markets. The supply of old ingredients will need to be phased out and new material inputs brought on stream. So far we have considered the direct effect of marketing strategies on material requirements. We need now to look at the effect of marketing strategies upon production and further consequences arising from production plans for purchasing.

- **Production strategies and implications for purchasing.** Plans affecting the output of finished products have direct implications for the production facilities needed to produce them. An increase in output will need an increase in capacity to produce the required volumes. Thus, additional equipment, buildings, and even new factories may be required, and old equipment may need to be replaced during the period covered by the corporate plan. Plans for capital investment will create a demand for the purchase of necessary plant and machines. The search for and installation of efficient modern equipment can make a valuable contribution to the effective implementation of the corporate plan. Changes in the level and methods of production will also affect the demand for consumable supplies needed in the conversion processes. Expansion plans may require the construction of a new factory, which leads to the problem of location (Fung, 1999). It is essential in analysing this problem to take into account not only marketing factors and labour factors but also an assessment of supply conditions. The location of suppliers and the cost of transporting supplies can significantly influence the economies of the location decision. For example, the high costs of transporting a large volume of low-value goods or a high consumption of energy can attract factories close to the supply sources. The relative costs of transporting supplies and transporting the finished product thus need to be studied to find out whether the factory should be located near the market for the finished goods or near the sources of supply. When opening up new markets in other countries, the possibility of building new factories in those countries may arise. It is essential, particularly when possible sites are in relatively undeveloped countries, to investigate the supply situation. Do such countries have potential suppliers who have the necessary skills to produce the right quality goods, at the right price, at the right time? If not is it feasible and economic to import supplies? There is evidence to suggest that companies have ignored these factors when taking investment decisions and have been faced with unexpected supply difficulties as a result. Corporate plans to implement marketing strategies can affect the demand for future supplied of bought-out requirements. We can now turn to the problem of devising purchasing strategies that are designed to ensure that those requirements can be satisfied. If insurmountable supply constraints are foreseen then the corporate plan, if it is going to succeed, must reflect this. However, if future supply difficulties are anticipated in advance, then solutions to overcome them can, in most cases, be found.

Purchasing Strategies

The influence of purchasing strategies on performance is enormous (Janda & Seshadri, 2001). To be effective, the strategy needs (real) resources. In order to provide the required resources to support the corporate plan, it is necessary to assess the existing supply situation and then devise strategies to ensure that these resources can be obtained. This approach is more rational than merely reacting to emergencies on an ad hoc basis. First, the existing supply environment must be appraised and trends, threats, and opportunities identified regarding the availability, design, and prices of future supplies. Strategies need to be developed to exploit these opportunities and to find ways of overcoming threats regarding possible shortages and adverse price movements. There is a need to consider such aspects as the development of new materials, the opening up of new

Figure 11. Results of good buying practice

- The cost of purchasing as a %age of turnover reduces
- Purchases keep within budgets
- Operational, process, & product cost relations
- Scrap, reworking, obsolescence costs reduce
- Better supplies cooperation & responsiveness

sources of supply, and negotiating strategies in supply markets. Make-or-buy will be considered in depth as another important strategic decision in what might be called "resource management." The results of good buying practise by operating purchasing as a profit centre are clear (see Figure 11).

The Development of New Materials and Equipment

There are two reasons why buyers should be concerned with identifying and helping suppliers to develop new materials and equipment. First, innovations are an important source of cost savings and of improvements in performance. Second, the substitution of new materials and equipment for products bought on previous occasions can overcome anticipated shortages and adverse price movements. The development of new designs can take a long time, in which materials have to be investigated and tested. Purchasing personnel need to work closely with their own research and development engineers as well as the technical experts of supplying companies. Plans need to be drawn up to control the development and to introduce the changes on the basis of forecast lead times. The initiative in the development of new materials can arise either from the suppliers firm or within the buyer's firm.

The Development of Supply Capacity

Changes in supply conditions and changes in expected demand for materials may create a gap between existing capacity and the volume required. Buyers, therefore, need to take steps to increase supplies in line with the corporate plan. This may be done either by arranging for existing suppliers to expand their facilities or by developing new suppliers. Discussions should be held with suppliers regarding long-term requirements, so that suppliers can also plan ahead to meet their customer's needs and install new plant and equipment if necessary. A programme of supplier development can also be drawn up to create new

Copyright © 2006, Idea Group Inc. Copying or distributing in print or electronic forms without written permission of Idea Group Inc. is prohibited.

Figure 12. Factors purchasing needs to consider

- Single or multiple sourcing
- Supplier appraisal methods
- Supplier performance
- Finding new suppliers

sources of supply, which have the correct production and quality-control facilities to supply goods of the desired quality. Suppliers should, therefore, be closely involved in the corporate planning process so that both supplier and buyer can benefit from symbiotic growth. Suppliers are stakeholders in the purchaser's business and need to be viewed as such. See Figure 12 for the scope of what needs to be considered.

Price Strategies and the Structure of Supply Markets

An audit of existing supply market structures may show that they buying company may be in an unfavourable position. Monopoly and oligopoly situations could restrict competition and thus weaken the power of the buyer as regards choice of suppliers and the negotiation of prices. Purchasing departments, especially in the larger organisations, therefore, need to develop strategies to control the flow of supplies at favourable prices. "Counter" power can be developed in the following ways:

- Develop price-cost analysis techniques to improve negotiating ability with existing suppliers
- Allocate business to more than one supplier as a means of preserving competition
- Encourage new suppliers to enter the market or develop foreign sources of supply to increase competition
- Contact the director general of fair trading to investigate monopolies and restrictive agreements if the public interest is considered to be in jeopardy
- Consider the possibilities of the buyer's own company making the product
- Investigate the possibility of takeover or merger with a supplier in order to increase control of essential supplies

- Develop substitute materials from other suppliers to overcome shortages and resulting price rises

It can be seen, therefore, that buyers should not merely adapt to changes as they occur in the supply environment but should take positive steps to ensure that developments are favourable to their needs and protect their interests. The pursuit of short-term price advantages may have unfavourable consequences in the long term if the price-cutting tactics of suppliers are designed to drive competitors from the market and to build up a dominant position.

Flexible Strategies

The dynamic character of the world means that it can be difficult to forecast future conditions and, thus, flexible strategies may be needed to cope with uncertainty. Consider flexibility in the context of having several suppliers available and the possibility of maintaining flexibility in the choice of materials.

Single vs. Multiple Sourcing

Multiple sourcing can be seen as a response to the uncertainties of relying on the deliveries of one supplier, which can be delayed by such contingencies as strikes, transport problems and fires. A further advantage of multiple sourcing arises from maintaining contact with research and development undertaken by several suppliers. In addition, there may be tactical benefits from being able to alter the division of business between them to encourage a high performance as regards delivery and quality. Purchasing strategy, therefore, involves a policy decision regarding situations in which multiple sourcing should be adopted. Essentially, this should include items that are critical in the production process and that incur high costs if the production lines are stopped. The higher unit costs that might arise as a result of splitting the business can be seen as an insurance against the higher total costs of stopped production.

There is also a need to guard against buyer inertia. It is never possible to forecast future trends with complete accuracy and, in the face of a high degree of uncertainty, a plan that allows a flexible response is preferable. A good example arises in the choice of fuels. Technological change and competition between producers, as well as other disturbances, such as strikes and OPEC-controlled price rises, has made it difficult to forecast future price movements. A flexible approach, therefore, is to invest in equipment that can use more than one type of fuel. Such a strategy relegates the choice of fuel to a tactical problem of choosing the lowest cost fuel when an order has to be placed. A second example concerns the development of new materials and components. Predicting the time needed to carry out research and development projects is hazardous and plans may thus be needed to carry on using previously tried materials as an alternative. When developing the RB211 jet, for example, Rolls-Royce had to consider using fan blades made out of conventional metal material as well as the development of the new material, carbon fibre. Insurmountable obstacles meant that the new material could not be used in the end.

Plans for Stores and Stock Control

It is also important to consider the implications for stores and stock control when developing the corporate plan. Changing demand rates for materials and other goods and consequent changes in supply rates put different pressures on the stores function. Changing lead times are also relevant. It is necessary, therefore, to draw up plans to provide the physical facilities for the anticipated scale of operations. Problems such as what to stock, how much to stock, and where to stock need to be analysed, as well as defining the levels of service that are required. Materials handling techniques have evolved rapidly and, thus, methods need to be investigated and improved. Finally, the major aspect of costs, which can be as high as 25% of average inventory value, must not be ignored. Forecasts of working capital needed to finance planned inventory levels must also be prepared. Thus, the objective of planning in this area is to provide a least-cost service to meet the planned levels of production.

Elements of Supplier Partnership

To compete successfully in world markets, you need to be better than the competition and source suppliers who can both add value and reduce cost. Partnership sourcing is where a buyer and supplier develop such a close and long-term relationship that the two work together as partners in a win-win arrangement, as both have a vested interest in the success of the other. The cynic will argue that in a competitive sport, there is only one winner (e.g., the 100 metre sprint at the Olympics or the World Cup in football), but winning per se is not the issue. Perception of winning with the success of the other in mind is the key to partnership. Building a supplier partnership takes into account elements such as cost versus price, long term versus short term, quality control versus checks, and single versus multiple sourcing.

Make or Buy

For many companies, particularly in the engineering industries, "make or buy" problems are important strategic issues. This type of problem can arise as a short-term question when spare manufacturing capacity is available in times of slack demand. Technical considerations may be similar, but the financial aspects differ according to whether it is a long-term strategic issue or whether it is a short-term tactical difficulty. The former situation is of prime importance.

In the past, companies frequently have not taken a serious look at what should be made in the company and what should be bought from outside suppliers. Manufacturing policy has been determined by previous traditions and has not taken into account the present and future possibilities. The make-or-buy decision is not one that the purchasing function can take in isolation. It is important that both purchasing and production information is considered together, and thus a committee approach that allows all interested parties to express their view will be advantageous. Some important decisions may need to be resolved at board level. Nevertheless, the purchasing function should play a significant part in finding the right answer.

First, the strategic problem needs to be clearly stated. It may relate to the question of how existing production facilities should be used in the future, or it may relate to whether an investment should be made in additional plant or equipment. The tactical short-term problem, however, relates to how spare capacity should be used, or, indeed, what to subcontract if existing capacity is fully utilised in times of an unexpected jump in demand for the finished product. The company must first make a full appraisal of its technical capabilities with respect to proposals of what should be manufactured. This should cover existing strengths and weaknesses as regards knowledge and skills, availability of labour, materials, and finance, as well as suitability of plant and equipment. If there are any deficiencies (i.e., if the company cannot produce the products in the required volumes), then a further appraisal must be made of the feasibility of acquiring the extra resources.

Some larger organisations try to close any competency deficiencies or gaps when major projects are undertaken. They (a) set up a strategic plan, (b) nominate pilot sites, (c) commission a pilot framework, (d) identify the gaps from a pilot report, and (e) review available options; not unnaturally, work continues to close the gap in competencies required. At the same time the purchasing department should make a similar assessment of the supply market. Have there been difficulties regarding quality, delivery, and price that can be solved by internal manufacture? Are there any particular advantages that external suppliers have regarding research and development expertise, long production runs, and specialist equipment? The volume required by the company may be insufficient to benefit from the specialisation that suppliers can indulge in when supplying to a much wider market.

The purchasing function can make a valuable contribution to the decision-making process with regard to make-or-buy problems. It should also be prepared to initiate proposals to reverse previous policies if changes in supply markets indicate that the company can gain from doing so. The corporate plan should be based upon a careful analysis of what it should produce and what it should purchase from outside. Finally, assuming that there are no major technical barriers to making the product, a comparison of the total cost of manufacture needs to be compared against the cost of acquiring the product from external suppliers. It may also be possible to compare the alternative costs and savings from a number of "make" proposals. When the issue is a strategic question, full costs of internal manufacture (i.e., capital or fixed costs as well as variable costs) should be taken into account. In the tactical situation, however, a case can be made for leaving out fixed costs for use of machinery and equipment. This approach is based on the assumption that equipment will remain idle in the short run, if the particular product in question is not made internally, but that overhead charges will, nevertheless, be incurred by the company. The financial analysis will, therefore, reveal whether it is more economic to purchase from an outside supplier or whether it should be made internally.

International Trade: Implications for Purchasing Management

International factors may have a significant effect on a company either directly (in relation to the products that are bought or sold overseas) or indirectly (by influencing government actions and the activities of suppliers and customers). Purchasing management is more involved with influences affecting supplies, though changes in demand for the finished products cannot be entirely ignored. The changing pattern of world markets affects the availability of goods that can be purchased abroad. It is necessary to study changes in supply and demand and to identify new products and new markets as they develop. As a result of improvements in transport techniques, of changes in the relative competitiveness of overseas producers and of technological advances made elsewhere, the potential for sourcing overseas has increased. However, it is also important to be aware of factors which may reduce availability; for example, political changes in a country, adverse weather, exhaustion of resources, and official or unofficial quota restrictions. Finally, it must be emphasised that buyers should be looking for possible overseas sources for not only raw materials and foodstuffs but also for manufactured goods. Factors influencing the supply of aforementioned goods will also affect the prices of such goods. Thus, reductions in supplies will lead to price rises, as will a growth in demand. The opposite trends will lead to the reverse effect. There may be time lags before adjustments in supplies can be made to adapt to changes in demand. Thus, price fluctuations can be large, particularly for foodstuffs and raw materials on the commodity market

Government measures can also have a direct effect on prices of imports through tariff policies and international trading agreements. It is essential for buyers to take into account tariff and exchange rate considerations when analysing overseas opportunities and to assess the implications of changes in these factors. Devaluation, for example, may lead to a significant increase in costs if a company purchases a substantial quantity of imports from overseas.

Indirect Factors

Suppliers

A purchasing department may use suppliers located within the United Kingdom, but those supplier's operations may be affected substantially by international factors if they depend on overseas supplies. The effects of international events cannot be insulated from their customers, therefore, and thus prices and deliveries of goods will be affected. It follows, therefore, that buyers need to take international matters into account when analysing home markets in which goods have a substantial imported content.

Government Economic Policy

International factors and, particularly, balance of payments difficulties may influence government economic strategy in managing demand in the domestic economy. The implementation of government strategy via fiscal, monetary, and prices and income measures can affect home markets. If the strategy is aimed at expanding the economy at a faster rate, the growth in demand may lead to supply shortages, lengthening lead times and causing higher prices. A deflationary policy, on the other hand, may make supplies more easily available and prices may fall. The expansion of international trade has increased the opportunities of sourcing overseas, but it is also important to remember that difficulties may arise when using a foreign supplier that would not affect domestic suppliers. Taking the United Kingdom as an example, these problems should not be ignored:

- Communication problems that arise because of differences in language, distance, and time factors that may be more costly
- Increased transport problems because of increased distance and because the United Kingdom is surrounded by water
- Full transport costs, tariffs, and exchange-rate factors must be considered when comparing prices with suppliers in the United Kingdom
- Difficulties of obtaining spares and replacements quickly
- Difficulties in visiting suppliers
- Complications with administrative procedures needed for imported goods to pass smoothly through customs

Specialist knowledge and expertise is useful in handling imports, and if a company is not large enough to develop this expertise, it may be advisable to buy foreign products through distributors and agents. Larger companies have shipping departments that are responsible for organising transport (unless arranged by the supplier) and for handling importing procedures (Fawsett & Magnan, 2002). The international environment is an extremely important influence and cannot be ignored in the development of a purchasing strategy. For some multinational organisations, however, it may be necessary to develop a purchasing strategy to provide supplies for locations in many different parts of the world. International factors have significant effects of the national economy, in which the intervention of a government has become a significant feature. Variables compose three broad categories: (a) the human factors of culture, leadership, motivation, organisational infrastructure, and deployment of technology; (b) the contextual variables of globalisation, industry, market size, the nature of competition, and customer needs; and (c) the public sector. For example government restrictions on trading with specific countries, the aftermath of terrorist attacks, local legislation, or disaster regulations such as those imposed as a result of the foot and mouth epidemic. This can be summarised in Figure 13 in terms of the variables affecting procurement strategies as organisations strive for competitive advantage.

The need for national and in some cases global competitive advantage is essential, and it is leading to customers of all shapes and sizes developing and implementing corporate strategies that entail integration and development of their supplier bases (Winser & Tan, 2000).

Figure 13. Factors affecting procurement strategy

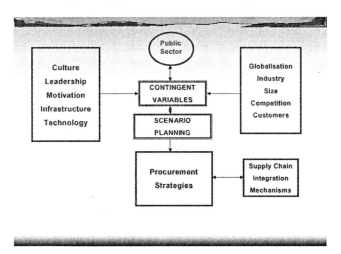

Ethical Purchasing

As the importance of the purchasing function in corporations increases, there has been a concurrent increase in the importance of ethics in the purchasing environment. The purchasing linkage is critical to the effective operation of corporations, as high-quality raw materials and supplies available on a timely basis are required for global competitive success. Bottom-line productivity and profitability, as well as long-term viability, dependent directly on effective functioning in the purchasing arena. The traditional organisational structure of the purchasing function has the potential to encourage unethical employee practices. Viewing the relationship between an organisation and its suppliers as adversarial creates conflict as well as inherent ethical dilemmas in the purchasing function. (See, e.g., Haynes & Helms, 1991; Wood, 1995.) Ethical purchasing can of course mean buying locally, particularly in the context of local economic development. This can be an emotive subject, but Figure 14 makes the point quite well.

The definitive guidelines on all aspects of ethics is provided by the UK's Chartered Institute of Purchasing and Supply (CIPS; 2003). The guidelines covering all aspects of ethics are regularly updated (see *www.cips.org*). The need for a policy on ethics is axiomatic.

Figure 14. We buy locally

Procurement Agencies

Contrary to what one might expect from an industry working at the leading edge of technology, not all companies' business fully appreciates the benefits of procurement agencies. However, although there is some resistance to it, the conclusion is still that procurement agencies are "alive and well" and are slowly developing alongside other techniques. Particularly relevant here is whether to outsource procurement. On balance, there is a relative immaturity within the public and private sectors with regard to the use of procurement agencies. There appear to be no real barriers to explain why use has not progressed further than it has. The constraints seem to lie within the cultures and attitudes of those it affects most. Imperatives for skills development and retention within organisations has meant that strong, functional "silos" have been built. Dealing with procurement agencies requires a project function that cuts across — and therefore threatens — these boundaries. Use of procurement agencies has the best chance of succeeding when conditions enable and support the performance of fully empowered teams focused and motivated on a "deliverable" basis. Organisation, if inappropriate, is a main factor in impeding use of procurement agencies. Too many reporting layers can fuzz communications, disempower individuals, and slow down decision making. Lack of clear accountability — heavyweight and lightweight management — can cause the team to lose focus and purpose. It is a paradox that small companies are better able to use procurement agencies and gain quicker paybacks while suffering few constraints. Large companies often fail to involve supplier companies properly or to prevent them from contributing effectively. Often this is made worse by their tendency to develop specialist information technology systems, thereby increasing communication and data exchange problems. Outsourcing procurement can sometimes lead to total abdication of the process. The attitude and the cooperation of people are crucial. Effective career progression is needed to ensure that commitment, skills, and knowledge are enhanced, not restricted. Effective communication is needed to break down barriers. Effective training is needed to cope with the cultural change and allow new roles to be performed within a new environment, resulting in benefits in time cost and quality. Effective rewards, not necessarily financial, are needed to motivate the individual and the team. Using procurement agencies will unlock and maximise vital resources. It will help organisations to stay at the leading edge of their sector. It is a key to survival.

Food for Thought

Purchasing as a function can sometimes be invisible. There is no single organisational form that could be argued as the best. I have no real problem with that however, sometimes I ask myself "where was purchasing?" This is in the context of major projects that have or are having difficulties. Such projects can find themselves in difficulty caused by greed, egotism or simply incompetence. Some recent United Kingdom and European examples include the Millennium Dome, the Channel Tunnel, and the new English soccer replacement stadium (Wembley). All have been or are troubled by cost overruns and delays. It seems to me that, in many cases, professional purchasing would have obviated the difficulties. Its competence would ensure that it is well able to deal with changes and rapid variations in business conditions that are often conveniently blamed by the business community and, indeed, governments. Within the United Kingdom there is a great opportunity for professional purchasing to get it right. The opportunity is the award to London of the Olympics 2012. The predicted spend is 3.8 billion pounds sterling. What is required to stage an Olympics is well known and hardly rocket science. The target date is not movable. Professional purchasing can make it happen on time and to budget.

This chapter has covered particular purchasing strategies that can be considered in the corporate planning process. It is vital that purchasing activities should be concerned with long-term plans as well as immediate operating problems. The next chapter is concerned with purchasing and supply chain policies to implement the strategy.

Chapter III

Purchasing Policy

Policy Issues

In this chapter I will cover purchasing and procurement policy, definition and structure, centralisation vs. decentralisation, consortia and associated issues, possible departmental structures, and benchmarking. In addition to the various strategies described in the previous chapter, there are several policy issues that can influence the operations of the purchasing department. A typical exemplar of a procurement business strategy can be found at the end of this chapter. The exemplar will place this chapter in context.

Policies regarding reciprocal trade, intracompany, and purchasing ethics should be established as part of the plan for purchasing management. Allied to selecting the policies, the structure of the purchasing function, centralise or decentralise activity and interface with materials management, sourcing policy are all relevant to effective purchasing and supply chain management.

Reciprocal Trade

Reciprocity involves a two-way flow of trade between companies so that each is both a seller and a buyer. A potential reciprocal trading situation is one that can cause conflict within the company between the purchasing department and the selling department. Let us consider a hypothetical example. Company A will only buy from Company B as long as B will agree to buy goods from A. The sales department in Company B will therefore apply pressure on their purchasing department to buy from A. How should buyers react to such an attempt to restrict their freedom of choice as regards source selection? As long as the product offered by Company A is satisfactory, competitive from a price point of view, and if A is reckoned to be a reliable supplier, there is no difficulty and they can be given the contract. Buyers should, however, insist on carrying out a full market appraisal to identify the strengths and weaknesses of all the possible suppliers. Any disadvantages of using Company A can then be clearly presented and weighed against the possible gains to be made by making the sales to Company B. The ruling criteria should be "what is right for the company," not what is right for purchasing or marketing in isolation. Thus, a policy decision should be made concerning the approach to be adopted in analysing reciprocal trading situations. If supplier A is chosen, even though they are not seen to be the best supplier in the market, then the reason for such a decision needs to be recorded and their performance needs to be monitored. A final point is that a decision should also be taken with regard to the provision of information from the purchasing department or the marketing department concerning the values of purchases from particular suppliers.

Intracompany Trading

The growth of multiproduct companies has increased the opportunities for internal trading between different parts of the same company. A policy decision is needed to state how such possibilities should be handled. There has been a tendency in the past for arbitrary policies to be established giving preference to internal sources and, thus, restricting the choice of the buyer. However, a preferable approach is one by which each case is examined on its merits to find where the balance of advantage lies. The cost of using an internal source should be compared with the costs of using an independent supplier. A profit-centre approach, which regards each manufacturing division or subsidiary as a separate accounting unit, means that each must be self-supporting and should not receive subsidies from other parts. In effect, if a subsidiary buys from another part of the company at a higher price than from an external supplier, then the difference, in the prices can be regarded as a subsidy. If the supplying division is not competitive, therefore, it should not be given the business (at least in the long term). Where there is no external supplier to act as a check on price, negotiations should be conducted to identify the true costs of manufacturing the product, and to set realistic "transfer" prices. Further difficulties regarding quality and delivery can arise in intracompany trading situations and the manufacturing division may give preference to independent suppliers. The correct policy should be to buy from the best source inside or outside the company. Additional complications can arise in multinational companies due to the fact that supplies may cross international boundaries. Setting transfer prices will involve the consideration of exchange rates, tariff duties and tax differentials in the various countries. An overriding objective in this case may be to minimise the total tax liability of the company. Decisions may need to be taken at headquarters in such companies, as only there may all the necessary information be available. It is important that a long-term view of activities should be prepared and that this should provide a framework within which day-to-day problems can be tackled. It is especially important for large companies to develop conscious long-term strategies in order that their monopolistic powers should be used wisely. Concentrated buying power may be able to dictate to smaller suppliers in the short term, but it is essential to estimate the long-term effects. The pursuit of low prices may bankrupt suppliers and such tactics may, therefore, alter the market structure and reduce competition. Other detrimental effects, albeit less severe, such as poor service and a high rejection rate may also arise as unwanted side-effects of the pricing policy. Purchasing, therefore, must decide whether their long term objective on continuity of supply is more important than achievement of price objectives in the short term. The dominant buyer should seek to maintain 'effective' or workable competition that produces fair prices in relation to cost, prompt service and a reasonable rate of innovation. The buyer must also remember the five rights of purchasing, shown in Figure 15.

If you do not get the five rights correct, then disaster is more likely than success!

Figure 15. The five rights of purchasing

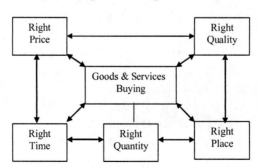

Selecting Overall Policy

The ability of the organisation to develop and apply effective purchasing policy depends partly on the perceptions of managers at all levels. The manager charged with the development of a policy should recognise that these perceptions are affected by the existing company structure, the quality of its internal communication system, the past experience of the company and its managers, and the resources available.

As has been suggested earlier, the development of a policy involves company-wide considerations. These considerations differ by industry and by company. What should be common, however, is the need to develop advantages over the competition and use them effectively.

The ability of the organisation to develop and apply effective purchasing policy will be conditioned by several factors, and there are roles for a purchasing manager that relate to the development of policy. Among these are:

- generating alternative solutions to procurement problems,
- protecting the cost structure of the organisation,
- minimising purchasing costs,
- assuring long-range sources of supply, and
- maintaining good relationships with suppliers.

Each of these has a strategic as well as an operational facet. This emphasises the important point that development of a policy necessitates a coordinated operational response. It is of little use defining and developing a policy unless the day-to-day actions of the organisation are geared to the strategic approach. This is a deceptively simple concept, for it is not uncommon to find companies that purport to have policies where the behaviour of managers is contradictory to the stated approach.

Structure of Purchasing Organisation

An essential part of policy development and selection is to devise an organisation to carry out the activities embodied in the policy.

Classical management writers have emphasised the importance of the activity of organising as a key function of management. Whilst their views have been modified in many respects, this function is still important and, therefore, the purchasing manager should pay close attention to the development of the organisational structure for the purchasing function. Organisation is concerned with the division of work and the delegation of authority and responsibility in such a way that the objectives of the organisation can be achieved. It also involves defining the duties of personnel and the relationships between them.

The task of developing an organisation structure has become a complex one, and there is no longer a simple prescriptive model that can be applied in all situations. The business environment is now populated by a wide variety of different types of organisation. It is recommended, therefore, that an organisation structure should be tailored to the particular circumstances of the particular organisation. What is suitable for one organisation would not necessarily be copied by another. In discussing organisational problems for purchasing management, it is essential to take into account some of the important differences. Of course, the development of an organisation for the purchasing function is but part of a general problem of developing an organisation structure for the organisation as a whole. Thus, purchasing considerations will reflect the needs of this broader framework as well as internal factors.

Structure of the Purchasing Function in Simple Organisations

In this example it is necessary to concentrate upon the organisation of a centralised purchasing function within a relatively simple, single product, single site firm; assess the advantages of specialisation and then map out the possible range of activities that could be included. Having portrayed a typical structure diagrammatically, the place of the purchasing manager within the overall management structure of the organisation will be examined.

Benefits of a Centralised Purchasing Function

In very small firms the scope for specialisation is limited and purchasing activities would not be sufficient to occupy a person full time. Once a firm employs around a hundred or above, however, it should be possible to introduce purchasing as a specialist job. As the volume of work expands so the number of purchasing personnel will grow and the opportunities for specialisation within the function increase. Parallel with this growth, therefore, the problem of organisation assumes greater importance.

The introduction of a specialist department to handle purchasing activities means that its members see purchasing as their major responsibility and can develop expertise in conducting their work. Previously, purchasing jobs were done by other people for whom purchasing was a major activity for which they had no particular skills. Thus, full-time specialists can develop their abilities and use progressive purchasing techniques to obtain better value for money. The department can coordinate the previously fragmented purchasing pattern and can introduce a common system of procedures. Knowledge of supply markets can be built up, an efficient record system introduced and negotiating skills can be applied. What may have started as a simple clerical function can become a sophisticated independent department.

The basic argument for the development of the centralised function rests upon the point that efficiency in controlling the flow of inputs to the firm is increased by the application of specialist expertise. The opportunities to make such improvements in efficiency can be found in different types of organisations in all sectors of the economy. Most large organisations already appreciate the advantage to be gained by effectively controlling purchasing activities, but many medium and small organisations have yet to reap the full rewards because insufficient recognition has been given to this function. The purchasing function can make a major contribution towards the achievement of corporate objectives in both the public and private sectors.

Activities in the Purchasing Function

A wide variety of arrangements can be found concerning the activities that should be included under the control of the purchasing manager. The most effective pattern is one in which the purchasing manager is given authority for all those activities which lead to the supply of goods and services to user departments. Such a range might include:

- **Categories of goods purchased**. With reference to basic categories of goods purchased by an organisation we can point out that the area of authority concerning this range varies in different organisations. In manufacturing companies, the purchase of industrial materials is regarded as the major area of expenditure to be controlled, but many purchasing managers have no control over the purchase of plant and equipment at all. In spite of this difference in delegation of authority, the arguments in favour of the application of specialist purchasing skills are relevant to all purchases. It follows that the purchasing department should be given responsibility for purchasing all bought out goods that are required. This does not mean that other departments should be excluded from the decision-making process, but that the purchasing department should contribute its commercial expertise to this process to complement the technical skills of the other departments. A purchasing research team should also be attached to the buying area to provide information to the buyers, which may include cost analysis.

- **Progressing or expediting.** An essential phase in the purchasing process, for the more important needs at least, is the progressing activity, to ensure that goods arrive at the desired time. The organisational problem here revolves around whether buyers should also progress the orders they have placed or whether a specialist or specialist team should be formed to carry out these duties. The division of work between buying and progressing sections allows each to develop its own particular skills for the different activities. The buyer can concentrate attention on market analysis and contract negotiation and the expeditor can build up contacts and persuasive skills to obtain deliveries from suppliers. On the other hand, others argue that having to do the progressing work helps to discipline the buyer in selecting reliable suppliers. On balance, the first approach is preferable (as long as the workload is sufficient), as long as the buyers are informed about poor delivery performance.

- **Purchasing in distributive organisations.** Whilst the principles of purchasing management apply equally to the wholesale and retail sections of industry as to manufacture, procedures differ. Because there are normally no production processes involved (the raw material stockholder may offer a cutting or shearing service), sales and purchasing personnel are involved in product selection and programming as a total merchandising operation. Many large organisations are headed, as far as supplies are concerned, by a merchandise executive or director, who is responsible for sales and purchasing, and who organises and coordinates the expertise and information available to both. In a dynamic, consumer-demand situation, such as retail multistores or supermarkets, purchasing requirement forecasting and expenditure based on product sales, subject to changing preferences, promotions, and seasonal peaks and troughs, require continuous updating to data and flexible purchasing arrangements. Product knowledge, ability to interpret sales data, short and long term, allied to continuous supply market research, are essential to successful buying for direct resale to the consumer.

- **Stores and stock control, including goods receiving.** It can be argued that there are advantages to be gained by grouping stores and stock control activities under the control of the purchasing manager. The achievement of the objective of lowest cost of supply implies that both purchasing and stock

Figure 16. Supplies organisation structure

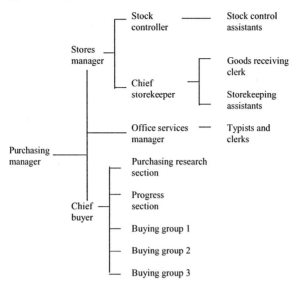

control considerations are relevant in deciding how many and when to purchase goods required to reprovision the stores. It is easier to develop an integrated system of procedures and exchanges of information in a unified purchasing organisation than it is to develop them in two separate departments. Goods receiving activities complete the purchasing cycle and transfer the purchases to user departments or, more frequently, to the stores. These, too, should be integrated into the purchasing organisation.

It can be seen from the foregoing information that the structure of the purchasing department can be varied to give an assortment of different configurations. Figure 16 is a typical structure for a supplies organisation in a medium to large sized company.

Division of Work amongst Buying Groups

Negotiating Links

It is worth remembering that there are many links in the negotiation chain. These include bidding, bargaining, and agreement; they include introductions, negotiation research, and planning. The information flow may be complex, partnerships may be under consideration (or existing), and there is a need for continuous

Figure 17. Negotiating links

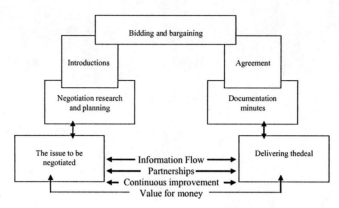

improvement allied to value for money. This is illustrated at Figure 17, where each link is reviewed and assessed in order to develop the full strength of the whole chain.

The division of work between buying groups and buyers should be made on a logical basis. In single product, single-site organisations the major principle adopted is to divide purchasing work according to commodities. Each section and each buyer would be given responsibilities for particular groups of products. Thus, Buying Group 1 might be authorised to purchase all the industrial materials, Group 2 might be responsible for industrial equipment, and Group 3 might be given industrial supplies and services. Individual buyers would then be given narrower ranges within each section. However, a second principle might also be followed in so far as more senior buyers would be responsible for high-value orders. Specialisation on a commodity or product basis allows buyers to build up expertise in a limited number of markets and they have the opportunity to get to know the nature of these products and the characteristics of the suppliers.

In more complex multiproduct, multisite companies, however, two further principles, which can be adopted in the division of work, may arise. Buyers may be appointed to handle purchases for a particular product line or manufacturing division. In addition, workloads can be divided up according to geographical locations.

Arrangements in the Automotive Industry

The nature of the large volume production systems and the methods of control adopted throughout the organisation have led to the emergence of a different type of structure on the purchasing side in the automotive industry. The method of control is based upon a set of interrelated computer programmes linking market forecasts, production programmes and materials schedules (i.e., lists of products required to meet the production programme and which also take into account stocks on hand). A scheduling group is responsible for obtaining the necessary quantities at the required time from suppliers by sending out delivery schedules (usually on a monthly basis). A purchasing group has responsibility for initially arranging "blanket order" contracts with suppliers when the items are first introduced as part of a new or modified model programme. These contracts over the specification and price arrangements with the suppliers and provide the framework for subsequent scheduling operations. Some companies have a third group concerned with supporting research and development projects for new designs and prototypes. Finally, other purchasing groups control the acquisition of equipment and supplies following more conventional practices. Within this scheme there are variations as to whether the scheduling group is part of the supplies department or whether it is part of material control (embodying production control and inventory control) and falling under the jurisdiction of the production manager.

The Position of Purchasing Management in the Organisation

Where there is an integrated supplies organisation or, indeed, where there is a significant purchasing team, a case can be made out for the purchasing manager or director of purchasing to have a high position within the management structure. This allows the manager and his or her department to give full weight to commercial aspects of purchasing decisions. If the purchasing manager is subordinate to the production manager, there is a danger that too much importance will be attached to technical matters. As an independent department, the supplies department can make its full contribution towards the achievement of corporate objectives. It can be argued, therefore, that the purchasing manager should be a member of the senior management team, with a direct reporting

Figure 18. Management organisation

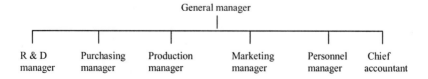

responsibility to the general manager. The purchasing manager may also be a member of the board of directors. Thus, the management organisation might be shown at Figure 18.

The position of the purchasing manager within the organisation hierarchy is an important determinant of the impact that the department can have. A high position and high status enables an effective, progressive approach to purchasing work to be implemented. Support from the general manager helps to increase recognition for the function and to encourage good horizontal relationships with other departments. In the 21st century we should have more purchasing managers at board level. In the last analysis, however, it is successful performance that earns the respect of others in the organisation.

Structure of the Purchasing Function in Complex Organisation

The emergence of large multiproduct, multisite organisations, and marketing strategies that can alter product as they seek growth. They have, therefore, moved away from the relatively simple situation of operating one production site to manufacture one product line. Thus, some have diversified into other product areas on one or more sites and others have duplicated production facilities by opening establishments in different geographical locations. Policy decisions that have brought about these transformations have also influenced the development and adoption of different organisational structures to cope with the added complexity. We have also seen the emergence of huge multinational conglomerates, in which international differences magnify the problems of geographical dispersion. One of the major organisational innovations of the 20th century has been the introduction of the multidivisional structure

In the simple organisation, the basic breakdown of tasks was achieved by splitting work up according to the main functional activities in the multidivisional organisation function tasks are grouped around different product lines. Thus, several quasi-independent organisations are created and each has a reporting relationship to a central headquarters organisation. Each product organisation might be a separate limited company, with as headquarters a holding company. In others, each division and the head office may all be part of the same legal entity. At both divisional and head office level, further divisions of work can be made on a functional basis (see Figure 19).

Each division may have a management structure, and the same functions may be present at head office level to act in a coordinating capacity. However, the extent

Figure 19. Division of work by product

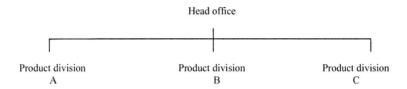

of head office activities of the divisions tends to vary. Some multilevel organisations are relatively centralised and head office personnel play a detailed part in the activities of the divisions. Other decentralised arrangements, however, give more autonomous powers to the divisions. These are established as separate profit centres, with minimal interference from headquarters, and the relationship between the division and the headquarters is mainly a financial one. The division is responsible for achieving satisfactory profit figures and must apply for approval of corporate plans and investment finance. It can be argued that, the more unrelated in terms of technology, materials requirements, and markets the divisions are, the more decentralised should be the method of control. There is little scope for central coordination as each division operates in an entirely different sphere.

The opportunities for central coordination are greater in situations when organisations are manufacturing the same product or offering the same service at multiple locations. Production technology, marketing problems, and purchasing problems are similar and there is potential for more centralised control of operations. In this multilevel situation, therefore, more power and more activity will be located at headquarters. Indeed, some of the functions can be located solely at head office.

Alternative Structures for the Purchasing Function in Complex companies

There are three possible solutions to the problem of organising the purchasing function in complex organisations. Each will be examined in turn to establish the advantages and disadvantages inherent in each solution. The three solutions are as follows:

- Complete centralisation — one central purchasing department controls the purchasing of all supplies for various scattered units or factories.

- Complete decentralisation — each separate unit or factory has its own purchasing department and is responsible for obtaining its own requirements.
- Multilevel structure — each unit has its own purchasing department, but a central purchasing department has some powers to coordinate the activities of the local departments.

Advantages of Centralisation

The advantages to be gained from the establishment of one central purchasing department are as follows:

- Economies of bulk buying of items commonly used at each unit. The central department can negotiate cheaper prices on the basis of total consumption throughout the company.
- Avoidance of "competitive" buying by individual departments of materials in short supply.
- Opportunities for development of greater knowledge about products because buyers can specialise in a narrower range of commodities which can be handled more expertly (i.e., buyers place orders for the whole company for a small range of products), whereas local buyers have to handle a more general range of local requirements.
- Savings in operating costs. Fewer, but larger orders are placed and hence a reduction in administrative costs can be made.
- Development of common procedures, forms, standards, and specifications.
- Simpler relationship with suppliers as a result of single, direct contact.
- Investigations of new products and materials can benefit all units in the company.
- Centralisation of stock control can reduce overall stock levels through greater flexibility and establishment of strategic reserves (i.e., flow of stocks between factories to meet shortages).
- Development of improved support services made possible (e.g., purchasing research and statistical information services).
- Enhanced importance of the supplies department and higher position of the supplies manager in management hierarchy.
- More scope for purchasing strategy and contribution to corporate plans.
- More scope for manpower planning in the function and development of training programmes.

Advantages of Decentralisation

The advantages of decentralisation can be seen as a remedy for the weaknesses of centralisation. The main advantages are as follows:

- Closer coordination with local organisation and buyers can build up close contacts with other departments.
- Buyer is in direct touch with the problems where they arise and can handle emergencies more easily than a distant office.
- Local buyers are better informed about local markets that may offer possibilities to a local customer which could not be offered on a national basis.
- Clear responsibility of buyers to local management.
- Local plants may need a different range of products, and thus a local buyer may have a more specialised knowledge of these.

A Multilevel Structure for Purchasing Management

The multilevel approach attempts to obtain the advantages of both the previous models. The division of duties between the two levels which is designed to achieve this are as follows.

Central Office

The following tasks may be allocated to the central office:

- Determination of purchasing strategies and development of purchasing policies
- Standardisation of procedures, specifications, codes and forms
- Negotiation of contracts for commonly used items against which local departments can place delivery orders for supplies as required
- Purchase of major plant and equipment
- Importation of supplies from overseas

- Responsibility for legal matters
- Interplant stock transfers and stocking policy
- Responsibility for training
- Research and information service

Local Offices

- Responsibility of placing orders for "noncontract" items
- Place delivery orders for contract items

In this group purchasing system, the manager at the local level would be responsible to his or her local line management. The manager at the central office would usually act in a staff capacity; that is to say, the latter would not have executive authority, as such, over the local manager, but would act in an advisory capacity.

A number of difficulties can arise in this multilevel approach. First, there is a danger that local initiative will be stifled by having group contracts imposed by a remote head office. The relationship between the two levels may be difficult to control. The local department may resent interference and there may be a conflict of interest between local interests and head office views. The staff/line division of responsibilities does not successfully resolve the problem of the local purchasing manager who has dual responsibilities to his local management team and to the group purchasing manager, when the latter has a more senior position, but no executive authority.

In spite of these problems, however, where a large range of items are commonly used, the benefits of having a central office outweigh the difficulties. When the range of commonly used items is small, other methods of achieving a common approach have been devised. These methods do not involve the formation of a permanent central department as such.

Sourcing Form

Whatever the form of organisation, the choice of sourcing is a complex issue. Arguably there are contingencies such as the individual, markets, products and organisations; there are criteria such as economic, power, risk and social factors; the contingencies and criteria prevailing at the decision point will result in single of multiple sourcing (see Figure 20).

Figure 20. Factors resulting in sourcing form

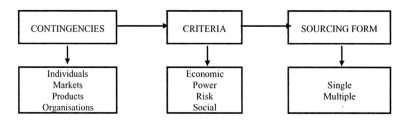

In larger organisations policies of single or multiple sourcing are often set; often where purchasing is "centralised," the sourcing form is left to the "decentralised" units.

Other Methods of Achieving Coordination

Several other approaches have been developed to take advantage of the purchasing power of large companies without developing a central purchasing office. These include the use of a "lead buyer" strategy and the use of committees of local purchasing managers.

- **Lead buyer contracting**. The essential feature of this strategy is that the major user division or factory negotiates a contract, which is made available to the other parts of the company to use if they wish to do so.
- **Committee of purchasing managers**. Regular meetings of Purchasing Managers can be held to discuss common problems and to coordinate activities. Tasks of negotiating bulk-contracts can be allocated to individual departments.
- **Informal communication**. Informal communication between local departments can also lead to the formation of common policies.

These three approaches can be seen as being of a less formal kind than setting up a permanent central office. They also lack the scope of the central office for providing all the additional services indicated previously. In some cases local purchasing departments may be large enough to afford some of the specialisms we have given to head offices.

The Selection of an Appropriate Structure for Particular Circumstances

There is no single method of organising the purchasing function that is appropriate for all complex organisations. In developing a suitable structure, it is important to analyse the circumstances of the particular organisation for which it is intended. Perhaps the key question that needs to be asked is how common are the purchasing problems that have to be faced at each site. The greater the similarity of purchases the greater is the potential for centralising control. Conversely, the greater the variety, the greater the opportunity to decentralise activities. Four different situations are worth examining:

- Single Product/Multisite operations
- Multiproduct/Multisite operations in which products are related
- Multiproduct/Multisite operations in which products are unrelated
- Very large multiproduct/multisite operations in which there is scope for multilevel structures in each division

Single Product/Multisite Operations

Where each factory is concerned with manufacturing the same products, the purchasing requirements are the same. Demand arises for the same products that are purchased from the same markets. There is scope for a fully centralised purchasing function, therefore, to gain the maximum benefit of the purchasing power of the company and to provide common solutions to common problems. In the tertiary sector, a central purchasing department would be able to control the purchasing for individual branches of a retail or distribution network and organise central storage points from which supplies of many items could be delivered. Buying consortia for several local authorities base their arguments on such a premise.

Multiproduct/Multisite Operations in Which Products are Related

In organisations that have several product divisions but whose products are related, in the sense that similar technology and similar materials are used, a multilevel purchasing system could be used. Sufficient common items and associated purchasing problems exist for a central department to make a valuable contribution, whilst local supply departments maintain close contact with local factories.

Multiproduct/Multisite Operations in Which Products are Unrelated

Conglomerate or diversified organisations may consist of manufacturing divisions that are entirely different in terms of technology and materials used. In such a situation, few common problems arise and there is little to be gained, therefore, from having a central department. Each divisional purchasing manager, however, should be given a high position of responsibility within the divisional management structure and should play a significant part in the planning process for the division.

Very Large Multiproduct/Multisite Operations

In very large organisations, individual divisions may themselves have a multilevel organisational structure. In such a situation, there may be local purchasing departments under the control of a divisional purchasing manager. On top there may be a corporate purchasing department to coordinate the activities of the divisions, depending on how similar their needs are.

Multinational Supplies Structures

The multinational character of big organisations creates additional complications. Wide variations in terms of political, economic, social and industrial conditions may exist in the countries in which operations are located. It may be necessary, therefore, to allow a local purchasing department wider latitude in determining its own supply policy and controlling its own supplies. Nevertheless, if there are opportunities to be gained from closer coordination, such objectives should not be ignored and the local department should be encouraged to follow group policy. The central office could be used to organise the supply of goods being imported into other countries for local factories.

Public Sector

Both in central government and local authority purchasing, the emphasis is on public accountability. This is not to underestimate the vital necessity for efficiency in purchasing, as in the private sector, and the move towards centralisation is evident in both central and local government. Examples from the UK and Europe (EC) may assist understanding here.

Best value scenarios (which replace compulsory competitive tendering) exist United Kingdom wide and the EC is considering modifications to procurement directives to ease perceptions of bureaucracy. Overall, however, whilst much progress has been made by the public sector procurement agencies, there is still a long way to go. The public sector plays an increasingly important role in the UK economy. In Wales, for example, some 345,000 people depend directly on this sector for their employment and the public sector accounts for approximately 27% of Welsh GDP. The public sector is facing the challenges of modernisation and is being increasingly exposed to the commercial environment and its cultures. Couple this to the political 3-year UK budget cycles which, have become a feature of national government strategy for the public sector, and it is apparent that the gap between public and private sectors in terms of practice and ideology has considerably narrowed. Given this perceived convergence does the Welsh public sector for example have greater or lesser strategic awareness than their private sector counterparts in the 21st century. What control mechanisms are used and what awareness exists of a selection of strategic tools and techniques? Are the drivers for this perceived convergence actually supported by data on collaborative activity between sectors? Is the private sector seeking to add value while the public sector is seeking best value by cutting costs? The majority of the public sector use strategic objectives as their management control mechanism whilst the majority of the private sector respondents still use their financial budgeting system. The public sector's strategic awareness and performance may be helped by better strategising skills. Although the vast majority of the public sector feel that collaboration between the public and private sector is a good thing, only 71% of the public sector organisations regularly collaborate with the private sector. Just over one third of public sector use strategic alliances. This suggests that those public sector organisations that have been exposed to collaborative activity could have a positive role to play in dissemination of information concerning their experiences and help those who have yet to move into the 21st century. Consequently there is a general perception of a dynamic private sector and more conservative public sector. The public sector use of recognised strategic tools and techniques is disappointing. Only four are widely used by the public sector these being mission and vision statements, SWOT analysis, and benchmarking. Of these four strategy tools all except benchmarking are simple instruments, and, even here, benchmarking could be argued to be lacking in originality as a mechanism for strategic development. One significant factor is that only 38% of public sector employers train their staff in creative problem solving. This is an area where opportunities may present themselves in terms of education and training to enhance and make significant contributions to the UK economy. Education and training are central planks of the generic knowledge economy and the "learning country" that lie at the heart of government policy. It therefore follows that attitudes toward management initiatives and strategic thinking are crucial in the achievement of this policy. The strengths and shortcomings in public-sector thinking are germane to education and training provision. Much work needs to be done in "lifting up" the use of strategic management tools (including procurement professionalism) by public sector management. The public sector needs to lead the push — the private sector does not have the critical mass to make a genuinely competitive nation. Creativity, innovation and knowledge management principles demand action if a nation is to compete on a global scale. Technical skills are holding the public sector back in long-term approaches to innovation. The public sector needs to meet the challenges of corporate responsibility, and the need to utilise a wider range of strategic decision-making tools is axiomatic.

Benchmarking

One method of shaping an organisation is to benchmark from a strategic and tactical perspective.

Types of benchmarking:

- Internal benchmarking is a way of identifying best practise within a group and share it perhaps resulting in cross-functional and/or cross-site teams.
- Competitive benchmarking is literally comparisons with competitors; data collection and reliability may be a problem and there is a need to ensure similarity (e.g., size).
- Functional or generic benchmarking compares specific functions (e.g., logistics); the comparison is with the best in class or best in the industry. It is easier to obtain information and often there are "clubs" that share data openly.

The benchmarking process:

- There needs to be planning. The subject needs to be identified, data collection methods agreed upon, and agreement to the plan by those involved. The need to be realistic about the scope of the process is paramount.
- The data needs analysis — is the competition better, and by how much? Why are they better? What can be learned? How can the learning be applied?
- The data gathered should be used to define the goals to establish or maintain superiority; these should then be incorporated into the overall planning process.
- The plan should be an action plan identifying clearly who will do what and establish completion dates; similarly, a monitoring process should be embodied in the plan to measure progress and ensure benchmarking becomes integral.

The Rank Xerox Experience

Rank Xerox provides an interesting example of the use of benchmarking to identify weaknesses and the means of improvement and the incorporation of benchmarking into a continuous improvement process. *Benchmarking: A Strategic and Tactical Perspective* (Cross & Leonard, 1994) is the definitive work on this subject.

In the 1980s, when faced with increasing competition from Japanese manufacturers, Rank Xerox assumed that, because they were cheaper, the Japanese products were of poorer quality. This belief, due largely to the culture of the organisation that led to a failure to perceive the nature of the threat to their survival, made the organisation extremely vulnerable. The decision to benchmark against their competitors revealed the truth — that the organisation was vulnerable in almost every business area. Japanese manufacturers such as Fuji were producing machines of equivalent quality and selling at a price close to Xerox's cost of sales. Xerox had nine times more suppliers, was rejecting 10 times as many machines on the production line, and taking twice as long to get products to the market. These competitive benchmarking findings brought home the reality of the business and forced senior management to acknowledge both the size of the problem and the nature of the change required to reestablish the company's position. External competitive and non competitive benchmarking was then used in almost every business area as the means of improving business

Figure 21. Rank Xerox benchmarking process

PLANNING	1. Identify benchmark outputs
	2. Identify best competitor
	3. Determine data collection method
ANALYSIS	4. Determine current competitive gap
	5. Project future performance levels
INTEGRATION	6. Establish functional goals
	7. Develop functional action plans
ACTION	8. Implement specific actions
	9. Monitor results/report progress
MATURITY	10. Recalibrate benchmarks

performance with very high levels of success. The process is illustrated in Figure 21.

The Rank Zerox approach to benchmarking was to incorporate it into a total quality strategy, which they called "Leadership Through Quality." This involved converting benchmarking into a process of continuous improvement which had five phases 10 ten steps.

The five phases were planning, analysis, integration, action, maturity. Within each phase there are specific steps or actions that are required. Note in particular that step 10 is the recalibration of benchmarks and the restarting of the whole improvement process, for example, a continuous improvement process. Clearly, benchmarking can determine the preferred organisation and indeed, functional operation required to gain competitive advantage.

Materials Management

The materials management concept is based on the potential advantages to be obtained from controlling the flow of materials and goods from supplier through stores and production to despatch. The overall control would thus embrace the following:

- Purchasing
- Stores
- Inventory control
- Production planning and control
- Physical distribution

The functional managers would operate under the coordinating expertise of a materials manager or director. There has been a strengthening "lobby" for some time to give inventory control responsibility to purchasing, and materials management appears as a wider aspect of this development. Arguably, both functions could be part of logistics management. Alternative structures can emerge, based on functional managers responsible for:

- *Purchasing* — With responsibility for supplies research and acquisition
- *Inventory* — Stores, warehousing, movement of materials, inventory management
- *Production* — Control of programmes, work schedules, material quantities
- *Physical distribution* — Limited either to inwards and despatch transport facilities or the wider concept of external warehousing and customer service

The benefits of this wider concept of *materials management* are reflected in:

- Higher levels of departmental cooperation
- Efficient communications
- Improved inventory control by centralised non duplicated records, with the possibility of data-processing support
- Personnel development with wider experience
- Strengthened support for purchasing

There are no simple prescriptions to help designers prepare a plan for the organisation of the purchasing function in a complex organisation. It is necessary to examine the conditions in which each is operating. An additional determinant will be the view of senior managers as the corporate level who are the key decision makers regarding the structure of the organisation as a whole. A further feature which may require diplomatic treatment is the relationship between the parent company and newly taken over subsidiaries. Personnel in the latter are often reluctant to alter systems and procedures and to adopt new policies. Even within old established organisations, plans to restructure an organisation can also cause much conflict unless the task is carefully carried out.

This chapter has been concerned with the problem of policy and organisation with respect to the purchasing function. There are no simple solutions which have general applicability for all organisations. It is, nevertheless, extremely important to design an effective structure if purchasing activities are to make a significant contribution to the success of the company. Structural arrangements have a significant effect on the performance of individuals in the function, because it is these arrangements which circumscribe the duties to be carried out by them. It is individuals who select and implement policy.

Exemplar Case Study: Procurement Business Strategy

PROCUREMENT BUSINESS STRATEGY

The MQ Group plc

Introduction

Increasing emphasis is being placed within the group on the need to enhance the return on assets. Improvement in the process of procuring materials and services offers a unique and in many cases unexploited opportunity to improve returns significantly with little or no additional capital investment. The large expenditure on materials and services by companies in all industries has made their management address this area as a means of not only reducing costs but of gaining and maintaining competitive advantage. Examples of these instances are given throughout this strategy.

Controlling production in business is an essential day-to-day task, but effective management of the resources purchased is equally important. It is simply no longer acceptable to treat the supply of goods and services as an administrative issue — it can and should be a potent force to make competitive gains and generate significant financial benefit. In particular, the recognition of suppliers as an external resource to the Group highlights the benefits to be gained from taking full advantage of their technical and commercial strengths.

The new procurement business strategy moves the group into a challenging era that focuses on the proactive management to the procurement process from design, through acquisition and supply to monitoring the performance of materials and services once in use. In doing so it recognises the benefits to be gained for all of the Group's businesses, its suppliers and the environment.

This document sets out the strategies that will be supported by business processes to be developed during this decade. It identifies specific benefits to the business that will be gained from improvements in the procurement of goods and services. Gaining these benefits must rank high in our management priorities.

The Challenges

The management of modern business requires a new set of values, based on the certainty that change is the only constant. The new millennium is proving to be a decade of turbulence, with significant changes in cost structures resulting from the opening up of global markets and global competition, the contracting out of activities which are no longer essential to core business, the move to more flexible workforces, and the focus on improving productivity through investment in technology. These pressures are already forcing a very much sharper focus on the skills required for the successful management of external resources, coupled with a demand for faster response times and product innovation.

Companies in many industries are therefore recognising the need to anticipate and capitalise on change. However, managerial initiatives in the past have ensured that few major opportunities for improving overall effectiveness in the traditional business areas remain, and attention has turned to the management of procurement as a means of providing significant competitive advantage.

The large expenditure of money on procurement of goods and services within companies, coupled with an almost habitual feeling of frustration with the reactive and fragmented processes typically associated with procurement, have led management's to recognise the advantages to be gained from managing *total* procurement as a clear business objective. Common goals must be identified for all parties involved, including customers, user departments, purchasing organisations and suppliers, with emphasis being placed on performance measurement and customer satisfaction. World-class procurement needs to exist in a proactive rather than reactive environment.

This challenge not only provides the background to the future development of procurement activities but also highlights the magnitude of the contribution that can be made to the overall business through the efficient and effective management of procurement in every area of the Company.

Issues

Issues the group will have to consider in the future conduct of its procurement include:

- **Changes in the marketplace**. Dynamic changes are taking place in world markets such as:
    - the increasing number of global suppliers, which are being formed, either in pursuit of the economies of scale or in an effort to match the changing requirements of customers,
    - the evolution of trading blocks resulting in a rearrangement of traditional commercial relationships,
    - new competitive sources of supply from nontraditional countries in Southeast Asia and the restructured economies of Eastern Europe, and
    - terrorist activity.
- **Decentralised world**. The breadth and geographical spread of its businesses together with the decentralised nature of the company's structure will continue into the future and must be accommodated when considering procurement, standardisation and leverage initiatives.
- **Pressure on cost effectiveness**. In all parts of the company the continuing requirement to respond to competitive pressures highlights the drive for cost effectiveness and is leading to an acceleration in the outplacement of activities now judged to be noncore to the organisation. This in turn focuses on the need to manage the external resources on which we increasingly depend.
- **Toughening societal expectations**. The heightened expectations of society regarding standards of behaviour of large businesses, emphasised both by the increasing public pressure being applied to companies in the environmental debate and the proliferating influence of regulation, raises the importance of both corporate and individual responsibility for the conduct of our procurement business in the market place.
- **Communication and information technology**. Information technology presents new opportunities to break down traditional barriers and accelerate application of "paperless" business transactions and information exchange.
- **People**. Staff are clearly a key asset, but social, political and business changes are impacting both individual expectations and the requirements of the company.

Consequently, the new procurement business strategy seeks to meet the challenges associated with managing external resources in these times of accelerating change; it requires the building of commitment at all levels and across all functions and departments to achieve the totality of the benefits available.

World-Class Vision of Procurement Strategy

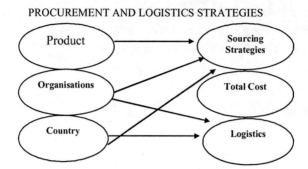

Our strategy takes into account the product material costs, our organisational costs and expertise, and, the infrastructure of the country in which we do (or wish to) source. The sourcing strategies per se will take full account of a make or buy analysis. The subsequent logistics strategy needs to take account of delivery reliability and the need to enhance supplier communication. The total cost of ownership (referred to elsewhere in this strategy document) cannot be overstressed.

The Procurement Vision

These business challenges of change require an innovative response, practical rather than abstract, all embracing rather than piecemeal, and above all affording measurable results.

This procurement business strategy in addressing these challenges, stresses the importance of recognising that the management of procurement should be seen as a business issue. Clearly, in overcoming the fragmented processes imposed by the traditional departmental barriers, all parties involved should gain immense benefit from working together as a team, united by a common set of goals. The existence within the company of an identifiable procurement function represents a unique opportunity to facilitate this harmonisation. In so doing, this infrastructure will promote and support the strategies by exploiting the opportunities, particularly in regard to the management of external resources that the challenges provide. In fulfilling this role, the procurement function will pursue the following strategic vision:

> To be recognised as a world-class procurement organisation in the sector through the provision of strategic professional services for the benefit of the company.

Leadership

Competitive advantage can only be realised as long as the business activity being undertaken is managed in a way that is not only different, but contributes more to profit than the same activity does to a competitor. These strategies are a comprehensive package that reflect the best procurement practices used both inside and outside the industry, chosen specifically to be complementary to the overall business plans of the company and to address the evident shortcomings of the traditional approach.

Outperform Competition

It is already clear that our competitors are also aware of the need to enhance the procurement process with such initiatives as:

- Developing common coordinated procurement systems and centralising in particular their European purchasing to exploit their leverage
- Reducing their supplier base, for example in their chemical division by 60% in the last 3 years
- Introducing quality awards for key suppliers
- Publicly recognising suppliers as key stakeholders in their business
- Developing supplier quality management programmes
- Introducing coordinated procurement and cataloguing systems

The principal message from these initiatives is that we will experience increasing competition for the output of a diminishing number of top class suppliers. Whilst this is clearly a key area for competitive concern, of equal importance is that advantage can also be gained by us if greater value is derived from the ownership of material, in terms of higher cash generation and lower costs, than by our competitors.

Professional Services

Meeting this competitive challenge will require the procurement process to be undertaken by professional staff:

- capable of improving performance and responding to changes in global economic conditions,

- whose core expertise lies in procurement and managing the relationships with key external resources,
- performing quality work safely and with complete integrity in environmental matters and business relations, and
- using high quality systems and other communication aids to ensure effective team working throughout the company.

Benefits to the Business

The principal benefits to the business are identified as being:

- generation of competitive advantage
- maximisation of the contribution to net income and return on assets by improving the value received from purchased materials and services
- improved resource management
- measured response to changes in global economic and environmental conditions.

The Objective

The acknowledged key factor in maintaining competitive advantage is the competent management of procurement in its widest sense, from design through purchasing and utilisation to final disposal — *the concept of Total Procurement*. In recognition of this factor, the procurement function has set itself four strategic objectives, which are not mutually exclusive but interrelated:

- To promote the effective management of procurement for materials and services
- To outperform the competition in ensuring continuity of supply commensurate with the needs of the business
- To ensure the materials cost impact and total cost of acquisition is minimised
- To develop new sources of supply to match the dynamics of the economic situation in which we operate

Total Procurement

For many years Procurement has been an undervalued activity in its contribution to corporate performance improvement and value for money management. Inadequate planning, poor communication between departments involved in the procurement of materials and equipment, and weak performance measurement have resulted in delays and compromise on materials acquisitions. The acceptance of total procurement as a business process that embraces all disciplines involved in the activities of the company, directly addresses these issues.

A significant consideration in the change from the traditional approach to materials supply to the concept of total procurement is the recognition that the value generated by a purchase can be enhanced through effective management of the process. Moreover the cost of owning materials or services is always more than simply the purchase price.

Benefit only accrues to the owner of purchased materials or services if the value added to the business, while in use, exceeds the cost of ownership. Good procurement should therefore aim to target both sides of the profit equation, by maximising the ability of an item to contribute revenue on the one hand, and by minimising the cost of owning it on the other. Clearly, competitive advantage is only gained in this process if these related objectives are achieved more effectively by the company than by our competitors. Benefit of ownership is only achieved if:

Increasing the Value of Ownership

The principal target on the revenue side is availability, both in terms of on-time delivery and of continuity of service. The duration of the acquisition process can often be a critical success factor. For example, the need to bring production on stream at the earliest possible moment can be a major element in determining the return on capital employed. Time wasted by a maintenance technician waiting for spare parts impacts operational costs. Consideration of all the elements of total procurement allows the balancing of price with the potential added value brought to the business during the use of a resource. For instance, additional expenditure to ensure the necessary delivery may be fully justifiable on this commercial basis.

Continuity of service itself has two aspects: first, freedom from deficiency in terms of an item meeting its specification, and secondly the assurance of resupply of materials (often spare parts). This can have measurable impact on both cost and reliability of operations.

Reducing the Total Cost of Ownership

The cost of manufacturing an item or supplying the labour component of a service is embraced to a greater or lesser extent in the contractual price. The cost of acquisition, however, begins with in-house design and specification and ends with delivery to the user. The cost of installing, operating, maintaining and finally decommissioning, are all associated with the life span of these items or services. The three components of price, acquisition activity cost and life cycle cost represent the Total Cost of Ownership.

The objective of procurement therefore is to minimise this total cost of ownership by addressing each of these components. Some activities within the procurement process are clearly more capable of contributing to cost reductions than others. For example, a team effort at the design stage between the various disciplines involved in the acquisition part of the process will often lead not only to a lower price being paid but also to the possibility of reduced costs associated both with the preparation of the specification and the requisition and even the later installation and operation. The total cost of ownership can sometimes be further reduced by involving the supplier in design and in eliminating unnecessary or redundant acquisition activities.

Continuity of Supply

To achieve advantage in this wider view of procurement, we need to recognise the wider range of competition that exists:

- Not only direct competitors but also the increasing array of international organisations
- Other companies not directly in our sector but who share similar needs either for a commodity or for manufactured supplies and with whom we must directly compete in times of short supply

Both of these types of competitor may attempt either to monopolise or at least to gain priority access to a supplier's resources, research, and development. This, allied to the constant terrorist threat, means *appropriate relationships must be developed with suppliers so that our strategic requirements are recognised by them as being paramount.*

Profitability

Most capital expenditure and an increasingly significant proportion of operating expenditure involves procurement activity, whether managed through an established procurement function or devolved to individual profit centres and line managers. The opportunity to improve performance in the hitherto under valued area is substantial and can produce value for money improvement on all expenditure with third parties with a direct contribution to bottom line profits.

Reduced Acquisition Activity Cost

The principal component of the procurement process, which can be directly influenced by the procurement function, is the cost of acquisition. This need to achieve ongoing performance improvement will only be met by a reconsideration of the process, particularly in contracting, and must be a high priority. A principal aim must also be to reduce acquisition time.

This will involve a fundamental review of resent business practices involved in the procurement of goods and services, and re-engineering the process to the most cost effective in the industry. Areas for attention include vendor stocking programmes, e-business and the associated electronic funds transfer, Just-in-Time contracts, and statistical process control to eliminate both rejects and inspection costs.

Supporting Strategies

In support of "the objectives," the following strategies are being promoted:

Procurement and Supplier Management

The development of a procurement business strategy must inevitably delineate overall supplier management policies. Certainly the progression from adversarial dealings and a win-lose relationship has not yet fully taken place. Suppliers should be seen as a valuable external resource with whom a win-win partnership brings overall benefits to both participants and should be actively sought. In certain cases, where the materials involved are considered of critical importance to the company, a long-term relationship based on a high level of trust and communication may be formed. In other cases, traditional competitive bidding may be appropriate. Regardless of the way in which goods or services are purchased, we must acknowledge our responsibility to quality suppliers if mutually beneficial associations are to be formed. Equally, suppliers must recognise the contribution that such relationships can make to both their own and the company's success. Accordingly, the supporting strategies need to be used to improve active management of the supply chain.

- **Exploitation of leverage**. Our buying power if fully exploited can benefit the profitability of the company. The sharing of information and standardisation of requirements will extend the ability to gain procurement benefits based on our total knowledge, volume, and image.
- **Procurement targeting**. Procurement targeting is an approach designed to elevate purchasing from the cost-attracting routine of order placement to a level of planned activity which concentrates resources on those areas that add value to the procurement process through the adoption of differentiation in procurement techniques. The same principles can equally be applied to the procurement of services. Successful execution of the procurement targeting approach for developing commodity or service buying strategies requires a coordinated team effort involving all disciplines.
- **Identification of quality and critical suppliers**. Some suppliers are chosen because they consistently contribute to a higher quality of performance than others, some because their product or service is necessarily critical to our requirements. Both features must be appreciated in the procurement process and appropriate emphasis given to optimise the relationship. As with procurement targeting, suppliers should be categorised according to their criticality to us. The type of commercial relationship established should be based in turn on this classification.
- **Supplier rationalisation**. By the same token, removal from the supplier base of those who do not offer any benefit in either area will reduce the overall number of suppliers thus enhancing procurement efficiency and operational value. In parallel, our business becomes more valuable to the remaining supplier base.
- **Widen process involvement**. Many of the far-reaching cost implications of a procurement exercise take place early in the process — external

research suggests that in-house design and specification has by far the greatest influence on the cost of ownership. Cross-functional cooperation at this early stage can ensure that all the benefits of effective procurement are obtained later in the acquisition process and life cycle.

- **Standard measurement of performance**. Only through the measurement and rating of supplier performance can contracts be awarded on a true cost basis. These ratings can be used to qualify suppliers' quotations by allowing for nonproductive costs to be considered for example an inspection and delivery performance. This enables real comparison to be made between suppliers.
- **Material standardisation and variety control**. Similarly, a rationalised approach to procurement, by making the maximum use of external standards and rigorously selecting the optimum number and types of products or services to meet prevailing needs, leads to gains both from increased leverage in the marketplace and the greater availability of materials. In turn this provides added value through a reduction in the need to maintain investment in extensive inventories.
- **Services procurement**. In the drive for cost effectiveness an increasing share of non-core activity is being contracted out to suppliers who can either offer better quality service because of specialisation or lower overall cost. Although contracting out can often be a source of short term cost reduction, it can only be a long-term source of competitive advantage if the business relationship is properly managed to ensure the supplier's technical and commercial competencies are fully utilised. Procurement of services has been limited in the past largely to those areas directly related to their traditional business — inspection, storage and transportation. As contracting and supplier management skills are developed and business information systems are designed to support total procurement, it is envisioned that we will have an increasingly active role in adding value to the procurement of services in general and in managing relationships with contractors.
- **General note**. The wide knowledge assembled in the procurement function over the years has on many occasions shown the benefit of a coordinated approach to procurement. By monitoring market changes, we can provide advice on the optimum response to price movements and market trends.

Focus on Core Activities

The priority for procurement to always focus on those parts of the process in which maximum value can be added. Activities that are unnecessary or capable of being performed more effectively elsewhere should be either eliminated or contracted out. Examples of this concept include using agents to purchase low value, simple orders; having inventory held by stockists and allowing end users to order directly against price agreements. Core activities in the materials area can vary significantly depending on our business objectives. For example, project procurement may be handled more efficiently by a contractor. However, as discussed earlier, full value is added to the business only where the total cost of ownership, particularly life cycle cost, is considered. In the contracting out of project procurement, the core activity shifts for the actual buying to one of ensuring that the materials related activities are properly specified and executed by the contractor.

Conforming to conditions imposed by joint venture partners or governments can also affect materials procurement activities. For example the need to develop the local market or to employ local staff may be overriding objectives. While the procurement principles should not change, different strategies may be emphasised. Procurement training for company staff and educating selected local suppliers in quality improvement techniques may be critical to supporting overall company objectives.

Improve Inventory Management

The test of good inventory management must be that items are only stocked if the benefits of direct availability outweigh the cost of holding them as stock. As a result, increasing emphasis is being placed on stocks being held by suppliers or third parties. The thrust therefore has to be towards zero stock holdings and the provision of materials by quality suppliers at the time of requirement. Particular considerations are that:

- the determination of the need for stock items, the initial quantity and take off rates are significant factors in the concept of total acquisition cost of that item over the lifetime of its usage,
- the availability of surplus or slow moving stock represents waste both in terms of capital employed and resources devoted to their acquisition and care, and
- the introduction of the concept of service level inventory control will enhance the quality of inventories by ensuring stock levels are directly commensurate with the criticality of user requirements.

Provide Supportive Systems

In the past procurement systems have been transaction rather than business orientated. Common systems will be designed therefore to provide for the future information needs of the procurement process in addition to purchasing and inventory administration details. The emphasis must be on systems to support the business processes, not the adaptation of the business processes to the capabilities of the system. Easy availability of information to both end users and materials management staff is paramount for business decision making. Specific requirements are:

- the ability to exchange information between decision makers regarding supplier and product performance and materials specifications,
- the exploitation of available technology to improve the basic efficiency of the processing of materials transactions, and to facilitate communications to and from key suppliers, and
- the provision of value added networks which enable the ready exchange of information between business units.

Networking

Working together in areas such as procurement coordination, systems development and training, enhances efficiency and cost effectiveness by sharing the expertise available within the company. This can either be on a worldwide or regional basis, or in relation to special interest areas. Direct commercial advantages can be gained by treating geographically separated purchasing resources as though they were centralised.

Sponsor Safety and the Protection of the Environment

Safety and the environment are essential factors in procurement decisions and these factors and the provision of a safe place of work should be fully appreciated in the total ownership cost calculation. The principal aim in this area is to conduct its activities safely and to contribute to environmental protection.

Particular goals are that:

- the procurement process should be seen to include managing the purchase and storage of hazardous materials and arranging disposal of waste and depleted materials; and
- the understanding and selection of acceptable materials is to be actively encouraged, including the choice of all packaging, in order to assist in avoiding acquisition or holding of environmentally unacceptable materials in the first place.

Organisation: Focus on Customers

It is essential that procurement adapt to changed business processes. Facilitating the procurement process for end users through e-business, supply agreements, JIT (Just in Time) delivery, and zone stores is important. However, to gain the advantages of total procurement, the process must be coordinated or managed at the highest level possible. If this is not done the added value to be obtained through a coordinated approach to procurement and materials management will be lost. In pursuit of this objective, three areas must be addressed – processes, systems and skills.

Procurement activities have to be managed in a manner that allows easy access to the services required by end users through the provision of processes and systems that are designed both to optimise the value to customers and to minimise the cost of acquisition. Equally, the quality of skills and breadth of management understanding required, leads to the need for the enhancement of the job content of procurement staff, emphasising personal growth and skills requirements to actively participate in business management. As new ways evolve of doing business and the attention focuses on the need to manage more effectively the contracting of services, so the processes, systems and skills being promoted by procurement can be applied to equal advantage in managing the procurement of services. Opportunities should be constantly sought to add value to all contracting whether for materials or services.

Develop Human Resources

Clearly the key to the successful application of our procurement business strategies is the continuing development of professional staff with the required mix of business, managerial and specialist skills.

The strategies are therefore aimed at continuing the process of recruiting high calibre graduates and seasoned professionals and of providing appropriate training, or retraining, to enable new and existing staff to develop the capability of the evolving procurement business.

The company works in a decentralised manner, but in the eyes of many, is a single entity with a single reputation. Therefore, what may seem purely a local issue can easily impact critical supplier relationships around the world. Accordingly, it is essential that the ethical behaviour of all individuals involved in the Procurement process is beyond reproach and in full compliance with the company's general business ethics.

The strategies further highlight the need to identify and develop the high-calibre regional staff that will be required to manage the procurement process within their own regions in the future whilst also recognising that increasingly we will seek to meet our international obligations with regional staff wherever in the world they are based.

Performance Measurement

The application of these strategies will clearly enhance procurement effectiveness. Well-managed procurement will not only lead to lower costs and the optimal meeting of supply requirements, but also contribute to improvements in net income and return on assets.

The successful achievement of any business objective, however, can only be judged if goals are set and progress measured towards the goals. Experience in many world-class companies has indicated that by utilising best practices, it is possible to achieve previously unrecognised savings which directly contribute to net income. On the bases of this experience, we will set goals in the areas highlighted below. The percentages shown are an indication of the improvement that could be achieved in overall company performance and are expressed in real terms.

- **Cash generation**. Reduce the procurement process (thereby accelerating or prolonging cash generation) to a maximum of 6 weeks.
- **Price**. Generate savings of 5% in the cost of goods and services.
- **Acquisition activity**. Lower acquisition activity costs by 10% for example by reducing:
    - incoming defects on material received by 50%,
    - inventory levels by 20%, and
    - invoice processing costs by 10%.

Such substantial benefits cannot be obtained simply through the efforts of procurement — it requires a concerted and coordinated approach by all functions in the organisation involved in the procurement process. The steps to be taken, however, require careful consideration. Both an analysis of the business processes and an assurance of the completeness of each step taken is essential. Use of the techniques associated with the concept of reengineering and with quality management may greatly assist in these areas. In order to ensure the participation of all relevant functions, we will establish a procurement steering committees at the most senior level. Indeed it must be stressed that achieving the financial gains associated with the new procurement strategies requires real commitment from all levels of management within the company. I think most larger organisations do see purchasing as a "strategic weapon," whose value stretches beyond cost reduction. Even NASA procurement, where in the past, money had been no object has entered the 21st century. Sometimes procurement does get itself isolated and does not, for example, interface with marketing to ensure customer satisfaction. In the 21st century professional and effective procurement is axiomatic. This procurement business strategy will ensure we continuously improve our effectiveness and build on our professional reputation.

In the next chapter we examine quality management, which is a fundamental content of effective procurement and supply chain management.

Chapter IV

Quality Management and Customer Service

This chapter provides a brief overview of a lengthy aspect of the supply chain — that of quality. After defining quality and the costs of failure, methods of getting it right such as ISO 9000, ISO 4000, quality management, and efficient consumer response, are covered. Quality is an essential ingredient of the supply chain.

Defining Quality

The reputation attached to an organisation for the quality of its products and services is accepted as a key to its success and to the future of its employees. To prosper in today's economic climate, any organisation and its suppliers must be dedicated to never-ending improvement and more efficient ways to obtain products or services that consistently meet customers' needs must constantly be sought. The consumer is no longer required to make a choice between price and quality, and competitiveness in quality is not only central to profitability but is crucial to business survival. In today's tough and challenging business environment, the development and implementation of a comprehensive quality policy is not merely desirable — it is essential. Quality is often used to signify "excellence" of a product or services — we talk about "Rolls-Royce quality" and "top quality." In some engineering companies, the word may be used to indicate that a piece of metal confirms to certain physical dimension characteristics, often set down in the form of a particularly "tight" specification. If we define quality in way which is useful in its management, then we must recognise the need to include in the assessment of quality, the true requirements of the "customer." *Quality* is simply meeting the customer's requirements; this has been expressed in many ways by others:

- "fitness for purpose or use"
- "the totality of features and characteristics of a product or service that bear on its ability to satisfy stated or implied needs"
- "the total composite product and service characteristics of marketing, engineering, manufacture, and maintenance through which the product and service in use will meet the expectation by the customer"

Reliability is another word that we should define properly. "Why do you buy a Volkswagen car?" "Quality and reliability" comes back the answer. The two terms are used synonymously, often in a totally confused way. Clearly, part of the acceptability of a product or service will depend on its ability to function satisfactorily over a period of time, and this aspect of performance is given the name "reliability." It is the ability of the product or service to continue to meet the customer's requirements. Reliability ranks with quality in importance, since it is a key factor in many purchasing decisions where alternatives are being considered. Many of the general management issues relate to achieving product or service quality are also applicable to reliability. Quality requires that both the needs of the customer and his/her perceived needs are explored. Frequently, a choice of product or service is made upon apparently irrational grounds; identical offerings, presented in different ways, will sell in vastly different quantities, and will have different qualities ascribed to them. The detergent that sells better in a blue box than a red one, the bank account that has a higher status because of the leather chequebook wallet, are well known. Similarly, a quality judgement is often related to the price paid without any regard to the discernible properties being purchased. The reasons for a purchase may be difficult to identify, yet their reality must not be denied.

The quality of products and services is important not only for users but also for suppliers. For manufacturers, quality deficiencies result in additional costs for inspection, testing, scrap, re-work, and the handling of complaints and warranty claims. In the service industries, errors, checking, enquiries, and complaints account for losses in efficiency and productivity. Repeat sales and future market share will also be affected, with significant effects on profitability and survival. Quality must therefore be taken into account throughout all the areas of marketing, design, purchasing, production or operations, and logistics. It must be controlled in all these functions, and their activities coordinated to achieve a balanced corporate quality performance. Quality performance will not just happen; effective leadership and teamwork is the only sure recipe for success. Real understanding and commitment by senior management, together with explicit quality policies, lead to an improvement throughout the entire organisation, which in turn generates a momentum for the improvement of products, services, and performance. Achieving quality relies upon consideration of both the external environment and the internal resources: The identification of the customer's requirements must be matched by the ability to produce a product or generate a service which will be recognised as satisfying the needs. In the event of a conflict between these two determinants, the intended market segment may have to be changed, or the internal resources may have to be re-examined. The customer's perception of quality changes with time and any organisation's attitude to quality must change with this perception. The skills and attitudes of the producer are also subject to change, and failure to monitor such changes will inevitably lead to dissatisfied customers. Quality, like all other corporate matters, must be reviewed continually in the light of current circumstances.

A traditional approach to many transformation processes is to depend on production to make the product and quality control to inspect it and divert that output that does not meet the requirements. This is a strategy of detection and is wasteful because it allows time and materials to be invested in products that are not always saleable. This postoperation/production inspection is expensive, unreliable and uneconomical. It is much more effective to avoid waste by not producing unsaleable output in the first place — to adopt a strategy of prevention. The prevention strategy sounds sensible and obvious to most people. It is often captured in slogans such as "Quality — right the first time." This type of campaigning is, however, not enough on its own. What is required is an understanding of the elements of a systematic control system that is designed for the prevention of products or services that doe not conform to requirements. Management must be dedicated to the ongoing improvement of quality, not simply a one-step improvement to an acceptable plateau.

A quality policy then requires top management to:

- establish an "organisation" for quality,
- identify the customer's needs and perception of needs,

- assess the ability of the organisation to meet these needs,
- ensure that supplied materials and services reliably meet the required standards of performance and efficiency,
- concentrate on the prevention rather than detection philosophy,
- educate and train for quality improvement, and
- review the quality management systems to maintain progress.

The quality policy must be publicised and understood at all levels of the organisation.

Design and Conformance

We have defined quality as the degree of satisfaction of customer needs. So the quality of a motor car, or washing machine, or a banking service is the extent to which it meets the requirements of the customer. Before any discussion on quality can take place, therefore, it is necessary to be clear about the purpose of the product, in other words what those customer's requirements are. The customer may be internal or external to the organisation and his/her satisfaction must be the first and most important ingredient in any plan for success. The quality of any product or service has two distinct but interrelated aspects:

- Quality of design
- Quality of conformance to design

Quality of design. This is a measure of how well the product or service is designed to meet the customer requirements. If the quality of design is low, the product/service will not satisfy the requirements. The most important feature of the design, with regard to the achievement of the required product quality, is the specification. This describes and defines the product or service and should be a comprehensive statement of all aspects of it that must be present to meet customer requirements. The stipulation of the correct specification is vital in the purchase of materials and services for use in the transformation process. All too frequently, the terms *as previously supplied* or *as agreed with your representative* are to be found on purchase orders for suppliers. The importance of obtaining quality inputs cannot be overemphasised, and this cannot be achieved without adequate specifications. A specification may be expressed in terms of the maximum amount of tolerable variation on a measurement, the degree of finish on a surface, the smoothness of movement of a mechanical device, a particular chemical property, the number of times the phone rings before it must be answered, and so on. There is a variety of ways in which specifications may be stated and ingenuity must be constrained in order to control the number of forms of specifications present in any organisation.

Quality of conformance to design. This is the extent to which the product or service achieves the quality of design. What the customer actually receives should conform to the design, and direct production or operating costs are tied firmly to the level of conformance achieved. Quality cannot be inspected into a product or service; the customer satisfaction must be designed into the whole system. The conformance check then makes sure that things go according to plan. A high level of final product inspection or checking of work is often indicative of attempts to inspect in quality, an activity that will achieve mostly spiralling costs and increasing viability.

The area of conformance to design is largely concerned with the performance of the process, which transforms a set of inputs, including actions, methods and operations, into desired outputs — products, information, services, and so forth. In each area or function of an organisation there will be many processes taking place, and the output from one is often the input to another. Clearly it is essential to have an effective system to manage each process. The recording and analysis of data play a significant role in this aspect of quality.

The Costs of Quality

Manufacturing a product or generating a service that meets the customer requirements must be managed in a cost-efficient manner, so that the long-term effect of quality costs on the business is a desirable one. These costs are a true measure of the quality effort. A competitive product based on a balance between quality and cost factors is the principal goal. This objective is best accomplished with the aid of competent analysis of the costs quality. The analysis of quality costs is a significant management tool that provides:

- a method of assessing the overall effectiveness of the management of quality, and
- a means of determining problem areas and action priorities.

The costs of quality are no different from any other costs in that, like the cost of maintenance, design, sales, production/operations management, information and other activities, they can be budgeted, measured and analysed.

Having specified the quality of design, the task is to achieve a service or product that matches it. This comprises activities that will incur costs that may be separated into the categories of failure costs, appraisal costs, and prevention costs. Failure costs can be further split into those resulting from internal and external failure.

Internal failure costs. These costs occur when products fail to reach designed quality standards and are detected before transfer to the consumer takes place. Internal failure includes the following:

- *Scrap* — A defective product that cannot be repaired, used, or sold
- *Rework or rectification* — The correction of detective output or errors to meet the required specifications
- *Reinspection* — The reexamination of output that has been rectified
- *Downgrading* — A product that is usable but does not meet specifications and may be sold as "second quality" at a low price
- *Waste* — The activities associated with doing unnecessary work or holding stocks as the result of errors, poor organisation, the wrong materials, and so forth
- *Failure analysis* — The activities required to establish the causes of internal product failure

External failure costs. These costs occur when products or services fail to reach design quality standards and are not detected until after transfer to the consumer. External failure includes the following:

- *Repair and servicing* — Either of returned products or those in the field
- *Warranty claims* — Failed products that are replaced under guarantee
- *Complaints* — All work associated with servicing of customer's complaints
- *Returns* — The handling and investigation of rejected products and services, including any transport costs
- *Liability* — The result of product liability litigation and other claims, which may include change of contract

- *Loss of goodwill* — The impact on reputation and image which impinges directly on future prospects for sales
- External and internal failures produce the costs of getting it wrong

Appraisal costs. These costs are associated with the evaluation of purchased materials, processes, intermediates, products, and services, to assure conformance with the specifications. Appraisal includes:

- *Verification* — Of incoming material, process setup, first-offs, running processes, intermediates, final products and services, and includes product/service performance appraisal against agreed specifications
- *Appraisal activities*
- *Vendor rating* — The assessment and approval of suppliers of all products and services

Appraisal activities result in the costs of checking that it is right!

Prevention costs. These are associated with the design, implementation and maintenance of the quality system.

- *Quality audits* — To check that the quality system is functioning satisfactorily
- *Inspection equipment* — The calibration and maintenance of any equipment used in prevention costs are planned and are incurred prior to production

Prevention includes the following:

- *Product/service requirements* — The determination of quality requirement and the setting of corresponding specification for incoming materials, processes, intermediates, finished products, and services
- *Quality planning* — The creation of quality, reliability, production/operation supervision, verification and other special plans (e.g., trials) required to achieve the quality objective
- *Quality assurance* — Creation and maintenance of the overall quality system

- *Appraisal equipment* — The design, development, and/or purchase of equipment for use in appraisal
- *Training* — The development, preparation and maintenance of quality training programmes for operators, supervisors, and managers
- *Miscellaneous* — Clerical, travel, supply, shipping, communications, and other general management activities associated with quality

Resources devoted to prevention give rise to the costs of making it right the first time. Total direct quality costs, and their division between the categories of prevention, appraisal, internal failure, and external failure, vary considerably from industry to industry and from plant to plant. The work of Juran (1974) suggested that total quality costs in manufacturing average 10% of sales turnover. Another writer on quality, Freigenbaum (1983), introduced the idea that in the average organisation there exists a "hidden plant," amounting to approximately one 10th of productive capacity. This is devoted to producing scrap, rework, correcting errors, replacing defective goods/services, and so on. Thus, a direct link exists between quality and productivity, and there is not better way to improve productivity than to convert this hidden plant to truly productive use. A systematic approach to the control of quality provides an important way to accomplish effective control.

ISO 9000. The ISO 9000 series are the national standards that promulgate, for use by suppliers and purchasers, the series international standards for quality systems. They tell suppliers and manufacturers what is required of a quality-orientated system. They do not set out extra special requirements which only a very few organisations can — or need — comply with, but are practical standards for quality systems which can be used by industry. The principles of are applicable whether you employ 10 people or 10,000. They identify the basic disciplines and specify the procedures and criteria to ensure that products or services meet the customer's requirements. The benefits of applying ISO 9000 are real: It may save money — because procedures may be more soundly based and more efficient; it may ensure satisfied customers — because you may have built in quality at every stage; it may reduce waste and time-consuming reworking of designs and procedures.

Constituent Parts

- Part 0: Section 0.1/ISO 9000 is a guide to the selection use of the appropriate part of the ISO 9000 series.
- Part 0: Section 0.2/ISO 9004 is a guide to overall quality management and the quality system elements within the ISO 9000 series.

- Part 1/ISO 9001 relates to quality specifications for design/development, production, installation and servicing when the requirements of goods or services are specified by the customer in terms of how they must perform, which are then provided by the supplier.
- Part 1/ISO 9002 sets out requirements where a firm is manufacturing goods or offering a service to a published specification or to the customer's specification.
- Part 3/ISO 9003 specifies the quality system to be used in final inspection and test procedures.

Purpose. ISO 9000 sets out how to establish, document, and maintain an effective quality system that will demonstrate to customers that organisations are committed to quality and are able to supply their quality needs. It is an internationally accepted standard and is simply common sense set down on paper in an organisation way. It has been broken down into sections to enable manufacturers to implement it easily and efficiently. Using ISO 9000 may bring real economies in its wake; economies in production because systems are controlled from start to finish, economies in resources and in time spent on replanning or modifying designs. You also have a complete record of every stage of production - invaluable for product or process improvement and in relation to any product liability claim.

Who Uses ISO 9000. Suppliers can use ISO 9000 when setting up their own quality systems; customers may specify that the quality of goods and services they are purchasing shall be controlled by a management system complying with ISO 9000 and customers or third parties may use it as a basis for assessing a supplier's quality management system and thus ability to produce satisfactory goods and services. In fact, it is already used in this last way by all major public sector purchasing organisations and accredited third party certification bodies. Exporting firms who have been assessed may find that assessment helps them to obtain reciprocal recognition of certificates where needed by overseas authorities.

Comments

A slavish adherence to sources being ISO 9000 approved can deny to the buyer organisations having the integrity and ability to deliver reliability. Bluntly it can deny access to "quality" companies, it can reduce choice and eliminate flexibility. A cynic might argue that it allows "ordinary" companies to masquerade as "quality."

ISO 14000. After the success of the ISO 9000 series of quality standards, the International Standards Organisation is nearing completion and publication of a comprehensive set of standards for environmental management. This series of standards is designed to over the whole area of environmental issues for organisations in the global marketplace. The ISO 14000 series emerged primarily as a result of the Uruguay round of the GATT negotiations and the Rio Summit on the Environment held in 1992. Whereas GATT concentrates on the need to reduce nontariff barriers to trade, the Rio Summit generated a commitment to protection of the environment across the world. After the rapid acceptance of ISO 9000, and the increase of environmental standards around the world, ISO assessed the need for international environmental management standards. The new series of ISO 14000 standards are designed to cover environmental management systems; environmental auditing; environmental performance evaluation; environmental labelling; life-cycle assessment; environmental aspects in product standards.

A set of international standards brings a worldwide focus to the environment, encouraging a cleaner, safer, healthier world for us all. The existence of the standards allows organisations to focus environmental efforts against an internationally accepted criteria. At present, many countries and regional groupings are generating their own requirements for environmental issues, and these vary between the groups. A single standard will ensure that there are no conflicts between regional interpretations of good environmental practice. The fact that companies may need environmental management certification to compete in the global marketplace could easily overshadow all ethical reasons for environmental management. The constituent parts of ISO14000 follow.

Standard	Title/Description
14000	Guide to Environmental Management Principles, Systems, and Supporting Techniques
14001	Environmental Management Systems - Specification with Guidance for Use
14010	Guidelines for Environmental Auditing - General Principles for Environmental Auditing
14011	Guidelines for Environmental Auditing - Audit Procedures-Part 1: Auditing of Environmental Management Systems
14012	Guidelines for Environmental Auditing - Qualification Criteria for Environmental Auditors

14013/15	Guidelines for Environmental Auditing - Audit Programmes, Reviews & Assessments
14020/23	Environmental Labeling
14024	Environmental Labeling - Practitioner Programs - Guiding Principles, Practices and Certification Procedures of Multiple Criteria Programs
14031/32	Guidelines on Environmental Performance Evaluation
14040/43	Life-Cycle Assessment General Principles and Practices
14050	Glossary
14060	Guide for the Inclusion of Environmental Aspects in Product Standards

Within Europe, many organisations gained ISO 9000 registration primarily to meet growing demands from customers. ISO 9000 quality registration has become necessary to do business in many areas of commerce. Similarly, the ISO 14000 management system registration may become the primary requirement for doing business in many regions or industries. For a comprehensive review of ISO 14000, see *www.quality.co.uk*, from which much of the foregoing material was drawn.

Efficient Consumer Response

Efficient consumer response (ECR) is all about managing supply and demand to ensure that the customer is never disappointed by an empty shelf where their favourite brand should be. Disappointed consumers mean lost sales and less profit. In 1993 approximately, ECR arrived in the United Kingdom from the United States via Europe, in an attempt to address poor distribution of groceries. ECR has high-level support from the major retailers and brand suppliers. They see ECR as a streamlined supply chain able to respond to the actions of consumers with cost-effective use of resources. This involves a programme of continuous improvement that embraces everything from electronic data interchange (EDI) to best practice in cross docking operations. ECR practitioners claim that gains have been realised across the entire business in terms of faster growth, improved margins, reduced stock levels, and increased integration with raw materials suppliers. This is where packaging companies have an important role to play whether it is getting their logistics operations up to speed or in developing products to ensure that new brands get to the supermarket shelf in the most appropriate container as quickly as possible. The guiding principles of ECR strategy are to:

- work constantly to provide better value to the consumer, with less cost throughout the total supply chain;
- involve business leaders who are determined to replace the win-lose trading relationships with mutually profitable business alliances;
- use accurate and timely information in a computer-based system to support effective marketing, production, and logistic decisions;
- ensure that the right product is available to the consumer at the right time, by implementing value-added processes as the product flows from the end of production/packing to the consumer's basket; and
- use of standard measurement and reward system that evaluates the impact of business decisions on the whole system.

ECR has spread to some manufacturing sectors but has not really taken hold with some viewing the concept as yet another fad. Arguably a total quality management approach is more effective (and yes, more appealing!).

Total Quality Management

Competitiveness is often measured by quality, price, and delivery. It is often a misconception that quality costs extra money in terms of inputs. The theory behind a total quality management (TQM) system is that, as quality improves, costs actually fall because of lower failure and appraisal costs and less waste. TQM involves much more than assuring product or service quality; it is a system of dealing with quality at every stage of the production process, both internally and externally. TQM is truly a system requiring the commitment of senior managers, effective leadership, and teamwork. The processes are shown in Figure 22.

The TQM system requires that every part of the organisation is integrated and must be able to work together. The main elements of the system are:

- **Teamwork**. This is central to many parts of the TQM system where workers have to feel they are part of an organisation. In addition, teams of

Figure 22. Key processes for TQM

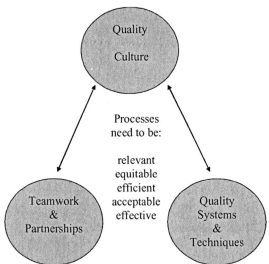

workers will often be brought together into problem-solving groups, quality circles, and quality improvement teams.

- **Commitment**. To be successful, TQM needs to be truly organisation-wide, and therefore commitment is required at the top from the chief executive as well as from the workforce. Middle management have an important role to play in not only grasping the concepts themselves but also explaining them to the people for whom they are responsible.

- **Communication**. Poor communication can result in organisational problems, information being lost and gaps occurring in the system. A good flow of accurate information, instructions and feedback is vital in maintaining the cohesion needed by the system.

- **Organisation**. A cohesive system needs to be an organised one, with clear channels of responsibility and clearly defined reporting procedures. Quality-related errors can be quickly rectified if an efficient organisational structure is in place.

- **Control and monitoring**. The TQM system will not remove the need to monitor processes and sample outputs, neither will it simply control itself. Many organisations use after-the-fact control, causing managers to take a reactive rather than proactive position. The TQM system needs a more anticipative style of control.

- **Planning**. Processes need to be planned carefully if they are to be efficient. This usually requires recording activities, stages and decisions in a form which is communicable to all. A clearly defined process reduces the scope for error, and provides the basis of an analysis into possible improvements that might be made.
- **Inventory systems**. It is in the storage of raw materials, components or the finished product that quality can diminish. The keeping of stocks is also physically expensive and can lead to cash-flow problems. An inventory control system is therefore required to keep stocks to a minimum, whilst ensuring that supplies never dry up. One such system is the Just-in-Time system.

A breakdown in any part of the TQM system can lead to organisational gaps where wastage may occur or quality be overlooked. Errors have a habit of becoming multiplied, and failure to meet the requirements of one part of the organisation creates problems elsewhere. The correction of errors is time consuming and costly. TQM can provide a company with a competitive edge. This means that managers must plan strategically both externally and internally, and that internal strategic planning has to involve everyone in the workplace.

Figure 23. The TQM diamond

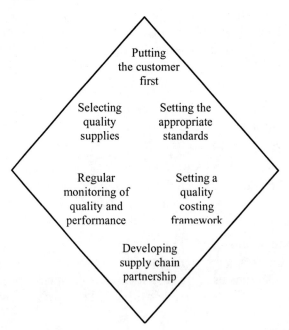

TQM is an approach aimed at improving the effectiveness and flexibility of business as a whole through the elimination of wasted effort as well as physical waste (i.e., improving the effectiveness of work so that results are achieved in less time and at less cost). The buying process is very relevant to TQM. If quality is priceless, then the TQM diamond at Figure 23 is appropriate!

Overall TQM appears to be a better integrative process. Here is a reminder of the benefits:

- Focuses individuals' roles on customers and constant improvement.
- Develops teamwork and commitment and innovation as vehicles for employee ownership of improvement process.
- Identifies and eliminates waste of resources and costs.
- Provides a basis for management development and training focused on company values and the shift from policing to enable style.

Generally, TQM may increase profits and market share — the positive way (i.e., by delighting the customer and doing it *right the first time!*).

Food for Thought

"Investors in people" is a worldwide process of ensuring that all employers are educated and trained to meet the business objectives; a clear business objective is quality. The business environment is changing. Emerging trends, such as increased global competition, new product and process technologies, increased concern for environmental impact, demands for more efficient and effective business processes, growing demand for quality and convenience and the diffusion of new information and communication technologies are influencing management strategies and tactics. Traditional management approaches that optimise specialised functional performance do not adequately address the challenges of today's competitive business environment. This is especially true in supply management where the focus is shifting toward the development of fast and flexible supply chains with renewed emphasis on quality, cost and convenient availability (Ferrin, Landeros, & Reck, 2001). In the next chapter, I will explore logistics and supply chain management perhaps demonstrating need for flexibility, and not one size fits all.

Chapter V

Supply Chain Management

If your international supply chain management is the weakest link in your organisation, your board or chief executive will say good-bye — without a winking eye. How do you know your supply chain in the age of globalisation and internationalisation is effective? Literature in its many forms contains a lack of clarity and completeness in the how to's of implementation. This chapter covers the nuts and bolts of what's required and what can go wrong. I've been there, seen it, done it and didn't get fired. Reality, therefore, pervades this chapter. Within this chapter, I will explore definitions and concepts of logistics and supply chain management, including the value chain, logistics management, global sourcing, and the bullwhip effect. Illustrations will be taken from the private and public sector along with a suggested interlock strategy.

The Role of Supply Chain Management

Where do you start? First, you have to accept there is no escape from globalisation and internationalisation of business in the 21st century. You also need to accept that in the Western world, organisations and businesses are more similar than different. What this means is that international logistics strategies are a substantial challenge for any management group. It also means these strategies must be tailored to suit the dynamic and frequently changing global environments. What changes, what environments? Remember the Soviet Union break-up; its effect still reverberates. Remember the European Union; it's about to get larger. Remember China with no money; well, they've got some now. Remember the imperial market of India; it's opening up. Remember the Middle East, all that oil money and no industrial structure; well, they've bought the technical know-how. Remember the Asian economic collapse; well, they've recovered. Australia and New Zealand businesses have world-class supply chains (Mollenkopt & Dapiran, 2005). Then there's the Internet. Convinced yet? Okay, let's move on.

Does a supply chain lead to improved performance? Yes, if you do it properly and if you understand what supply chain is. It arguably includes all activities required in order to obtain the product from the supplier and get it to the place where it is actually used. It encompasses the purchasing function, store, traffic and transportation, incoming inspection, and quality control and assurance. Some also include salvage and management of environmental issues (as they are related to materials) in procurement. What I am concerned with here is the complete supply chain. The message here is that there is a chain of events to be managed — the art is recognising that there is one and where it can be influenced in one form or another.

With major changes occurring in industry, the perception of supply chain in executive offices has failed to evolve in concert, principally due to continual changes in terminology. Nevertheless, business executives are increasingly questioning the supply chain potential for contributing to overall profitability. These questions are typified by the following comment from a chief executive of a leading organisation:

I now know what supply chain management can do to save money. Tell me what it can do to improve my profits, to increase my share of the market, to improve my cash flow, to open new territories, to introduce new products, and to get the stockholders and board of directors off my back.

Notice that the chief executive asks if supply chain can do anything important for profitability, and if so, what? Supply chain must make this profitability contribution if it is to expand its role in the company.

Expenditure on purchasing goods and services in a company may account for between 30 to 75% of total costs. Expenditure on storing and distributing materials may absorb a further 10 to 20% of total costs. Using some very different benchmarks, stock as a proportion of total funds employed can account for anything between 30 and 50% (see, for example, Quayle, 2002). Total distribution costs expressed as a percentage of sales, range from 9 (industrial manufacturing) to 34% (wholesale consumer goods). Despite this, and whilst some organisations focus on efficiency, there is little evidence of integrating logistics processes (McAdam & McCormack, 2001). The effective sourcing of material (embracing raw materials, components, assemblies and finished goods), and the subsequent management of that material through a production or value-adding process and on to the end customer, is therefore critical to the success and on to the end customer, is therefore critical to the end customer, is therefore critical to the success of most businesses. Moreover, these activities have a major impact on some of the main strategic problems facing many businesses today. Such problems will often include:

- how to reduce costs and best add value to products and services,
- how to sustain the highest quality standards,
- how to improve customer service, and
- how to adapt to ever increasing environmental pressures.

Supply chain management is a powerful means of resolving these problems. Understanding and management of the logistics supply chain is critical to any company's drive to improve productivity and profitability.

What is Supply Chain?

The underlying philosophy of supply chain management is straightforward and can be defined alternatively:

- Supply chain is the process that seeks to provide for the management and coordination of all activities from sourcing and acquisition, through production, where appropriate, and through distribution channels to the customer.
- The goal of supply chain is the creation of competitive advantage through the simultaneous achievement of high customer service levels, optimum investment, and value for money.
- The detailed organisation and implementation of a plan or operation.
- A term that was originally used in the military sphere to describe the organising and moving of troops and equipment. It is now applied to any detailed planning process in an *organisation*, which entails the *distribution* or redistribution of resources.

Supply chain concepts invoke a strategic view of thinking which seeks to account for all links in the flow of materials and related information in a flexible but integrated manner so that they perform in unison to achieve an overall optimum result for the business.

Just as marketing grew in the 1960s to encompass sales, retailing, advertising, customer relations, product design, and market research and in so doing encouraged an overview that then revolutionised the approach to serving the customer; so supply chain has evolved to encourage a similar integration of materials-related functions. Moreover, and what is perhaps more important, the supply chain approach recognises the importance of those functions both individually and collectively and the need to manage then in totality. Supply chain management coordinates and integrates all of the materials-based functions inherent in planning and forecasting, coursing, manufacturing or servicing and processing a product, and its distribution. The agile supply chain in particular is market sensitive.

- The aim is to enable businesses to keep ahead of market changes where quality, price, response time, and service are crucial factors.
- The goal is to link the market place and its distribution channels to the procurement and manufacturing operations in such a way that competitive advantage can be achieved and maintained.
- The benefits accrue in cost reduction, sales generation, much improved service levels, and increased profitability.

The Supply Chain Mix

The business functions which fall within the scope of supply chain management are included in what is commonly known as the supply chain (or logistics) mix:

- *Planning and marketing strategy* — The major influences of design and marketing on materials requirements and distribution requirements
- *Purchasing* — Source research and selection, negotiation, building supplier partnership programmes
- *Production planning* — Plant capacity, location and layout, scheduling, manufacturing resource planning, and the control and support of work in progress

- *Storage and materials handling* — The handling and storage of goods, utilisation and packaging
- *Inventory management* — Control over inventories, sustaining minimum practical stock levels, minimising holding costs, wastage and obsolescence
- *Warehouses and stores* — Location, capacity, mix and operation
- *Transport* — Mode decisions, scheduling, routing, and operation
- *Customer service* — Demand forecasting, service levels, order processing, parts/service support, and aftermarket operations
- *Technical support* — The provision and management of the systems needed to support these activities

Not all of the elements in this mix will necessarily coincide with all business interests. The logistics concept however, actively concentrates on those elements that do. Again, as examples - for the retailer of fast-moving consumer goods (FMCG) distribution, sourcing and distribution are likely to be the key elements. For the manufacturer, purchasing and production planning are naturally more dominant. Rarely will all of these elements be of equal importance to a business, but depending on its characteristics a number may be identified as having a major impact on the bottom line as well as having a critical interrelationship that requires skilful management to secure the most profitable results:

Market strategy and product design: In combination determine the nature, volume and timing of demand to be met by the purchasing operation. Additionally, marketing and engineering functions can greatly influence the extent to which the product to be procured or manufactured is "supply chain friendly."

- **Materials management**. This embraces all aspects of materials flow from determination of requirements and capacity planning through purchasing, source search and selection, and scheduling — the latter including the planning and control of production processes, applicable most commonly when manufacturing is central to the business. Tools employed to achieve effective planning and execution may include manufacturing resource planning (MRPII), Just-in-Time (JIT; i.e., the elimination of waste) and optimised production technology (OPT), as appropriate to the individual needs of the business.
- **Inventory management** (often seen as part of material management in manufacturing enterprises). Determination of stocking policy to ensure continuity of suppliers with minimum investment costs — including the effective control and execution of that policy.

- **Storage and materials handling**. This covers the safe, secure, and disciplined handling of materials as initial receipts, as parts awaiting processing, as work in progress during manufacture, and subsequently as finished product. Embraces packaging design, unitisation and the full range of simple to sophisticated aids to storage.
- **Distribution**. Includes warehousing and both inbound and outbound transportation: all strongly influenced by demands for higher levels of customer service, JIT requirements and the evolution of contract distribution. With an estimated 500,000 vehicles dedicated to freight movement in the United Kingdom alone, distribution is under increasing pressure for greater control on environmental grounds.

The Scope of the Supply Chain

The basic nature of business is that it procures or buys something, whether goods or information: changes its form in some way that adds value and then sells a product or service onto someone else. In manufacturing industries in particular, this sequence may occur a number of times:

Inbound	**Core business**	**Outbound logistics**
raw materials	process or refine	supply others
refined materials	manufacture	components/assemblies
components	assembled	finished product
finished goods	distribute	customer

At a similar albeit oversimplified level, within a manufacturing or processing organisation we can identify three basic operations:

- *Change of form* — Production or process
- *Change of ownership* — Marketing or internal transfer
- *Change of time and place* — Logistics

But these three operations are not clear-cut and do not stand alone. Taking overpackaging as an example of a process. It does not strictly change either the form of the product or its time and place, but rather its outward appearance. Packaging must, of course, be designed with a change of ownership in mind (i.e., unitisation to suit an industrial customer's needs), or display packaging for marketing. It must also be designed for movement (i.e., protection against damage, ease of handling) or for security in transit. However, the requirement that takes priority not only has a major influence on the costs of the packaging but also distribution costs. There are some apparently discrete activities that can be influenced by a number of individual functions or management areas. The supply chain concept aims to capture and to analyse such activities.

Supply Chain an Integrative Process?

The organisational emphasis of traditional business is normally on vertical line management within individual functions. Such a framework actively promotes suboptimisation, as many of the trade-off opportunities outlined previously are not visible. It is essential to highlight the pattern of materials and information flows and their interdependence. An example of the strategic process of planning integration is shown in Figure 24.

Each of these planning functions are discussed throughout this text with an emphasis on the need for integration as part of the logistics process. The key steps in the planning and integration process, highlighted in Figure 24, are as follows:

1. The organisation sets up a corporate strategic plan and mission statement
2. The supply chain/logistics element of the corporate plan (identify the broad logistics strategy and improvement targets)
3. The logistics management team accepts the challenge of developing and managing the process
4. Logistics strategic management team identifies the full supply chain/logistics base profile and mission statement
5. Mapping process, SWOT analysis, strategic review. Where are we now? Where are we going? How do we get there?
6. Start the organisational and structural review and change plan.
7. Reengineer each element of the logistics map and the supply chain process.
8. Identify the best practice "gaps," overcome the obstacles, improve the elements of effective management and processes
    (a) Identify the best practice standards, develop personal competencies to bridge the gap
    (b) Develop and improve on relevant management information
    (c) Develop state-of-the-art communications within the supply chain

9. Set demanding targets for each mapping element within the total logistics service profile and plan
10. Manage the project; individual and group elements within the team plan

Manage the performance outputs and the process of continuous improvement at every level. Feedback to process 8 and rework as required. Feedback to process 4 and rework as required.

Figure 24. Supply chain planning process

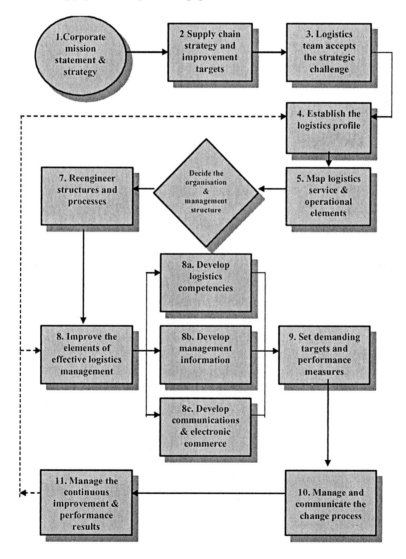

Bullwhip effect. The objective of supply chain management is to provide a high velocity flow of high-quality, relevant information that will enable suppliers to provide an uninterrupted and precisely timed flow of materials to customers. However, Kacheria (2003) suggested unplanned demand oscillations, including those caused by stock outs, in the supply chain execution process create distortions that can wreck havoc up and down the supply chain. There are numerous causes, often in combination that will cause these supply chain distortions to start what has become known as the bullwhip effect. The most common general drivers of these demand distortions are customers, suppliers, promotions, sales, manufacturing, and poor internal processes. This unplanned for demand results in a disturbance or lump of demand, which may be a minor blip for any one customer, oscillates back through the supply chain often resulting in huge and costly disturbances at the supplier end of the chain. Often these demand oscillations will launch a mad scramble in manufacturing with the need to acquire and expedite more raw materials and reschedule production. The bullwhip effect has in the past been accepted as normal. The negative effect on business performance, however, is often found in excess inventories, quality problems, higher raw material costs, overtime expenses, and shipping costs (see, e.g., Christopher & Gattorna, 2005; Kacheria, 2003). In the worst-case scenario, customer service deteriorates, lead times lengthen, sales are lost, costs go up, and capacity is adjusted. An important element to operating a smooth-flowing supply chain is eliminating the phenomenon. The most effective process for smoothing out is customers and suppliers understanding what drives demand and supply patterns and then, working collaboratively to improve information quality and compressing cycle times throughout the entire process.

The role of supply chain in today's and tomorrow's organisations will change as the value of products changes, and also as the value that buyers or customers ascribe to product changes. This statement represents a new concept for many supply chain managers, who were trained in transportation, warehousing, and other such functions to conduct their activities based on lease-cost or other hard measure priorities. Modern supply chain managers must find innovative ways to help their companies improve profits, increase market share, improve cash flow, open new territories and introduce new products. However, supply chain neither creates demand nor product. Supply chain management is the organisation that responds to demands, and creates a bridge between that demand and those who supply it. A professional and integrative approach is clearly needed.

Bottlenecks. Within any supply chain, bottlenecks are possible. For example, marketing accepting more orders than the organisation has the capacity to produce — a production bottleneck! The more a product or service is successfully marketed, the greater the number of requests for quotation — a marketing bottleneck! Purchasing, too, may not escape the bottleneck problem. Assuming production capacity is not exceeded, "late" orders can create a bottleneck by placing orders on suppliers and subsequent deliveries not in sequence with production needs.

The Value Chain and Interlock Strategy

A value chain identifies activities, functions and business processes that have to be performed in the designing, producing, marketing, delivering and supporting a product or service. The strategy making lesson of the value chain is that increased organisational competitiveness entrails concentrating resources on those activities where the organisation can gain dominating expertise to serve its target customers.

This section examines organisations failures and inability to maximise their value chains, and, suggests the value chain is like an orchestra consisting of a number of links. An orchestra develops its skills and value and there is need to develop an interlock strategy to fully utilise value chains skills and value to its constituent organisations. The design of an interlock strategy is discussed and a number of scenarios identified in order to understand what can be (and needs to be) done by both private and public sector organisations. The ultimate aims of interlock strategy are to reduce costs and increase security of supply as far down the value chains as possible in a turbulent world.

An orchestra is a collection of instrumentalists usually containing a substantial string element. The value chain is a collection of interrelated activities or strings. Both the orchestra and the value chain perform to add value. Both can perform well only if they have been assembled correctly and their constituent elements are fully understood. The intelligent orchestra practices and hones its elements to enhance its performance. The value chain once established, is often left to perform and receives little honing or enhancement. Clearly the intelligent value chain needs to learn from orchestral manoeuvres.

There is evidence that a well-managed value chain has a significant inverse relationship with average selling price. Organisations that create a greater level of trust among value chain members, communicate future needs, emphasise on time delivery and work throughout the value chain (i.e., beyond tier one) reduce their average selling price compared to competitors (see, e.g., Tan et al., 2002). The typical value chain is based on Michael Porter's model, shown in Figure 25.

Whilst the value chain is understood within (purchasing) organisations, its use beyond the organisation itself is unclear. Many would claim publicly that the Porter model is used throughout their value chain. However, in a credible survey, less than 2% of organisations participate in an "excellent" value chain and, remarkably, only 20% have a value chain strategy. A refreshingly honest view

Figure 25. Porters value chain

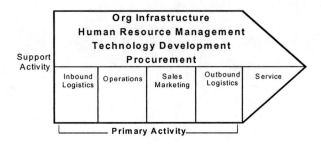

from 44% is that they see themselves as the main barrier, with some 64% of those citing lack of knowledge (training and education) as the primary cause. This all the more remarkable when cost savings, improved quality, accelerated delivery, and improved customer service have been achieved by over 60% of the small minority who have grasped the value chain opportunity. It appears that the notion that suppliers' value chains do matter; therefore, is not understood in the 21st century. To ignore the notion that costs and margins throughout the value chain are part of the price paid by the end user, whilst wonderfully attractive, is strangely naive (see, for example, Dekker, 2003; Earnst & Young, 2000).

Value chains are perceived to fail because of a lack of supplier integrity. In the global arena, they are perceived to fail for a variety of reasons including foreign exchange, quality, political instability, and logistics difficulties. These perceptions come from the purchasing organisation. It's never their fault. Is it not likely that value chain failures are more often due to not creating alliances within the value chain, not developing a listening system, not encouraging the value chain members to develop partnerships within their value chains, a lack of trust both internally and externally, an inability to broaden vision beyond logistics, and, a lack of genuine leadership?

Many organisations have clearly failed to realise the importance of (really) examining their value chains and identifying what is strategic in terms of supply exposure (Rugman, 2001). The strategic elements of the value chain are not too difficult to identify. They are those that are strategically critical and those that affect strategic security. Strategically critical elements have few major sources, no alternatives, may be safety critical and are likely to be high cost. Those that affect strategic security again have few major sources and may be safety critical but are quite possibly low cost. Both elements are likely to be supplied by the purchasers tier one suppliers and the purchaser is likely to abdicate responsibility for continuity and security of supply to that supplier. The abdication is sometime deliberate, sometimes tacitly, sometimes due to inertia. Overall, such abdication is reckless and naïve. Nevertheless, the need to be competitive and subsequent rush to be global has masked the abdication trait. The rush creates global value chains and with it an even greater tendency to abdicate responsibility for security of supply to tier one suppliers. Global value chains are inherently complex both in advanced economies and developing and transitional economies (Tan et al., 2002). With that complexity, uncertainty exists at every link in the value chain. This natural uncertainty has been enhanced by the tragic events of 11 September 2001. The mindset that drives globalisation is primarily to achieve competitive advantage. Organisations that have high operating costs and little investment in research and development generally pursue global value chains to achieve better quality, on time delivery, lower prices and if they are honest, the development of a problem solving capability or additional technology. Some pursue global value chains however, because "local" suppliers are perceived as incapable; some perceive the former Eastern European countries have a low cost base; some organisations simply want to emulate Japan. Some simply (as indicated previously in this article) do not understand their value chain (Sweeney, 2002).

Major organisations have been able to take advantage of relative peace prior to 11 September 2001 to maximise opportunities to purchase goods and services globally. This has created the long and complex value chains that are now threatened by both the worldwide terror campaign and the subsequent military response. The threat has occurred before — the oil crisis of the 1970s, in the Gulf War of the early 1990s, and the Millennium computer bug. None of these threats, although serious at the time, were long term. The war on terror however, appears to be a different proposition. Allied to this threat are other significant business issues. These issues can be categorised into the drive for competitiveness, critical factors that emerge from that drive, and power relationships. The drive for competitiveness is influenced by the instability of the world economic slowdown (which, arguably, was happening before 9/11). Fluctuations in oil and fuel prices and the sheer pace of technological change are relevant factors (Taninecz, 2000). Consequential activity has been opportunistic job losses as well as opportunities for some industries to consolidate in the market place. Critical factors that have emerged include the need to utilise the new technologies and meeting the logistics demands of the 21st century. Delivery on Thursday means delivery on Thursday, not the following Tuesday. These factors alone create pressure and significant hassle and are leading to the return of adversarial business relationships throughout the value chain.

Ironically, perhaps, those pressures led to globalisation of value chains in the first place. But what is globalisation? It is generally recognised to be the production and distribution of similar products and services on a worldwide basis — in more simple terms, providing the same output to countries everywhere. Some would argue that the reality is that globalisation has only stretched to the three continents. North America, Asia, and Europe (see, e.g., Rugman, 2001). In all some 31 nations, however, the United Nations has approximately 189 member nations and FIFA some 200 football (soccer) member nations!

The reality is that the largest multinationals are spread across North America, Asia, and Europe. Nevertheless, the war on terror poses a significant threat to both inbound and outbound logistics of companies that operate "globally." The terrorists themselves will undoubtedly carry out further atrocities that will threaten supply chains as well as kill people. The United States and allied reaction to 11 September 2001 suggests that action will be taken not only in Afghanistan. Countries such as Syria, Iraq, Lebanon, Iran, Colombia, Peru, Palestine, Somalia, Sudan, the Philippines, and Yemen could all be at risk. Europe and the United States are not immune from risk. Are organisations aware of the risk to their value chains? Based on informal contact with regional and national government agencies and with a range of companies in the Dow Jones, NASDAQ, FTSE 100, and Reuters Top 50 Scottish companies, the business priorities of today are security of supply, quality, capability to support, product reliability and time to market. These priorities are very clear, some at the expense of traditional business issues most notably price. It would appear that some organisations have at least recognised the potential threat. Some notable comments include, "Security of supply throughout our supply chain is now paramount, and we'll have to look more locally for sources of supply"; "We will probably increase centralised procurement to ensure we find more local sources of supply"; "Perhaps we need to look again at our value chain"; "My internal value chain doesn't add value, so I need to tackle the whole value chain quickly"; and, "I have no idea what happens beyond my tier one suppliers, I had better find out." Post 11 September 2001, there is arguably serious consideration being given to more "local" sources of supply.

The question becomes, what local sources of supply? A parallel question is, are these local sources strategically critical and are we simply creating a strategic security problem in our value chain if we switch to local sources? Before organisations pursue the local source policy, there is a need to examine the value chain. Within the value chain there will be an interlock link, and it is this link that needs most attention from organisations both in the private and public sector. An exemplar interlock strategy grid is shown in Figure 26, using one organisation producing three products and four tiers of the value chain. For the purposes of this discussion, tier one is an original equipment manufacturer (OEM), tier two is a supplier of subassemblies, tier three is a supplier of piece parts, and tier four is a raw material supplier. Service and support of the products are excluded. The grid shows routine single sourcing from tier one. At tier two, supplier 3 supplies all tier one suppliers. At tier three, supplier 4 supplies suppliers 1, 5 and 6 of tier two. At tier four, supplier 5 supplies suppliers 3, 4 and 6 of tier three. In this

Figure 26. The interlock strategy grid

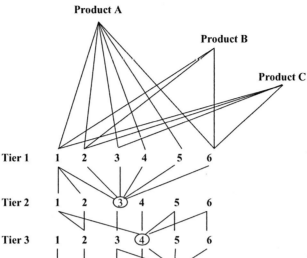

interlock strategy grid example (for one purchasing organisation's products) supplier 3 in tier 2, supplier 4 in tier 3 and supplier 5 in tier 4 are critical to the whole value chain. They are the common interlocks.

There are a number of scenarios to be examined here.

- **Scenario 1**. The purchasing organisation needs to evaluate if the respective suppliers in each tier are vulnerable and if the capacities are adequate or need protection. It would appear from the example if any or all of them ceased to exist or supply was interrupted for any length of time, it may not be possible for products A, B and C to be produced. The purchaser could therefore decide to takeover/buy out those suppliers, could decide to establish additional sources of supply and, perhaps, "free issue" material to suppliers to tiers 2, 3 and 4 of the value chain.

- **Scenario 2**. One or more of the suppliers are outside the purchasing organisation's country. The risk to the value chain needs to be assessed for example, in the context of terrorist attack/war on terror. This could be in terms of the country of origin or the logistics supply network. If the risk is unacceptable, the purchasing organisation should seek to establish a source of supply or additional capacity within its own country.

- **Scenario 3**. The purchasing organisation is an inward investment company into the host region, state, or nation. Having identified the unacceptable risk, the purchaser seeks assistance from the host regional, state or national government to develop a source of supply. This would apply particularly as part of or an alternative to scenario two. The government motivation is development of its indigenous supply base.

- **Scenario 4**. Neither the purchasing organisation or the government agencies can identify an alternative source of supply within their borders. The source of supply needs to become a priority target of the government agencies for inward investment — that is attracting the source of supply to their region.

- **Scenario 5**. From a government agency viewpoint, there is no reason for example, if product A, B and C are three separate companies, why they could not work with a range of inward investor organisations to identify interlock suppliers. They could then work with the companies to create additional capacity or if one or more of the sources of supply are not indigenous to the government's territory, develop a new source of supply. This could be achieved through investment in the indigenous supply base as part of either local economic development or regeneration agendas. The benefit in terms of new employment is clear. The benefit to inward investment companies of security and continuity of supply (to say nothing of good public relations) is also clear. This raises the question of who should design and execute the interlock strategy? The logical answer within the supply chain is the purchasing function, but much depends on the status of the function with the organisation. Figure 27 highlights the various dichotomies.

Figure 27. How management looks at purchasing (Lysons & Farrington, 2005)

Scope of Purchasing	Status of Purchasing	Purchasing Performance Measures	Focus On:
Purchasing is a clerical function	Low in organisation	Number of orders, back log, lead times, procedures	Efficiency
Purchasing is a commercial function	Reporting to Management	Savings, negotiation contracting, sourcing policy	Efficiency
Purchasing is a strategic business function	Integrated into strategic planing process	Supplier development value chain analysis, make or buy, e-procurement, outsourcing	Effectiveness

Clearly, if the organisation does not see its purchasing function as strategic, there is little point in purchasing taking the lead. Arguably, purchasing should be strategic and in the longer term should both design and execute the interlock strategy. In the short term, a multidisciplinary or cross-functional team would be a feasible option. The team needing to consist of purchasing, quality, and materials engineering and led effectively by a senior manager of the organisation — a value chain analysis project team. An alternative is to outsource value chain management and analysis where the internal skills needed do not exist internally. The interlock strategy needs to become part of every organisation's risk analysis of their supplier's portfolio. Indeed, a value chain risk analysis needs to be carried out for every new product. The strategy also needs to become part of regional, state, or national government economic development policy. Quite simply, the supply source needs protecting, developing, or creating. It is clear that when organisations endeavour to produce a viable value chain strategy, there are a number of variables to be taken into consideration. Some are more obvious than others but the scenarios dealt with in this section should help identify the variables.

Organisations who take value chain seriously need to be proactive rather than reactive. The rewards are clear — reduced cost and increased security of supply. The interlock strategy of course will become ineffective if those who are operationally responsible are incapable of executing it at the tactical level. In other words, the interlock strategy must ensure that operational capability is commensurate with the strategy. The interlock strategy is about people, expertise, and performance. It is not simply about process.

A primary aim of this section is to help both public- and private-sector organisations realise that value chain strategies are important and are not simply an add on to core strategy. There must be a value chain strategy and it must be an integrated strategy. One size does not fit all and scenario planning is important. Organisations need to shift the focus from efficiency to growth and strategic advantage. If this shift does not take place, then organisations are destined for mediocrity and at worst, doomed. Stock markets (worldwide) are beginning to realise this too, and it is one reason that share prices are moving in the negative direction. In the 21st century, organisations need to strive for a triple A supply chain — agility, adaptability and alignment (Lee, 2004). Having provided you with a number of supply chain scenarios, in the next chapter I will discuss managing the supply chain function.

Chapter VI

Managing the Supply Chain Function

The supply chain manager is concerned with not only managing the flow of materials and resources, he or she is also concerned with managing the human resources through which control of materials is achieved. In this chapter I will investigate the problems associated with staffing the positions or roles that have been defined in the structure. I shall consider aspects of recruitment and training and the preparation of job descriptions and operating manuals. People are probably the most important asset in any supply chain.

In addition to these elements of the staffing problem, I shall also focus attention on a closely related managerial requirement. This concerns techniques of directing and motivating the staff to achieve departmental and corporate objectives and to provide opportunities for members of the logistics function to satisfy their own individual goals at the same time. This topic is a controversial one and in the social environment of today, traditional views have come under severe attack. I shall consider these opposing views in the context of supply chain management.

Staffing the Department

Audit

In an established organisation structure, a periodic audit of company resources essentially must include a survey of personnel in terms of adequacy of numbers and skills to meet the needs of changing programmes, particularly in a period of growth. A responsibility rests, therefore, with the departmental manager to determine the effect of corporate plans on the department and in conjunction with the personnel department to arrange participation in the training and development programme and for recruitment where necessary. The audit will need to relate workload to current staff and assess future needs. A programme of training and experience obtained through job rotation (particularly an advantage to the specialist in developing product knowledge), visits to suppliers to obtain firsthand experience of industrial processes, formal education courses for professional training. Job evaluation for recruitment and grading requires a description of the job, and a job specification describing the personal skills and attitudes required by the duties and responsibilities (matching person to job and therefore important in recruitment and training).

Job Description

One of the classical principles of organisation is to carefully define the duties and responsibilities of each position in the organisation structure. Job descriptions specify what the holder of the position should do and they are a major determinant of the behaviour of the holder. They provide a broad statement of the purpose, scope, duties and responsibilities of particular jobs and allocate job titles. The need for such descriptions increases with the size of organisation, but even in smaller organisations it is important that the occupants of job positions know what is expected of them. They act also as a guide for recruiting staff and for the assessment of training needs. For organisations that have not yet developed job descriptions, the following steps should be taken. The first task is to prepare an analysis of existing jobs by a series of interviews both with job-holders and other staff. Job analysis is concerned with establishing why a job exists, its objectives, and how those objectives will be achieved. It is also necessary to establish its relationships with other jobs in the department, what supervision is given and received and what qualities are needed by the job-holder. On the basis of the information that is collected, job descriptions can be compiled. It is important to retain flexibility.

The following list includes the headings which could be included in a plan for the preparation of job descriptions.

- Job title
- Title of immediate supervisor
- Brief summary of the job
- Detailed description of duties
- Specific reports or information to be provided
- Decisions and recommendations made by the holder
- Responsibility for work of others
- Responsibility for accuracy of work and effect of errors
- Education and experience required

In many organisations, job descriptions form the basis for job grading schemes, which in turn are related to salary and wage structures. The ultimate objective is to prepare a rational salary scheme which gives similar pay to jobs of a similar grade throughout the company. In order to do this, it is necessary to compare the content of jobs in different departments. Various methods have been developed to evaluate jobs, such as ranking, points rating and factor comparison, with respect to such features as duties, supervision given and received, the nature of decisions taken, and the qualifications needed by the occupant. Such exercises are likely to be carried out by personnel or human resources departments, with the possible assistance of organisation and methods (O&M) specialists.

Exemplar Senior Post in Supply Chain Management

A leading innovator and provider of network and service solutions that create business opportunities for service providers and enterprises. Their solutions focus on enabling existing networks to profitably deliver and manage advanced services that are being driven by the diverse applications of today and tomorrow. The organisation has built an environment where individuals at all levels have an opportunity to assume responsibility, actively contribute, and be a part of a result-driven team. It is a fast and exciting atmosphere that lets you create your own success while helping to solve challenges for some of the world's largest networks. Will be responsible for the supply chain function relating to the supply-chain forecasting/planning, material procurement, supplier selection, inventory control, and financial reporting of the materials and products to meet organisational objectives and customer requirements. This involves the responsibility of directing and administering purchasing, sourcing, new product introduction planning and interfacing with production control, inventory control, shipping and receiving, and material stores. Oversees purchasing of inventory items, in addition to all materials, supplies, equipment, and services. Investigates and solves problems resulting from material shortages, however caused. Management of an annual material inventory spend in excess of $150 million across more than 10 product lines, with a geographically and technologically diverse supply chain. Take a leadership position for all cost-reduction initiatives associated with our material supply and sourcing activities. Responsible for defining all business processes relating to supply chain management, their documentation and ongoing assessment for efficacy of control. With the internal audit department, ensure compliance for all of these processes. Maintains optimum inventory levels to ensure on-time deliveries to meet customer requirements while minimizing carrying costs and premium transportation charges. Responsible for identifying and negotiating for new materials, suppliers, and implementing processes to achieve the best possible prices, quality, reliability, continuity and delivery. Establishes and maintains purchasing practices and policies to ensure honest, fair, and ethical relationships with vendors. Keeps informed on legal matters that affect purchasing policies. Keeps abreast of the relevant material/sourcing markets and pricing trends. Responsibility for the accuracy of product costing information contained within our MRP (Materials Resource Planning) system. Responsible for the motivation and development of subordinates to optimize their performance and their personal professional growth. Develop and cultivate executive level relationships with our key suppliers. Ensures proper contract with customers relating to releases and deliveries. Must have production control planning and scheduling program experience to meet sales forecasts. Make certain that deviations to the production schedule are investigated and properly followed up. Physical inventory procedures and implementation. Management of shipping and receiving functions and the storage of purchased parts and finished goods. Experience in managing a manufacturing plant and new product introduction processes. Requires proven track record in supply chain management and cost reduction. Well versed in current manufacturing/supply chain best practices. Capable of leading and developing a manufacturing team. Strong leadership and technical skills desired. Ability to work with executive peers to drive our business goals desired. A team player that will work well in a cross functional team environment desired.

Staff Appraisal

The staff appraisal meeting between manager and supervisor and between supervisor and individual staff member, gives an opportunity for:

- setting objectives and targets jointly in key areas of the individual's duties and responsibilities;
- the supervisor or staff member to participate in choice and setting of targets, promoting job interest and confidence in planning and in handling of problems;
- supplies the manager with facts on individual performances in support of personal judgements; and
- the setting of key objectives and the discussion and counselling involved at this stage and at the end of the period under review involves leadership and motivation, benefiting management and staff in a common purpose.

Examples of objectives agreed might be:

- a specified percentage of on time deliveries to customers;
- a specified percentage saving against standard costs within a given period;
- a reduction in administrative costs per £100 of expenditure on transport; and
- a warehouse stock reduction through improved supplier relationships and supplier development.

Operating Manuals

Many organisations have found it useful to prepare logistics manuals as a guide to company personnel. These act as a guide for employees in other departments and, for suppliers. Manuals describe the procedures to be adopted to achieve particular purposes and the rules for making particular decisions. They will also usually contain information about job responsibilities and reporting relationships, inform people about the service provided by the department and service as a guide to departmental policies regarding such issues as business ethics. The objective of such a manual is to provide a clear statement of how things are to be done and it is a useful help to newcomers. Also, it can help to resolve disputes. The drawback with this approach, however, is that it might lead to a stifling of initiative and a reluctance to tackle new problems which do not seem to be covered by the manual. Thus it is possible to argue that an operating manual is a more useful device in relatively static conditions, but less appropriate in a rapidly changing environment in which old methods and procedures may quickly become ineffective.

Qualities of Supply Chain Personnel

Discussion of organisational aspects of has indicated the wide variety of jobs that exist within the function. The desired qualities of job occupants need to be tailored to the needs of particular positions. In other words, it is not possible to prepare a simple blueprint of the ideal person for logistics work. Skill and personality profiles should vary according to the nature and complexity of the job. In spite of these reservations, however, we can make some general comments about the characteristics apparent in a member of the function.

It has often been said that the supply chain specialist is a "jack of all trades, master of none." In the sense that an effective specialist needs a sound general business knowledge this is true. He or she needs a thorough understanding of the commercial and economic background to supply chain work and must develop a detailed picture of the particular markets in which they are operating and be able to make a careful analysis of the abilities of suppliers within them. He or she must also develop sufficient product knowledge to gain an appreciation of the alternative possibilities and the commercial implications.

Technical Expertise

The extent to which detailed technical knowledge is required is a controversial issue and policies differ from organisation to organisation. One the one hand, it has been argued that the main contribution of is that of providing and analysing commercial information and of playing a leading role in the supply chain. Supporters of this view suggest that supply chain specialists should not attempt to become "pseudotechnologists" and take on the roles of designers and engineers. On the other hand, there is the belief that they can only make a full analysis of the commercial aspects of a supply chain problem if they have got a detailed knowledge of the technical features. Other departments may gain a greater respect and may cooperate more closely with a person who demonstrates an understanding of the technical problems. Thus, some organisations do see a technical training as an essential quality for some posts. It is not possible to make a judgement in this debate that would be valid for all situations. The degree of technical knowledge required can be expected to vary.

The expert will have a sound understanding of advanced techniques and should be able to apply a creative approach to supply chain problems. In applying such techniques, competence in accounting and financial areas is also important. Increasingly it is becoming more and more important to develop skills in mathematics and statistics for the purpose of undertaking analytical work. Finally, in this list of required skills and knowledge we can refer to the addition of managerial skills as individuals move into more senior positions involving supervisory and planning work. We can now consider personality traits.

Personal Qualities

It is apparent that one of the most important characteristics necessary is integrity. Communication skills play an important part in relationships. These skills involve the ability to perceive and understand points of view and points of information presented by other people as well as being able to express points in a concise and easily comprehensive manner. The supply chain specialist must be able to work closely with other people, both inside and outside the organisation and at times patience and diplomacy may be necessary when working under pressure. In situations that may threaten to stop an assembly line from operating because of supply chain shortages, individuals have to be able to cope under pressure.

Recruiting Personnel

In developing a personnel policy in the supply function it is important to plan for internal recruitment as well as external recruitment. Individual members of staff should be encouraged to develop their abilities by providing them with training facilities and an appropriate work programme with a view to future advancement to positions that will become available as a result of expansion and/or the retirement or promotion of existing incumbents. Records of existing members of staff should be kept and reviewed for training and recruitment purposes. Records showing education qualifications, specialised technical skills, appointments within the organisation and career experience with other firms, training received and a summary of appraisals and personal particulars should be maintained. Internal promotion can improve morale and act as a spur to better performance.

Careful planning should precede interview work, to decide what questions should be asked and how assessments are to be made. Many organisations like to use intelligence tests and aptitude tests as additional devices. It is important to get the applicants to talk and to provide an opportunity for them to ask questions. Two possible schemes for interviewing can be outlined.

The Seven Point Plan

The National Institute of Industrial Psychology (now defunct) has suggested a scheme for selection interviews, which covers the following still-valid features:

- *Physical characteristics*
- *Attainments* with regard to education, training, and previous experience
- *General intelligence*
- *Special aptitudes*
- *Interests*
- *Disposition* — Personal characteristics with regard to manner, and ability to get on with people
- *Circumstances* — Domestic situation

The Five-Fold Grading Scheme

An alternative scheme places more emphasis on the dynamics of personality and motivation. It also involves the use of a five-point scale for each of the five headings.

- **First impression and physical characteristics.** This covers appearance, speech, manner and personal method of dealing with others.
- **Qualifications and expectations.** This includes details of education, training and previous experience, but also expectations for the future.
- **Brains and abilities.** Much will have been learnt from qualifications, but the results of tests can also be included.
- **Motivation.** Concerned with finding out the type of work the applicant likes and the "interest pattern" of the candidate.
- **Adjustment.** This covers distinct qualities such as integrity, reliability, acceptability to others and behaviour under stress or difficulties.

If, after considering the internal potential, it is decided to recruit externally, the supply chain manager will, in most cases, call in the personnel manager to assist. External recruitment is expensive. Advertisements should be placed in the papers or journals that are likely to be read by the type of person that is required.

Especially in times of high employment, this is a competitive process and the advertisement must be carefully prepared to attract the right person by giving a clear account of the nature of the post and future prospects, as well as giving a specification of the required quality. If applicants are asked to fill in a standard application form, the task of comparison is easier. A short list of candidates for interview can be compiled from this initial screening. Recruitment is a costly process, and it is important, therefore, to fully utilise the abilities of staff once they have been recruited, otherwise they will leave. Further development of their skills is another objective; we can, therefore, now study training and education of staff as a further aspect of personnel policy in the supply chain function.

Training and Education

Successful training and development policies will enable the organisation to attract and retain able people. In today's rapidly changing world, with developments in knowledge and techniques, it is also important that staff at all levels in the organisation are provided with facilities to keep up to date. In the last analysis, better trained staff will give a better performance. No longer can organisations rest content that employees have received sufficient education and training before entry into the organisation. Many organisations have developed a training department to help in this area and to assist departmental managers in devising the right policy.

A number of steps are important in developing and supervising training. The first task involves identifying the training needs of individuals. An assessment of individual strengths and weaknesses in relation to existing and possible future jobs is a starting point. The emergence of new knowledge, new techniques and new legislation must also be monitored. Having analysed the needs, a programme of how these training needs can be met must be drawn up. The training programme, once in operation, must be evaluated in terms of the benefit accruing to the individual and the organisation. In discussing the various types of education and training that can be given, it will be useful to distinguish between in-house or internal training and external training, although some schemes combine aspects of both.

Internal Training

As regards internal training, we can first consider commercial, undergraduate or graduate apprentices. Such programmes are run mainly for employees upon entry into the organisation and are concurrent with attendance on external courses. The training in the organisation may commence with an induction course to introduce the newcomer to the structure and activities of the company as a whole. This will be followed by special work assignments under the supervision of senior staff to provide experience in the different types of work involved in the function. Commercial apprentices may be on sandwich degree courses. In addition, they may be involved in specialised courses such as that offered by the appropriate professional body.

Other internal training courses can be devised for other members of the supply chain function. The emphasis of these courses, usually intensive and short duration, would be placed on specific aspects relevant to the particular needs of the organisation. These courses, frequently of a participative kind involving case studies and role-playing exercises, can be used to develop knowledge and skills, but also to influence attitudes and encourage cooperation. Courses can be organised and run by the organisations personnel or by consultants and can be tailored to the particular needs of the organisation.

External Courses

External courses can take several forms. First, there are part-time or full-time courses provided by the state education service. These cover undergraduate and postgraduate degree courses in business studies as well as the specific courses by professional bodies. These provide a general education in commercial aspects of business and a more specific education in logistics management and the techniques used in this field. Many universities now offer doctoral and master's degrees covering supply chain management. In addition, courses in technical subjects may also be considered. Correspondence/distance/e-learning courses provide another route by which the student can gain these qualifications. The importance of providing the right training in order to operate an effective supply chain department is crucial. Attention must also be given to the qualifications of employees upon entry, but these abilities must be supplemented and built upon by further programmes tailored to their needs and the needs of the company. The human resources of the organisation and of the department should be regarded as valuable assets that need to be carefully cultivated. The maximum benefit can only be gained from providing the right environment in which the knowledge and skills of personnel can be properly applied. Often the benefits of training courses are lost because those attending are not permitted to practice what they have learnt.

Managing the Department

When considering the managerial function of directing or guiding and supervising the work of subordinates, we move into one of the most controversial topics in business. The relationship between managers and their subordinates is at the heart of what have been called industrial relations. Whilst attention in the media tends to concentrate on industrial relations on the shop floor, relations in the "white collar" work are just as significant. In addition, social changes have taken place so that attitudes affecting the expectations of employees towards their jobs have been transformed. In particular different views concerning the nature of authority in organisations have emerged and the importance of employee interests has received increased attention. We shall consider:

- the classical and neoclassical management tradition,
- the human relations tradition, and
- more recent ideas concerned with participation.

The Classical and Neoclassical Management Tradition

The school of writers and ideas that can be labeled in this manner has been and still is extremely influential. Indeed, the framework of ideas upon which this chapter has been based has been drawn from this tradition. Many of the ideas concerning the functions of management, with regard to planning, organising, staffing and controlling, remain as key thoughts in organising an employer in general or a supply chain department in particular. However, the major weakness in these traditional ideas lies in the area of manager/worker relations and the somewhat naive ideas of earlier writers concerning motivation and leadership.

The cornerstone of this tradition with regard to industrial relations lies in the view of authority and the prerogatives that this appeared to confer upon managers. Authority within the structure of organisations in the private sector was seen to be derived from the shareholders and this delegation of authority gave the board of directors and the executive managers authority to issue instructions and direct activities designed to enhance the interests of the shareholders. In turn, they were held responsible for the achievement or failure to achieve the objectives of the shareholder. In return for the material rewards of the wage or salary agreement, employees were expected to accept without question instructions that were given to them. The pursuit of efficiency and the pursuit of profit were conducted with little attention to other interests of employees. In the public sector, managerial authority was seen to be derived from either parliament or the local council and ultimately from the electors. Strict adherence to this hierarchical view of authority has led to what might be called an "authoritarian" or "dictatorial" style of management. However, this view of an arbitrary style of management has come under fierce criticism for a number of reasons.

First, the view of authority itself has been challenged. The essence of this opposition is that insufficient attention is given to the rights of employees, and these need to be protected, particularly through collective bargaining processes. Other ways of extending the powers of the employees, such as representation on boards of companies, works councils, and an extension of collective bargaining, have been put forward. Around the world, government legislation has already been passed to protect the rights of employees and it is possible that other measures to increase industrial democracy will emerge in the near future, particularly in view of existing legislation.

Second, the authoritarian style of management has been attacked on the grounds of expediency. It is argued that it is based on a misconception of human nature and that it does not contribute to maximum effectiveness. Indeed, this view classifies authoritarian or dictatorial rule as being inefficient and warns that undesirable results will emerge, such as strikes, poor performance and a high turnover of staff.

The Human Relations Tradition

The foundations of the human relations tradition are generally accepted to rest upon the Hawthorne Studies, which were conducted in the United States during the 1930s (Mahoney & Baker, 2002). The essential finding of these studies, conducted by Elton Mayo, is that individual performance can be affected by the attitudes formed by informal work groups in which the employees are located. It was discovered that the morale and attitudes of such groups could be either favourably or unfavourably disposed towards the achievement of corporate objectives and the acceptance of managerial instruction. Furthermore, it was suggested that workers were concerned with obtaining not only monetary rewards, but also satisfaction of social needs from belonging to the group. The implication for management of this point of view is that attention must be given to techniques of supervision. Instead of relying on coercive methods, using only financial incentives and punishments, supervisors are recommended, by this school of thought, to develop ways of influencing group attitudes and gaining the support of employees for organisational objectives. The emphasis is placed, therefore, on the social skills of supervisors, designed to remove any antagonism in informal groups toward the formal requirements of the organisation. Importance was attached to communicating a sense of purpose and developing teamwork. However, difficulties attached to this view have become apparent; it tends to underestimate the importance of material rewards and it ignores some of the factors that can influence group attitudes. In particular, it ignores the influence of external forces, such as trade unions. Nevertheless, the development of this tradition was a useful counterbalance to the instrumental view of employees adopted previously.

Participative Approaches

New ideas have emerged during the last 10 years or so which have their origin in both the findings of the human relations school and in the more general opposition to authoritarian rule in society as a whole. These ideas are also based upon a different conception of the basis characteristics of human nature. The thrust of these views is to allow individual employees greater scope to exercise their basic talents and sense of responsibility. Instead of giving a rigid prescription of what job-holders should do, it is advocated that more discretion should be allowed so that they can use their initiative in solving problems. This extension of responsibility has been called "job enrichment," and to it others have added "job enlargement." The notion, underlying this second term is that jobs should not be divided up into too narrow a task, which might lead to boredom and monotony. Furthermore, the roles allocated to employees should include participation in the setting of objectives and the making of decisions that affect them. The essential feature for management in this school of thought is that managers should adopt a consultative style and encourage a joint problem solving approach.

Psychologists agree that this participative approach allows individuals the opportunity to develop the full potential of their abilities and satisfies their wishes to exercise more control over their work. It is argued that this desire for autonomy is increasing in advanced industrial societies. On the basis of this analysis, managers in designing organisations should establish a less rigid structure that creates an environment in which abilities can be developed. Too much reliance on prescriptive and coercive techniques will not utilise the full potential of employees. Rewards should be closely related to the achievement of objectives, but employees should be given freedom to select the means of achieving them. They should also be allowed to participate in the setting of the objectives in the first place.

The right of the manager to manage following these later ideas is justified less in terms of managerial prerogative and more and more in terms of expertise. Acceptance of managerial authority by subordinates may also, therefore, be based on the competence of the managers. Concern for people as well as concern for results is important in motivating people according to this third school of thought. The drawback with these later ideas concerns the problem of whether all people want, or feel happy with, the participative approach. Some people prefer to be given detailed instructions of what to do and experience stress if they are left to decide for themselves. Also, in situations that are straightforward and unchanging, there is evidence to suggest that firm decisions taken by the managers are more effective.

Implications for Supply Chain Management

In the dynamic and rapidly changing environment that exists today, there are no simple prescriptions in directing the work of the department. It is necessary to develop a sensitive perception of the needs of both the organisation and of subordinate staff. Attitudes need to be based on an analysis of the situation that exists, and situations vary from organisation to organisation. In some organisations, in which unions play an important part, a different approach is required from others in which employees are accustomed to a more authoritarian style. However, it is possible to argue that the task of the supply chain staff is one that can be done more effectively by people who are permitted to exercise initiative. Very often, within their particular commodity range, they are the ones with the most expertise. There is scope, therefore, for encouraging a participative approach, at least in the higher levels of the department. It is important that the supply chain manager maintains awareness of new developments and, in particular, an awareness of new legislation. Many people have suggested that social technology lags behind advances in other forms of technology. Nevertheless, it is of fundamental importance to develop a personnel policy and a managerial style that effectively utilises the talents of members of staff and that satisfies both organisational and individual objectives. In achieving this ideal, managers need to develop a sensitive awareness of the factors influencing performance. It is important to provide the appropriate training support to increase the value of these human resources.

Management and Implementation of Change

In order to achieve objectives within an organisation, changes are likely to become necessary from time to time. These changes are achieved through staff.

The outcome will depend upon the effectiveness with which this process is managed.

Strategic Change

Internal and/or external factors are likely to signal the need for change.

External factors might include legal changes, socioeconomic, technological, and so on.

Internally, it might be a change of objectives or mission, new staff with different ideas. Managing strategic change is concerned with a change in the "culture of the organisation." One can identify two main stages in the process of change:

- Unfreezing or breaking down previously held beliefs and assumptions
- Reformation of new sets of beliefs

Recipe for Change

The recipe is a set of beliefs and assumptions which form part of the culture of an organisation, and have been called

- paradigms,
- recipes, and
- interpretative schemes.

Unfreezing Process

We can identify from the above, a number of ways of unfreezing the existing recipe; for example:

- signal (downturn in performance),
- challenge and exposure of the existing recipe,
- reconfiguration of newer structures, and
- intervention of an outsider (i.e., someone with little commitment to the existing recipe).

Other Methods

We can implement change by:

- changing formal control mechanisms;
- structural changes;
- symbols of change (e.g., ICI [Imperial Chemical Industries] change; Harvey Jones, a flamboyant character, bright ties and not in the traditional ICI mould); and
- organisational structures, because they communicate "readily understood" visions of the organisation's mission or role.

Political Nature of Change

Management of change has political implications. If change is to be successful, you will need to manage and manipulate the political power structure.

Supply Chain and Change

Increasingly, proactive organisations are recognising that the supply chain, far from being just another operational variable, is uniquely placed within the organisation to manage the interrelationship of all the factors which affect the flow of both information and goods necessary to fill orders. This flow begins when the customer decides to place an order and ends when the order is fulfilled and monies collected. Organisations that believe that the single output of any organisation is customer service understand the strategic significance of logistics in this process. They know that, to succeed in today's environment, they must adopt a disciplined and systematic approach to the market, create carefully considered priorities, allocate resources in the strictest possible manner and make often difficult trade-off decisions. It is not yet common for the supply chain manager to be involved with the initial phases of an organisations strategic planning. However, the size of the corporate profit slice that supply chain affects is sufficiently large to suggest that the supply chain manager should be a key figure at the strategy formulation stage. In describing strategic planning as the process of formulating plans that ensures the long-term profitability of an organisation, we earlier referred to actions taken in anticipation of customer needs. The supply chain manager is the only person in the organisation charged solely with managing all flows of information and materials in the conception to consumption chain and their interactions. It is this unique position that provides the logistics manger with an appreciation of the organisation's capacity to respond to expectations.

Strategic planning forces management to reconcile two almost contradictory tasks: long-term (visionary) planning with short-term responsiveness to customers. To achieve this seemingly impossible balance we must focus on the "strategic" side of planning and not consider strategy to be just another word for *long term*. Strategic planning covers three steps as far as supply chain is concerned:

- *Vision statements* (what we stand for)
- *Aims* (directions we want to go in)
- *Objectives* (specific quantified targets)

The chief executive is in the best position to understand the expectations of "stakeholders" (shareholders and employees) and the organisation's long-term goals. Accordingly, he or she must be the one to articulate the vision statement. The difference between aims and objectives is the difference between quantitative and qualitative analysis. Aims are the qualitative statements, the expression of desires and goals. Objectives are quantitative and therefore must be measurable. It is not enough to set an objective as "increasing sales" because there is no way to determine if the objective has been met. Increasing sales may be the aim, but increasing sales by 3% within 6 months is the objective. This gives a finishing point and a specific target. Once the aims and objectives are established, operational plans can follow.

Proper procedures for implementation, control and evaluation are needed to translate plans from mere words on paper to actions on the ground. This is where effectiveness of the logistics manager will determine the success or failure of the whole planning effort.

The creation of a strategic plan does not provide a guarantee of success; rather it provides a frame of reference against which changes in the environment external to the organisation can be evaluated. In this way the organisation can respond to both anticipated and unexpected changes in the external environment in a planned manner. It is this ability to evolve and adapt that distinguishes the strategically oriented organisation from its endangered counterpart. Remakably, managing the supply chain function and activity is essentially the same whether the organisation is public or private, large or small. The critical success factors are strategy and deployment of technology (see, e.g., Gunasekaran & Ngai, 2003). Getting it right is important and not easy (Slone, 2004). The strategic planning process points the way forward for organisations that aim to be progressive and proactive in the years ahead. Supply chains, and the role of the supply chain manager, are being recognised by strategically oriented organisations as key ingredients in successfully meeting the challenges of these increasingly turbulent times. Supply chain mangers must adopt a strategic approach if they are to be equal to the challenges that await them in the future. In the next chapter, I consider operating environments that create these challenges.

Chapter VII

Operating Environments

Understanding the supply chain and logistics in operating environments is important to understanding the total concept, and we need to examine a new method and compare it to or examine problems of existing methods. To illustrate this, a specific example of logistics support in the aircraft industry needs to be considered; the principles however, are the same for any capital equipment project. An overview of the 3-day car programme is an interesting comparator.

Integrated Logistic Support

Integrated logistic support (ILS) is a structured and coordinated approach to support planning that will produce the most technically efficient and cost effective support solution. ILS is an American concept that was introduced by the U.S. government in an attempt to combat their spiralling support costs and to give a structured approach to support planning so as to let it influence the design process. The concept was developed and became a military standard which provides a framework that can be tailored to suit individual projects and user requirements dependant upon budgets, time scales and project size. The reason for adopting ILS is that the customer will make it a contractual requirement of the project with the aim of meeting the same objectives.

Integrated Logistic Support: Main Objectives

What is wrong with present systems, and why do we need ILS? Past problems can be grouped together to give three main objectives.

- *Reduce support costs* — past project support costs have risen to an unacceptable level
- *Ensure support influences design* — so that the product is designed to be as supportable as possible at the first attempt
- *Ensure the timely development and acquisition of resources* — all the required resources are to be in the right place at the right time

Reducing Support Costs

What exactly is a support cost? It is the cost, incurred by the customer, through owning and operating a product (e.g., an aircraft). It includes repairable components, technical publications, aerospace ground equipment (AGE), petrol oils and lubricants (POL), and contractor site representatives. Largest of all is the customer's labour costs.

Previous Support Costs

As products have become more complex, support costs have risen. The effects of these high support costs seriously jeopardise the chances of a supplier being awarded further contracts.

Potential Export Contract Support Costs

An example of the effects of high support costs on circa £250 million an export contract would be useful. Assume the product is an aircraft. If we allow £20 million per aircraft, then the support costs, at present rates, come to around £11m for each aircraft. To keep costs within the customer's budget the present support rates mean that the customer is going to be limited to eight aircraft. A fleet of eight aircraft means no better then six aircraft being available on the line — and having only six aircraft means sortie patterns of three pair or one diamond four. The effectiveness of all this in air-defence terms, in relation to the total cost, is probably not a viable defence option compared to other national budget demands.

In any national budget squeeze an early cancellation of the aircraft sale is likely — and the loss of important export revenue to the manufacturer. To emphasise how support costs dictate the number of aircraft a customer can purchase let us look at support costs. The effect is that high support costs can affect the actual numbers of aircraft that the customer can purchase. These support percentages are expressed as a proportion of the cost of an aircraft.

At 100% support costs, the customer gets six aircraft for £120m and £120m worth of support.

At 50% support costs, the customer gets eight aircraft for £160m and £80m worth of support.

If we reduce the cost of support to 33% of the aircraft costs, then we could supply nine aircraft.

But the bottom line — where we should aim — is if we managed to reduce the cost of support to 20% of the cost of that aircraft, then we could supply the customer with 10 aircraft — a more realistic figure with which to form a defence policy. Manufacturers do not lose orders through poor product performance — they lose orders because prospective customers cannot afford to keep the product in service.

Costs: Initial and Recurring

Having established the effect the support cost can have on a project, and that they must be kept to a minimum, let us look at what support costs are made up of. Support costs fall into one of two categories:

- *Initial costs* — Those borne at the time of the initial purchase such as test equipment, training, spares, and publications.
- *Recurring costs* — Those costs that are continued throughout the life cycle of the project. The major cost drivers in recurring costs are usually the upkeep of documentation, the cost incurred by the need to keep training manpower, but invariably the major cost driver is labour in the form of maintenance and repair.

The more we can improve the reliability of the product, the less would be the requirement for maintenance and repair, thus the lower the recurring costs. The main reason for keeping recurring costs to a minimum is that they are subject to inflation and as such can considerably influence the support costs throughout the life cycle.

How Support Can Influence Design

It would help if the product were designed to be as supportable as possible. An example of how costs escalate because of a poor supportability design and the failure to rectify it follows. In this particular example, a small alteration is needed to make the fitment of an item easier by changing the size of a securing bolt. If, during the design stage, a possible alteration is identified that could make the product more supportable it would take £10 to alter the drawing and no more than that would have been required. Had the project been in the development phase a modification (mod) kit would have been introduced — and the drawings altered — it would have taken £100. During the production phase, the stores quantity would have been altered, the mod kit purchased — and the drawings altered — the cost would have been nearer £1,000. If the product had been in service and the same bolt size changed to improve the products supportability, by the time you take into account the modification kits, stores catalogues, stores changes, product downtime, retrospective fitting, and labour — the cost of the change is nearer £10,000. The costs quoted are fictitious, but the effect is not. If we can influence the design we shall end up with a design that has been influenced by support — not support that is influenced by design.

Acquisition of Support Resources

The date an aircraft will enter service on is called the *in service date — ISD*. Three months before this occurs, all the agreed support requirements, facilities, and equipment are to be in service and ready for use. This date is called the *logistic support date — LSD*.

To achieve the requirements for LSD, there is a large amount of work to be carried out. Try to imagine the planning that is required to ensure that everything is ready to go:

- All the necessary training has been carried out so that both aircrew and engineers are competent
- National Publications database is compiled and up to date, and publications are printed and are available, as required
- All support equipment has been identified, developed, and is in the place at the correct levels ready for use

This planning applies to all the support requirements for the aircraft or any other significant product. It is the job of ILS to ensure that the agreed support package is ready, in all respects, for LSD.

Three Main Objectives

There are three main objectives and areas to concentrate on:

- reduce support costs,
- ensure that support influences design, and
- develop and acquire resources in a timely manner.

As well as the three main objectives, mistakes made on previous projects should under no circumstances be allowed to happen.

Past Problems

Various support disciplines have often been left to their own devices in producing support plans for their particular area. These are just a few examples of what went wrong in a, fictitious aircraft programme. The initial intention, stated in-service repair, would be from day one (ISD). All planning for the provisioning of spares necessary to support his date was carried out only to find that the ISD had slipped 3 years. This may seem beneficial in the that it provided a lot more item; unfortunately, it also allowed numerous modification to be introduced that resulted in the support disciplines planning for targets that had long since changed. The technical publications department of the various partner companies were working together to compile a joint set of publications. Unfortunately, these partner companies were not interested in Batch 1 aircraft, as their respective air forces were not going to receive aircraft until Batch 2. Therefore the three partner companies were working to widely differing Logistics Support Dates. You can imagine from this the confusion that reigned. It is a prime objective of integrated logistics support to ensure that the lessons have been learnt and that these same mistakes are not allowed to occur again.

Uncoordinated Logistic Support

There has been very little use of automatic data processing systems, and when they have been used they have been used for individual needs rather than as a coordinated attempt to construct a common support database. This unstructured and uncoordinated approach to support planning has some disciplines "talking" to each other — and others not at all. This, along, with an unstructured approach to support project management, has contributed much to the problems encountered.

Coordinated Logistic Support

It is necessary to bring everyone together and to pool their efforts into one coordinated and planned structure. That structure is called "*integrated logistic support*." This focal point is the means of achieving the objectives of ILS, that is, *logistic support analysis* (LSA). We shall look at LSA in more detail later but first let us see how the structure of ILS management will help us achieve our objectives. For consistency, the example is an aircraft; the principles remain the same for any major product.

ILS Management Structure

Integrated logistic support management is divided into three groups:

- Aircraft support group
- Supplier control group
- Programmes and budgets group

The ILS manager can be responsible to two directorates; to the support director and to the project director. Although it may look unusual for a manager to be responsible to two different directorates, if we are to accomplish the objectives, then the ILS manager needs to be on equal standing with the technical managers on the project. This is normally a condition of the contract placed upon the manufacturer to ensure that ILS and the support directorate has equal standing along side the technical areas.

Aircraft Support Group

The aircraft support groups' main task is to ensure that progress towards the "total support of the aircraft" is kept in view at all times and that the support disciplines work towards this concept. To this end we undertake various tasks:

- Ensure that the costs of support are reduced and that only the most technically efficient and cost effective approaches are adopted
- Review the maintenance policies as produced by LSA
- Monitor the reliability and maintainability targets and help propose ways that we can recover from any shortfalls
- Carry out life cycle costing between comparable procedures and policies
- Introduce ILS procedures into aircrew synthetic training aids (ASTA) and groundcrew training aids
- To ensure that interfaces are established between disciplines using ADP systems
- Act as interface for queries, particularly from the customer but also from any section in the company involved in the support process

Supplier Control Group

Supplier control groups act as the ILS/LSA interface with the suppliers of aircraft equipments and, in due course, the suppliers of test equipment for these equipments. Their duties include the following:

- Control of vendor assessments relative to ILS
- Control of vendor supplied support information
- Production of line-item networks against each equipment vendor — their primary objective is to identify items of equipment that will become phased support candidates
- Planning and controlling the introduction into service of phased support items

Programmes and Budgets Group

The programmes and budgets group plans, monitors, and reports progress on ILS matters to management and, on behalf of the management, to the customer. It also issues the work directives to the ILS disciplines and manage the ILS budgets. To achieve this, it is split into three areas:

- Programming and reporting
- Budgets and directives
- Meeting and briefings

Let us look at how the work packages for the integrated logistic support disciplines are issued and how they link in with the programmes that are used to monitor the overall ILS progress.

Statement of Work and Work Packages

Initially, a statement of work (SOW) is issued from the customer detailing work packages that need to be undertaken for the project to be completed. The SOW consists of various work packages, all required to ensure that the required tasks are fully completed, on time. These packages are then discussed with the relevant disciplines and their contents and time scales agreed. Finally, the work package is issued as a formal directive. As tasks are completed and the project progresses there will be a need to update the directives and issue new ones as targets and requirements change. Once the directives have been issued we need to monitor their progress and ensure that they are completed by the required dates.

Integrating the Support Elements

We have outlined the main objectives and some of the short falls of previous projects. We have also shown you an organisation that can be set up to implement ILS and manage the support activities. Now, we will discuss the system that will integrate discipline and structure support planning activities. This system is called logistic support analysis (LSA). The aim of this part is to give you a working level view of logistic support analysis. It will not be an explanation on how each discipline should carry out logistic support analysis in their particular area or a guide on which computer systems you may need to employ. What it will be is an overview of how LSA works; how the information is generated, what happens to it once it has been compiled, and how each of the disciplines fits into the process.

Logistic Support Analysis

Logistic support analysis is used to:

- add discipline to the ILS task,
- integrate the support disciplines, and
- provide a structured process to achieve optimum supportability.

That is, it must be potentially repairable or that it causes a maintenance task to be carried out; an inspection, a removal or replacement, a functional test, and so forth. We have identified candidates for LSA, but how do we keep track of each them? We can assign each candidate an individual logistic control number (LCN). The LCN is made up of up to 10 digits depending on what level of the system you are looking at. First, a letter identifies the aircraft. The next two digits represent the appropriate system. Following that the subsystem and then the sub-subsystem. The next two digits represent the individual LRIs in the sub-subsystem. Following that we identify the modules within that LRI and, finally, the last is the submodule, which is normally a character.

If we look at a typical system — for example, the crew escape and safety system — we can see just how a system breakdown code and numbering conventions work. At the top is the system, numbered in this example 95. Below that we have the subsystem, designated the "Ejection Seat and Survival Kit." The first subsystem in the "Crew Escape and Safety System" is designated 951. The first sub-subsystem is the "Ejection Seat" (single seat and twin seat rear) and is therefore numbered 9511. The fourth LRI is identified by its LCN, which 951104 and in our example this corresponds to the "Parachute." So, you can see how each LRI has its own individual logistic control number and how that number is generated. Below this level, modules within the LRI would have the same LRI LCN, but they would have two further identifying digits. Finally, a submodule would have the full LCN for the module, but it would normally have a character rather than a digit at the end. This system breakdown structure and numbering system gives traceability — we can easily identify where an LSA candidate belongs within the aircraft. So, we have our list of candidates, and they have all been numerically identified, but how does this logistic support analysis work? The easiest and only way to imagine LSA is to forget whatever you have heard and to think of the most logical way in which you would analyse an item of equipment in order to identify what its support requirements will be.

First of all we take an item of equipment and tabulate all the basic information that is available for it. This information will come from the items' spec, the information supplied by the manufacturer of the item — the Use Study. The next step is to analyse this information. We need to identify maintenance tasks because it is only through knowing how we will maintain the aircraft that we will know what support requirements will be needed. To identify a maintenance task for an item we must anticipate how the item will fail. To this end we carry out a failure modes, effects and criticality analysis (FMECA) on the item and predict how it will fail and how critical that failure will be. It cannot be stressed enough how important the role of FMECAs play in any support requirement identification process. If we do not know what the potential failure modes of a particular item will be then we cannot identify maintenance tasks. If the mathematical part of the analysis is incorrect then the reminder of our Support analysis, and that of the provisioning activity that is based on "Mean Time Between Failures" and "Mean Time Between Maintenance Actions" will be incorrect. Provisioning is in essence calculating the quantity and type of spares required. The result of an RMECA allows identification of essential maintenance tasks to prevent failures occurring. Even if no preventative tasks are identified the fact that a failure mode exists means that at some point the item will fail and have to be replaced by a serviceable item. This action is called "Corrective Maintenance" because its sole task is to restore the system to a serviceable state. Having identified the maintenance tasks that are applicable to the item through analysing the failure modes effects, the next logical step we take in identifying support requirements is to group all the tasks identified together so that we can then look at each one in more detail. We can now take each task and carry out an in-depth analysis on it. Each step of the task is itemised so that a sequential description is documented. As we go through this procedure we may identify the need for support requirements. For example, if we are going to change a transfer isolate valve when it fails we would need tools to remove it — these would be identified. If the valve needed to be functioned after it had been fitted, then it would not be unreasonable to identify a training requirement if the function involved a new test equipment. We now have a list of tasks, described in full sequentially, and a list of proposed support requirements.

Now, the remaining support disciplines can become involved and analyse the support requirement, as applicable to their own areas. For example, support equipment can look at the requirements for tools for work on the removal of the valve and training can analyse the need for new courses to train tradesmen in the use of new test equipment to function the valve. Facilities will look at the requirements for providing the buildings and support to carry out the work, and so on.

So, to recap:

- We have itemised the maintenance requirements for the equipment under consideration.

- We can highlight potential failure modes. From these we can identify the corrective tasks and the preventive tasks after carrying out the maintenance analysis. We then list the tasks that are applicable to that item together.

- And last, we can analyse each task in full and identify the support requirements needed. The remaining support disciplines can now carry out their in depth analysis on their own particular areas and in doing so the complete support package for the valve will be generated. Part of this support package will be the level of repair required. Given industry's general inability to effectively manage repair(s), this area of analysis is particularly important.

Level of Repair Analysis

From the end of the support requirement identification, a basic supportability trade-off is carried out that will identify whether it is more economical to repair the item in service or to just discard it when if fails. Should we identify the fact that the item will be discarded when it fails, then the LSA process will be stopped here — there is obviously no need to carry out further in-depth analysis to identify support requirements when as soon as the item goes unserviceable it is thrown away!

Assuming the item is repairable, we can carry out a more in-depth level of repair analysis (LORA). If an item is identified as being more economical to repair then, as industry would provide all the support facilities, the LSA process will be stopped here. Normally it would be most unusual to find industry cheaper for a repair option over the life cycle of an aircraft because the customer has extensive repair and overhaul facilities. But should this be the case then the most economical support option will be implemented. LORA determines the most cost effective maintenance policy for each item in the system over the whole life cycle of the aircraft. Each combination of support options is examined for each item, both as an individual and as part of the overall system. In the absence of any overriding customer policy constraints the option showing the least life cycle costs is chosen. At times such as this we can provide the justification, through LSA to the design engineers that an alternative approach on their behalf is needed. If we can highlight the undesirable areas and point out the savings that can be made if we alter them, we have the ability to influence the design process. This is a main objective in integrated logistic support.

Life Cycle Costs: Early Design Influence

The need for early design influence by support is therefore clear. The major support decisions are made as the item is designed due to the inherent designing in of support requirements. In doing so they are committing the majority of our costs at an early stage. Unfortunately, although these costs are committed at an early stage they are not actually paid out until the items go into service and it is at this time everybody starts complaining about the costs of support. That is why we must influence design to reflect our supportability requirements. Whether the design has been changed or we have come up with an alternative approach or data is updated we shall have to reenter the data and re-analyse our analysis. At least with an LSA system we are able to change our minds and view the consequences over the whole of the support disciplines quickly and with a relative amount of ease. This process of refining data, known as *iteration* (a good LSA buzzword!), enables us to achieve the optimum support solution. To recap on the objectives of LSA:

- We can add *discipline* to the requirements of the integrated logistic support tasks by providing a process that is common to all disciplines.
- We can *integrate* the support disciplines.
- We can produce a *structured process* using the analysis steps that will ensure that all decisions are recorded and that an audit path exists for each decision.

This has been a basic and broad overview of the LSA process. Large areas of information have been discussed in a short period, and much of this has been stated in a very simplistic manner so as to ensure that you have had an insight into all the different areas of LSA. LSA is new method of carrying out what has gone on for many years, but it is here to make us more efficient and the product we sell more supportable. Integrated logistic support is a structured, coordinated and disciplined approach that will:

- harmonise all aspects of support or a product,
- optimise support levels to customer's policies at minimum costs,
- ensure that the product is fully supported to the required level at logistic supply date,
- produce a more reliable and maintainable product,

- ensure that the support costs are a much smaller proportion of the total costs and that recurring costs are as smaller a percentage of initial costs as possible, and
- lower the product life cycle support costs.

The adoption of ILS, working within its structure and cooperation between the respective functions will lead to greater customer satisfaction.

Logistics Information Systems

It would not be prudent to recommend a specific information system or database primarily because each business entity has its own needs. To effectively manage a concept such as ILS, each entity needs to establish its information needs; a method of establishing such needs is to carry out an information strategy planning project. The purpose of the information strategy planning (ISP) project is to examine the information needs of the business and to develop a plan to ensure that the Logistics function is effectively served with information systems that match the business, its needs and provide clear business benefits. It is fundamental that the ISP is driven by the business, this will be achieved by the following approach:

- Development of a partnership between the information technology (IT) function and business management who will direct and steer the process
- Development of a clear understanding (by the IT community) of the business, its needs and priorities as identified by the businessmen
- Identification of the business systems and supporting equipment infrastructure required by the business
- Development of an approved investment plan for the provision of the system identified, together with the respective costs and benefits

It needs to be recognised however, that in today's highly competitive environment, many organisations are going global to acquire market share and take advantage of higher production and sourcing efficiencies. A key determinant of success is the role of logistics. To compete effectively the strategic importance of logistics regardless of sector and manufacturing techniques (Doran, 2001; Sum, Teo, & Ng, 2001).

Methodology: Workshops and Questionnaires

It is important to allow everyone within the logistics and supply chain to discuss what they do, how they do it, and suggest ideas for improvement. Following the workshop, questionnaires covering objectives and strategies and information needs need to be completed by the same group of people. This is the key to prioritisations.

Detailed Analysis of Results:

This will involve:

- identification of all the business systems required by the business (this will be achieved by detailed analysis of the results from the workshop and questionnaires using formal systems analysis techniques for structuring information);
- identification of the coverage of current systems against the business systems required;
- deficiencies between the business systems required and those already in place will be highlighted and taken forward into detailed plans for the enhancement or replacement of existing systems; and
- equipment infrastructure required to support the findings will be identified and plans developed for its implementation.

It should be noted that the purpose will not be to replace the existing infrastructure and systems across the board. Although in some areas this may be necessary, it is envisaged that the plans resultant from the ISP will build on the enhance much of what is already in place. The foregoing is a brief summery of what is required. We need now to look at the workshop. The purpose of a workshop is to gain a collective understanding of the linkages between the business plan and the business information needs in the area(s) that the workshop is examining. Not surprisingly, these linkages are expressed using the same terminology of business plans and strategy (i.e., mission statement, objectives), but it should not be thought that they are redefining these elements.

Mission Statement

The business plan contains a mission statement briefly defining the overall purpose and direction of the organisation. This statement will not be changed as a result of the ISP analysis. A mission statement should "provide the customer with a total quality service and secure continuing and expanding profitable business to year 2010 and beyond." There may be lower level mission statements to give a particular group of business activities focus. For human logistics the mission statement could be identified as "to provide a quality proactive logistics service to enhance and support the programme aims to the customer." However, a local mission statement is optional.

Objectives

The business objectives are defined as the broad long-term results that the organisation wishes to achieve. Topically, objectives relate to the financial, market, customer service, quality, products and services, and people aspects of the organisation. They are likely to be represented in the form of a hierarchy. For example for logistics a key objective is to "to secure a measured improvement in the quality of Logistics services provided to the customer." This has supporting objectives: "Comply with the customers' support requirement both in terms of quality and timeliness in the supply of spares," and "work towards a marked improvement in the clearance of repairs." Typically, 10 to 20 key objectives would be identified at each workshop.

Strategies

The strategies will define existing, or planned initiatives, deploying the organisation's resources, to achieve one or more objectives. Strategies are the "means" by which objectives are achieved. The more specific the strategy, the more useful it is to the formulation of the IT plans. For example, the strategy "to improve clearance of repairs" is rather vague. The strategy "to improve clearance of repairs by wider product inspection and more selective testing" is stronger, pointing to specific information needs and activities and indicating where IT could provide support. For example, in relation to the logistics objectives "expand the content of 'hands on' training through extending the time operatives spend on the actual product" and "examine the speciality training standards and make adjustments where appropriate," there should always be at least one strategy supporting an objective and, in many cases, more than one.

Performance Measure

Progress in the achievement of objectives and the implementation of strategies is monitored by performance measures. For example, for the logistics objectives, "number of customer warranty claims" and "products delivered against products found faulty on delivery." It is possible for an objective or strategy to have many performance measures and a performance measure to support many objectives and strategies. It is a characteristic of a mature business strategy plan that a high proportion of objectives and strategies have performance measures. It is envisaged that in the region of 20 performance measures will be identified at each workshop.

Critical Success Factors

A critical success factor is a key area where things "must go right" for the organisation to achieve its objectives and goals and implement its strategies. An example of typical critical success factors are "must clear repairs within one month for all customers." By definition, the number of critical success factors is small. It is envisaged that in the region of 10 CSFs will be identified at each workshop. Their main use in the ISP process is to understand the overall priorities of the organisation.

Critical Assumptions

Associated with every business plan are critical assumptions. It is essential that they are made explicit and fully understood. Critical assumptions will usually relate to the organisation's structure, competitor activity, technologies market and economic conditions and legislation. For example, from logistics, "it is highly probable that the customer will move more and more towards incentive contracts to minimise defects found on product delivery."

Business Activities

The high-level activities (functions) performed by the organisation will be identified. The activities will implement the strategies identified, support the operations of the business and generate the information need requirements. It is anticipated that, initially, 50 to 80 activities will be identified. Example activities associated with logistics are repairs/spares management, employee administration, manpower planning and monitoring, logistics strategy and policy management, recruitment management, employee development, employee relations management, and health and welfare management. These can be divided into subactivities. It is anticipated that 30 to 50 business activities will be documented at each workshop.

Information Needs

Information needs are unstructured statements defining the data required to support the organisation. Information needs relate to a range of strategy planning objects including:

- Objectives
- Strategies
- Critical success factors
- Performance measures
- Business activities

This is why it is vital to identify these statements and gain an understanding of how they relate together. Information needs will be categorised by the type of need they satisfy (i.e., whether they satisfy strategic, planning and analysis, monitoring, or transaction requirements). Examples of information needs for the logistics area are:

- Number of repairs received in any given period
- Number of new spares orders received in any given period
- Number of vacancies to be filled, broken down by position and skill

It is anticipated that approximately 100 to 150 information needs will be documented at each workshop.

Issues and Problems

Issues and problems will include:

- current systems support for the business strategy,
- major planning concerns and issues raised by management,

- areas of business plan which are incomplete or are lacking in detail,
- conflicts between departments within the business, including incompatible strategies,
- major areas of uncertainty and risk regarding the business plan, and
- differences in perceived priorities (from the objectives and strategies priority questionnaire).

Each workshop will be run by members of an ISP core team, with a further ISP team member documenting the results. The results will be issued to all workshop attendees immediately following completion of the session. The ISP team members will ensure continuity between workshops, and more than one workshop may be needed so that the results from each workshop are progressively built upon.

End Product

An information system that will meet the needs of the business and not the desires of a salesman!

Logistics and Other Organisational Functions

The principal interrelationships between logistics and other organisational functions are:

- the relationship between the marketing function (or noncommercial equivalent) and the physical distribution subfunction of logistics, and
- the relationship between the manufacturing function and the physical procurement and materials management subfunctions of logistics.

However, for the organisation to be properly served by an effective logistics system, similar coordination problems have to be solved in both interrelationships. Logistics is concerned with activities from throughout the enterprise. These activities interact for purposes that are to the enterprise's benefit. Materials flows affect all parts of an organisation and its relations to other organisations.

The major difficulty is that the traditional functional orientation of managers put organisational activities into departmental boxes — production, marketing, purchasing — which tends to limit an overall appreciation of the management issues which affect the entire organisation. Logistics can only be efficiently and effectively conducted if it is seen by managers as being concerned with the *totality of related functions* within the organisational systems:

- Production
- Marketing
- Purchasing
- Finance
- Personnel
- Information processing

Also, logistics can only be efficiently and effectively conducted if it is seen by managers as being concerned with the *total subfunctions* within the logistics system:

- Materials handling
- Transport
- Warehousing
- Inventory control
- Unitisation
- Packaging
- Information processing

The twin objectives of logistics are:

- to *minimise* logistics costs, and
- to *optimise* customer service levels (and ideally to do both simultaneously).

These objectives are achieved by trade-offs between these subfunctions and functions so as to minimise total logistics costs and/or optimise total logistics service levels. To take the first objective, costs may be deliberately incurred in one function or subfunction in order that the performance across several functions or subfunctions may be optimised. To put it more simply, total logistics costs can be minimised by balancing individual logistics costs. For example, the more depots a company owns, the less its transport costs *but* the more its depot investment and running costs. Examples of possible trade-offs are as follows.

Trade-offs between *elements* of logistics *subfunctions*:

- Choice between more sophisticated and expensive packaging against reductions in other handling and warehousing costs
- Choice between improved efficiency in prediction of demand for inventory against the holdings of inventory levels sufficient to cope with uncertainties of demand
- Choice between the firm's own road freight transport ("own account") against brought in ("hire and reward") road freight transport (own account is more expensive per mile travelled but much more flexible so it might reduce overall logistics costs)

Trade-offs between logistics *subfunctions*:

- Choice between improved warehousing facilities and reduced materials handling costs and improved flexibility in modal choice
- Choice between improved cost control procedures in warehousing and reduced difficulties and costs in total logistics planning
- Choice between improved information processing facilities and reduced costs and improved service levels elsewhere through greater organisational intelligence

Trade-offs between organisational *functions*:

- Choice between more selective and distribution cost-conscious marketing initiatives and a rationalised physical distribution effort
- Choice between improved materials planning and control and rationalised requirement for warehousing space and materials handling
- Choice between improved order processing facilities and rationalised manufacturing planning procedures

- Choice between research and development investment in producing products that can easily be distributed and reduced logistics costs

Trade-offs between the organisation and its *sources and customers*:

- Choice between promoting improved materials handling
- facilities on the part of customers and improved possibilities for unitisation and palliation
- Willingness of suppliers to make deliveries within a "time window" convenient for the organisation and reduced costs for delivery
- Willingness of suppliers to deliver "Just-in-Time" and reduced organisational requirements for inventory holding and control

Total logistics management requires to be built around the search for cost and service trade-offs to improve efficiency. There is a need clear need for the development of information systems sophisticated enough to support the demands of comprehending the detail of costs trade-offs, cost versus service level trade-offs, and trade-offs within varieties of service. Equally as important is having the skilled personnel to conduct logistics management.

Logistics Action Planning

The example of aircraft logistics shows clearly the need for planning. Indeed, planning is almost a generic activity throughout the discipline (and this text!). Figure 28 displays an action-planning table for "inbound" logistics activities. In many ways the action plan reflects the messages in earlier parts of this text; it should not be viewed as "utopian" — without it effective logistics will be extremely difficult. Figure 29 displays the corresponding action planning table for "outbound" logistics activity. Again, all essential for an effective logistics service

Other Examples of Logistics Operating Environments

Symbol Technologies Limited (Wokingham, UK) and ICL have assisted the major high street supermarket Waitrose to introduce self-scanning to its stores to enable customer check out time to be reduced. Called *Quick Check,* the system began at Waitrose's Abingdon store. It does away with the tedious task of unloading and reloading goods at the checkout and allows shoppers to keep a

Figure 28. Inbound logistics planning

Customer Requirements Forecasting	Supplies Forecasting	Purchasing	Suppliers Vendors
Better customer sales/demand forecasts	Improve forecasting methods	More effective buying methods	Improve supplier relations
Quicker information flow	Better computer systems	Better purchasing research	More reliable suppliers
Improve customer information data	Use of EPOS (electronic point of sale)	Adopt better buying methods/techniques	More competitive suppliers
Develop customer partnering	Quicker flow of information	Apply VFM (value for money) criteria in buying	Set up supplier benchmarking
Clearer specifications	Better market trend and status data	Better qualified buyers	Develop supplier partnering
Better requirements planning	More regular updates of forecasts	Better Logistics management methods	Use TQM (total quality management) suppliers

Figure 29. Outbound logistics planning

Stores Management	Distribution to customers	Customer Service
Lower stockholding costs	Better distribution service	Match/Exceed customer expectations
Better use of stores space	Quicker Distribution Service	Improve existing service
Lower stores operating costs	Lower distribution costs	Deliver better Service
Better use of capital equipment	Improved distribution planning	Deliver faster Service
Higher stores service levels	Right first time	Get everyone's commitment to better service
Agree performance and levels & targets	Minimum of paperwork/admin. costs	Continuously improve service

running tally of their spending as they tour the store. The system is based around Symbol Technologies' Portable Shopping System (PSS). The hand-held terminal incorporates a bar-code scanner that allows customers to scan the bar codes of items they select, totalling their bills as they fill their trolleys. The customer then returns the PSS terminal to a special dispenser, where a bar coded bill is automatically printed for taking to a dedicated express checkout. Quick Check is also installed in four other UK stores (Reading, Ruislip, Wokingham, and Finchley) and roll-out to a further 16 branches is expected.

Securicor Omega Express has invested £3 million in a project that will radically enhance its existing proof of delivery service, via the implementation of 3,500 hand-held terminals to all its drivers. The largest company within Securicor Distribution, Omega Express is the United Kingdom's leading business-to-business parcels carrier, handling over 2 million parcels every week. Omega Express' next-day service operates from a national network of 98 branches, employs 8,500 staff, and runs a fleet of 4,000 vehicles. Central to the customer's decision to use Omega Express to despatch its consignments is the company's reliability, customer service and its ability to provide prompt and precise information regarding the whereabouts of all its consignments. Customers access this information, either through Omega Express' "Signline" customer service centres or automatically via their own IT systems. Symbol Technologies portable data terminals (PDT3100) and ring scanners (RSI) are speeding up the availability and accuracy of this information. This Omega Express initiative is in direct response to customer demand. The most admired logistics and supply chain systems in the early part of the 21st century are Wal-Mart and Dell.

Another example of a different operating environment is the work aiming to produce a 3-day car. The 3-Day Car programme aims to develop a process framework through which a new car can be ordered, manufactured, and delivered in just 3 days. This will require a number of changes that will have a significant impact on environmental management. The major areas of change will be the number of deliveries to assembly plants will increase to permit product flexibility without holding significant stocks. Batching for paint must not constrain vehicle assembly. Ideally, the paint process must be capable of colour batch sizes of one. This will increase pollution and waste from changeovers using current painting systems. The delivery of new vehicles to customers within one day will increase the kilometres driven for delivery per car. Design factors will impact on the recyclability of the product, both positively and negatively. For further information about the 3-day car programme and executive briefings, see their excellent Web site at *www.cf.ac.uk/3daycar*. See also Holweg and Miemczyk (2002). In the next chapter I will review provisioning and inventory control.

Chapter VIII

Provisioning and Inventory Control

Provisioning and inventory control is crucial to a wide range of organisations in ensuring a smooth operation of the supply chain. Getting it wrong can be disastrous.

Provisioning

Sainsbury's, a major supermarket chain in the United Kingdom, compounded four major errors. It introduced technology too quickly; the project plan was 7 years and they cut that to 3 years using a "big bang" rather than an incremental approach. The automated system did not meet expectations. It was a thought 2.5 million cases a week from around 2,000 suppliers to approximately 500 outlets every day would be no problem. In many outlets, however, only 19 out of a shopping list of 30 everyday items were actually in stock. Sainsbury's used Just-in-Time (JIT) predictive replenishment as opposed to sales-based replenishment. Availability and flexibility became very difficult. Sainsbury's followed ineffective strategies and worked against the market. For example, it specified pallet sizes that were markedly different from the industry norm. These four major errors put the Sainsburys supply chain out of touch with its customers. A necessary prerequisite of deciding upon provisioning and stock replenishment policies is to codify and classify stock.

Some 20% of stock items account for 80% of the value of stock held; therefore, if you strictly control stocks of these items, you are controlling the greater part of stock values. Classification enables these items and the remaining 80% of stock to be easily identified. This is sometimes known as pareto analysis, and it is illustrated in Figure 30. A system of reduction and the standardisation of stock items will reduce the number of individual items carried in stock and enable stock control to be more effective. First, consider what the term *provisioning* means, so that you have a clear definition in your mind. It is the determination of when to order and how much to order so that stockholding may be kept in line with management policy. The responsibility for provisioning will fall to different departments, depending on the size of organisation and the class of stock. In small organisations, provisioning will be carried out by the storekeeper who will raise requisitions against minimum or reorder levels, any items not stocked being

Figure 30. Pareto analysis

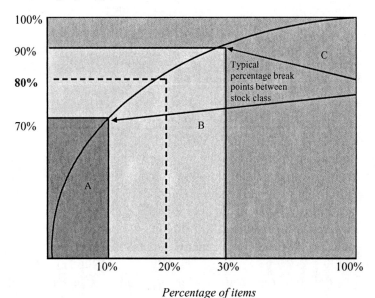

requisitioned by the user's department. As size increases so the responsibility moves to stock control, production control or planning departments, until you find separate provisioning sections in the largest organisations. It is impossible to generalise on where the provisioning function will fall in the overall structure. However, in one class of stock it will certainly be the responsibility of the stock controller, this being those items shown on a general stock list. A general stock list shows those items, which will be held in stock for common use and not for specific contracts. Based on a policy of this nature, the responsibility for provisioning must be with the stores manager, through stock control and provisioning staff.

General Stock Items

What are the two main points relating to provisioning? They are when to order and how much to order. The factors affecting the need for stock are shown in Figure 31.

When to order:

- When stocks fall to reorder levels.
- When an additional forward load has been advised.

How much to order? There are many links in the stores chain that should be reviewed and assessed in order to develop the full strength of the chain.

Figure 31. Factors affecting stock needs

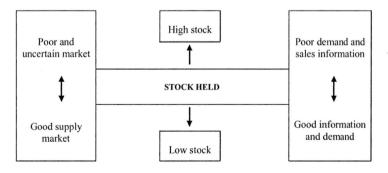

Order Quantities

There are five main considerations to remember when arriving at an order quantity, and these are the basis of any formulae.

The Accuracy of Forecasts

This will be of prime importance and every effort should be made to check as the period of a forecast passes, to compare actual usage with the estimated usage. Where differences occur, some action is required to adjust forecasts in order to increase the accuracy of these. An important point to keep in mind is that as the period of the forecast increases, so does the probability of error, a point that is obvious but often forgotten. Where long-term contracts are placed, close attention must be given to the rate of call-off as alterations are not always easy to arrange, particularly in the short term. Therefore if the rate is insufficient it may well be 2 or 3 months before an increased rate can be obtained, longer if further production equipment is necessary.

Storage Space

It is essential that all items provisioned have suitable storage facilities on receipt, bearing in mind that may overflow may have to be housed by an outside warehouse for which rent will be payable. The main point to bear in mind that any such extra facilities should be known in advance from careful consideration of the intake, and not be discovered when goods are left outside because there is no room in the storehouse.

Cost of Ordering

The cost of ordering is calculated over a year and averaged to give a nominal value of ordering each item; the cost encompasses enquiry, proposal, evaluation, and order placement.

Cost of Storage

The cost of holding stock can be represented in Figure 32.

Figure 32. Cost of holding stock

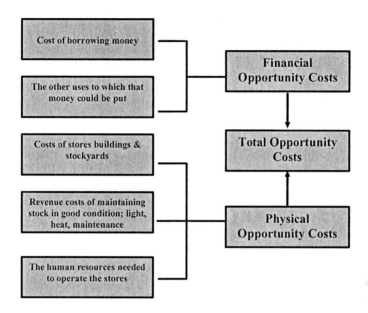

The cost of storage is calculated over a year and averaged to give a nominal value as a percentage of value of each item. It does not necessarily represent the true cost of stocking a particular item.

Acquisition Cost

The acquisition cost is the cost of storage plus the cost of ordering and if you consider this statement you will appreciate that there is a balance between frequent ordering and high stockholding. The following examples show this and the relevance of the value of the item.

Commodity X	
Purchase price	10p each
Rate of use	4 per week
Cost of storage	5 %
Cost of placing orders	£1 each

	Ordering every week	Ordering 1 year's stock
Purchase price	£20.80	£20.80
Cost of storage	NIL	£3.12
Cost of ordering	£52.00	£1.00
Total	£72.80	£24.92
= Price each	35p	12p

Commodity Y	
Purchase price	£20
Rate of use	4 per week
Cost of storage	15 %
Cost of placing orders	£1 each

Purchase price	£4160.00	£4160.00
Cost of storage	NIL	£624.00
Cost of ordering	£52.00	£1.00
Total	£4212.00	£4785.00
= Price each	£20.25	£23.00

These examples demonstrate that the higher the unit purchase price becomes, the lower is the relevance of the ordering cost. They also demonstrate that there is a relationship between the cost of storage and the cost of ordering.

Items not Contained in the General Stock List

There are still two questions which provide the key, how much to buy and when. Consider these two problems separately.

- *What quantity should be bought?* This must be governed by the programme laid down for production of the finished items, usually a function of top management. What are the factors affecting this?
- *When should the purchase be made?* Again, this must be governed by the laid-down programme, but there is room here for local initiative to decide when to purchase, ensuring that the material arrives by the required date.

Responsibility for Provisioning

In considering items not on the general stock list the responsibility for provisioning cannot rest with the stores manager. The opening paragraphs of this chapter provide some ideas as to where this responsibility may fall.

Methods of Provisioning

The provisioning department, or user if the item required is not a production material, raises a purchase requisition for the requirement. This requisition may take several forms. It will, however, contain the following information:

- *Code no.* — where these are used;
- *Quantity* — in standard unit of issue or accounting;

- *Description* — where this is not supported by a code number, it must contain all the information necessary for purchase. It may be dispensed with when code numbers are in use and the description inserted at a later date;
- *Standard price* — where these are in use, again this may be inserted at a later date;
- *Suggest suppliers* — this may be left blank or completed for special items to assist the purchasing department;
- *Job or contact number* — showing which works order the material is for;
- *Date required*;
- *Delivery address* — this will be within the organisation and indicates where the goods should be routed after inspection; and
- *An authorised signature.*

There may be other information required, depending on the needs of a particular organisation.

The completed requisition is then sent to the stores manager so that he or she can check that this item is not held in stores; he or she may also keep a record of recurring items with the object of putting them on general stock or offer an alternative. After this check it is passed to the purchasing department for action.

The provisioning department makes out planning sheets for each assembly or subassembly, giving details of material requirements. These will show the quantity of an item per unit, which has to be extended for a total requirement. In many instances, parts lists are used for this purpose. These provisioning sheets are sent to stock control, which action those items that are held in stores and forward the remaining items to purchasing department for action. It may well be that you will find a situation in which stores provisioning section do not pass on the planning sheets, but forward purchase requisition for action. There is a great disadvantage to this system where one item is used in more than one subassembly, as all the requirements will not appear on one sheet.

The provisioning department issues a complete list of parts, or bill of materials, to stores who action this in the same manner as a planning sheet. This gets around the problem of parts appearing in different subassemblies.

A computer issues a purchase requisition for those items not on general stock and a stores requisition for items on general stock. This is a very fast operation and has the advantage of being able to present the information in the most useful manner; for example, by presenting items by part number, supplier, or unit order. Keep in mind that, although the responsibility for provisioning does not rest with stores, all the items may require storage prior to use and therefore all purchase requisition activities may be carried out by this department. There are several classes of goods that will be provisioned direct from the user department to purchasing, stores being advised of their future receipt by a copy of the purchase order. The following are typical:

- Plant and machinery
- Office equipment and furniture
- Special items for the maintenance department
- Vehicles

A great deal of the information on which provisioning is based relies on forecasting., and so it is desirable to consider some aspects of the foregoing techniques used. An outline of the main foregoing techniques is given in the following section; however, bear in mind that they are relevant to many aspects of management and not only to stores and inventory control.

- **Graphs**. You will find many examples of graphs used to illustrate situations in which there are two variables. It is of course possible to present the historical data graphically and then project the future trend by draughting. This is useful to predict future trends in a general manner but not satisfactory for detail forecast. As an example, next year's financial needs could not be forecasted by this method, but the trend of future capital requirements in the succeeding years could be.
- **Exponential smoothing**. This is a technique by which a weighting factor is incorporated in the average demand. The weighting factor is known as alpha, written, with a value between 0 and 1. The basic equation is

    New average demand = D + (1 -) Old Average Demand

    D = the actual demand for the most recent period

    The use of this equation gives emphasis to the latest actual demand figures.
- **Forecast error**. Extending the principle in paragraph 2 the following equation is used:

    New average forecast error = Current Error + (1 -) Old Average Forecast Error

This forecast error is important when using statistical methods for determining future requirements, because it will influence the setting of minimum stock levels. The higher the forecast error, the higher the minimum stock will be for safety reasons.

Cyclical Provisioning

There is one method of ascertaining "when to order," which has not yet been covered, namely cyclical provisioning. Where items of a similar nature are in constant use. There is likely to be a constant flow of purchase requisitions resulting, for many instances, in uneconomic purchasing. This can be overcome by provisioning the whole group of items at the same time at regular intervals such as 1 week, 1 month, every 6 months, or possibly once a year. The following classes of items are typical examples of those suitable for this type of exercise:

- *Small tools* — drills, tool bits, soldering iron bits
- *Fastenings* — nuts, bolts, screws and washers
- *Toilet items* — soap, towels, toilet paper, disinfectant, items which can often be purchased from one source to advantage

Although provisioning of this nature is performed regularly, there must be protection against stock running out. To do this minimum levels are set and urgent action taken if stocks fall to this level, there must also be a maximum to prevent overstocking.

The Provisioning of Matching Items

Varying the principle of cyclical provisioning, there is one aspect that is often neglected — an appreciation of the need for a mating part, for example, the provisioning of a bolt without a matching nut or washer. Although this is not an easy problem to solve, attention can be given to lessen the likelihood of a stock imbalance, marking stock records to bring matching items to the notice of the provisioning clerk. This will also lessen the danger of an item being deleted from the general stock list without actioning the mating item. There is one danger in this approach that you may recognise, namely that a mating part may be used for several different parts. Going back to the example of a nut and bolt, the nut will almost certainly be used on several bolts of varying length.

Other Examples of Demand

A wholesaler holds stocks of products for retailers. Stock are held to satisfy the wholesaler's customers — the retailers. The demand for the products arises from outside the organisation. Therefore the wholesaler has no control on this

Figure 33. Solutions to independent demand

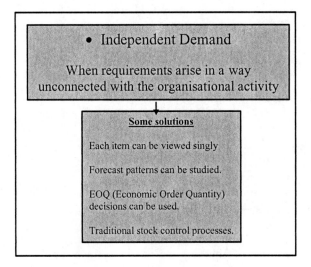

Figure 34. Solutions to dependent demand

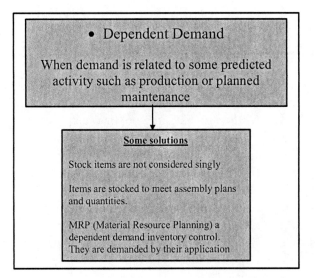

independent demand. However, the successful wholesaler forecasts the needs and demands. This is demonstrated in Figure 33.

A manufacturing company assembles components into a finished product; stocks are held to meet planned production quantities. These are items held against a dependent demand. The finished stocks offered for sale are, however, demand independent. This is demonstrated in Figure 34.

The use of computers can greatly facilitate the provisioning activity, particularly where mathematical formulae are used. This is an operation which is carried out at great speed. A computer also has a good memory and can rapidly assemble and compare data, a useful asset when provisioning mating parts.

Automatic Replenishment

This is an adaptation of the old "two bin" method of provisioning, when the storekeeper had two bins for an item. When both were full, it represented maximum stock, when one was empty this represented reorder level.

Today, under automatic replenishment methods, figures representing these levels are indicated on the stock record, and when the are reached the correct action is automatically set in operation. In practice this would be built into the computer programme, and the computer will print out wither a recommendation for action, or a purchase order if it is a routine item, appropriate purchasing information is also programmed.

The Use of Computers

The use of advanced electronic equipment is becoming widespread in many field. The use of computers is leading, and is particularly prevalent in, the accounting function couples with management statistics. Gradually the use of computers is extending into many activities — airline bookings, railway timetables and stock control are typical examples that make use of a special quality possessed by this equipment.

That special quality is memory, from which the machine can draw information and make decisions. Any decisions made will only be as accurate as the information and instructions given to the machine but they will maintain this accuracy when repeated. Remember, a computer can make decisions!

Information is an integral element of business management in general and the logistics process in particular. Systems support all key processes, finance, marketing, production, planning, design and all support services. Depending on the size and capacity of systems the links and outputs vary widely. Within logistics and supply chain management there is a vast range of systems available to operational and strategic managers.

Point of Sale

During the past 20 years, retailing in particular has gone through a period of continuous change as customer demands have intensified in a competitive world. The speed of change has been enhanced by e-commerce. The successful retailers have utilised e-commerce to great effect. Point of sale (POS) is the key link in e-commerce systems. This link has enhanced inventory management, reduced costs and increased flexibility (Weber & Kantamneni, 2002).

Case Studies of Computer Solutions

The Problem

Marston's, the UK brewers, needed a comprehensive warehouse management system for their bottled beers, wines, and spirits warehouse in Burton on Trent. In achieving the objectives for the new warehouse, all physical aspects of the operation had to be managed, with decisions made minute by minute, based on what is actually happening on the warehouse floor.

The Logistics Business warehouse management system was chosen. The software is configured from core modules and is designed to be adapted to the precise operational requirements of each user. At Marstons', a paper-based version of the system manages all aspects of the operation. In designing the solution particular attention was paid to ensuring the system meets current and anticipated future storage and warehouse throughput requirements of the warehouse. The software operates on a PC Novell network, linked to Marston's host mainframe computer system. Fastest moving items are picked from a forward picking face, which is dynamically managed addition of Radio Data Terminals, were also considered at the design phase. The system may also be integrated by *The Logistics Business* with other logistics operational software; for example, a proof of delivery system or vehicle scheduling and routing software.

The Success

Productivity has improved. Operators are directed to put away and picking locations. The operating disciplines of a computerised warehouse management system have improved stock accuracy and allow a true perpetual inventory to be maintained.

The Problem

At Europe's leading manufacturer and distributor of doors, window frames, and cubicles, Crosby supplies directly to builders', merchants, and construction sites. Deliveries were large, involving a full trailer travelling 2 or 3 days on the road to satisfy orders. An independent review of Crosby's logistics recommended the creation of stockless depots with more flexible delivery capacity. The required vehicle scheduling software. Optrak 3, the vehicle scheduling software supplied by *The Logistics Business* was the choice. Goods are trunked overnight on vehicles with draw bar trailers to the stockless depots. Onward delivery is by smaller vehicles with demountable bodies. The key to operating with Crosby's stockless depots, is planning the scheduling and routing of vehicles with Optrak 3. Crosby had a manual pigeon-hole system which was too slow and limiting for the new approach. Optrak 3 is a state of the art vehicle scheduling package designed for use with Microsoft Windows. The package is easy to use, with modules for both daily operational or strategic planning purposes.

The Success

More efficient load planning has helped to reduce distribution costs. The scheduling process is reduced to a short period each afternoon. Customer service has improved. Optrak automatically takes account of delivery time windows, vehicle access restrictions, vehicle's and drivers' hours regulations.

The Problem

Quaker Oats UK wanted to control and monitor the despatch of haulier loads and receipt of supplier deliveries at one their major production sites in London. They needed a system to book time slots on vehicle docks for deliveries and finished good collections. The system was also required to provide information on supplier and haulier conformance. *The Logistics Business* were able to supply Dock Manager, their yard management software to meet these requirements.

This is a networked, PC-based package that provides booking clerk, dock management, and gate functions. It can give a real-time overview of what vehicles are on site and on dock as well as providing key management information. The system was initially installed to handle the haulier loads only. It allowed the cheapest haulier for a given route to be selected from a database containing standard rates, contact names and telephone numbers. A booking time can then be agreed on and reserved on a dock. A terminal in the dock office is used to book the vehicles on and off the dock and to record the number and type of pallets received and despatched. As the security gates were not initially available, Quaker made use of a parameter that allows vehicles to be booked directly onto the docks. Once the gate was operational changing the parameter allowed vehicles to be booked on site and off site as well as on and off the dock.

The Success

Vehicle movements on site are efficiently managed, avoiding congestion. Haulier-billing is now just a matter of printing the appropriate report. Detailed reports on the performance of hauliers can be produced allowing poor performing hauliers to be identified. Vehicle turnaround times are monitored.

More information about The Logistics Business Systems and Software can be obtained through the company's Birmingham, UK, Office (++44 121 333 6303 or fax ++44 121 333 6407; *www.logistics.co.uk*).

The Objectives of an Inventory Control System

Whatever decisions have been made on stockholding it is essential that there is enough capital to back up policy. Because this capital will be tied up in stores, management will want this money to provide the maximum return or use. Consider the following points which can affect efficiency.

Efficient Control by Stores

- There is no need to stock large quantities of goods which are available at short notice. It may be possible to avoid any stockholding if stocks are under review constantly.

- Stores can ensure that any supplies received are directed to the location required and not routed for use on another project. You should note, however, that stores cannot ensure that an item is used for a particular job and that stores should forward items as directed by a responsible authority in the user department.
- Any materials which are lost because of their perishable or fragile nature or through theft, represent capital which has been expended to no purpose.
- A close watch on the rate of turnover can ensure that the minimum of working capital is required to finance stockholding.

How Controls are Exercised

- The basis of control is the setting of standards in stock levels, receipts, issues and rates of turnover. These standards are set in relation to a known programme. By regularly reviewing actual performance against the present standards, the success of the laid-down programme can be assessed. The system for setting standards must be flexible to allow for correction after each check.
- Various classes of items should be treated separately showing any variations that indicate that the inventory is out of balance. For example, the value of sheet steel held in stock has increased by 20%, but the value of paint used for finishing it has dropped 10%. This is worth investigating.
- Often, when studying the standards for various classes of goods, you will find that certain standards account for the bulk of the money held in stock. These should be given special attention to ensure that they have a regular rate of turnover. This does not mean that other classes should be neglected.

There is one important point to be remembered: Constant checks should produce some action when a departure from the plan is found. Remember, the ability of the organisation to control such activities can be a measurement of the success of the original budget or plan. For this reason, the budget must be flexible.

Why Do Controls Have to Exist?

Stock values have to be ascertained for the purposes of budgetary control, financial accounting and confirmation that items are priced correctly when issued.

This is done from stock records or a physical check of stock, more probably from a combination of the two. You must remember that those materials that have not been charged out, but which have been physically issued, should be included in the evaluation. Typical examples are materials which have been sent to a site and free issue materials sent to suppliers. These are sometimes missed. When a stock valuation has been arrived at for the various classes of stock, possibly covering different storehouses, the inventory control account is checked to see if the balances agree. However, discrepancies arise, even in the best of organisations, for any of the following reasons:

- Goods received notes and issue notes have been incorrectly priced and consequently entered at an incorrect value on stores or accounts records;
- Prices for issues have been made against standard costs;
- Prices for issues have been approximated to the nearest selected monetary unit (e.g., two decimal places). This often occurs where item are purchased at a price per 100 or 1,000, and the price of each unit does not coincide with a unit of money;
- Through an incorrect posting on a stock record (which will cause two errors; e.g., through a posting not being entered on any stock record); through incorrect reading of code numbers;
- When variations found during stock checks are not entered on records;
- Incorrect arithmetic causing the balances to be entered wrongly; and
- Errors made during any copying of the reports.

When you consider these points, discrepancies are bound to occur. If this is so, why bother to check them? You should think about this before going on.

When discrepancies occur the inventory control account has to be adjusted. This is done by a stock valuation adjustment entry, and a debit or credit note made to the balance. This entry has, of course, to be verified and agreed by the accounts department who will usually keep a separate subsidiary account for these entries.

Strategic Planning

What the previous sections reinforce is the need for a strategic planning process. This is shown in Figure 35.

Figure 35. Stores & inventory management strategic planning process

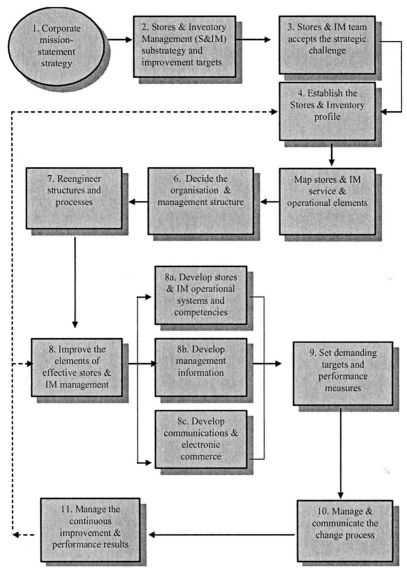

The key steps in the stores and inventory planning process, derived from Figure 36, are shown here:

1. The organisation sets up a corporate strategic plan & mission statement.
2. The supply chain/stores & inventory management element of the corporate plan:

Identify the broad logistics strategy and improvement targets.

3. The stores & inventory management team accepts the challenge of developing & managing the project & process.
4. Stores & inventory management strategic management team identify the full supply chain base profile and mission statement.
5. Mapping process, S.W.O.T. analysis, strategic review:

Where are we now?   Where are we going?   How do we get there?

6. Start the organisational and structural review & change plan.
7. Reengineer each element of the stores & inventory management map within the supply chain process.
8. Identify the best practice "gaps," overcome the obstacles, improve the elements of effective Stores & inventory management & processes.
    8a. Identify best practice standards, develop personal competencies to bridge the gap.
    8b. Develop and improve on relevant management information.
    8c. Develop "state of the art" communications within the supply chain.
9. Set demanding targets for each mapping element within the total stores & inventory management service profile and plan.
10. Manage the project — individual and group element within the team plan.
11. Manage the performance outputs and the process of continuous improvement at every level.

>   Feedback to process 8 and rework as required.
>   Feedback to process 4 and rework as required.

The Physical Aspect of Inventory Control

Because we are considering the physical aspect of inventory control, it will be useful to restate the main purpose of this aspect, which is to provide user departments with materials as and when they are required whilst making the most economic use of working capital and minimising storage costs.

The first problem to be considered when engaging in inventory control is deciding what items should be stocked. The following are some of the factors affecting this choice:

- Delivery — rate of usage
- Delivery — uncertainty

- Bulk purchasing
- Bulk manufacturing
- Insurance
- Work in progress
- Finished units

The following are some of the factors influencing the extent of stockholding:

- Operational needs
- Lead times
- Capital
- Cost of storage
- Insurance

The means by which the consequent inventory levels can be maintained. There are two means available: regulating input and regulating issue.

Regulating Input

Input can be regulated by advice to purchasing who can then contract outside suppliers to increase or decrease supplies. If supplies are obtained through internal sources similar action can be taken by liaison with the production control department.

Time is an important aspect of this control for the measures regulating output are seldom instantaneous. This means that control levels must make allowances for changes in input to have effect.

Regulating Issue

This is not an easy exercise to carry out because the main function of stores is to provide a service: Issues must be made to the requirements of the users. Regulating input usually takes time to have effect and the same is true of issues, although some regulation of daily issues is desirable. Some control of issue can be made by consultation with production control and any issues against schedules should be reviewed.

Method of Inventory Control

A stock record database and system is advisable. Typically, such as system is shown in Figure 36.

Visual

Here the level of stock is controlled by physically separating stock so that a remainder may be isolated. This can be done by:

- Partitioning a bin
- Tying a quantity of stock with tape
- Keeping a separate bin

When a storekeeper has to break into this separated stock he or she knows that a new order must be placed.

Figure 36. Stock record system

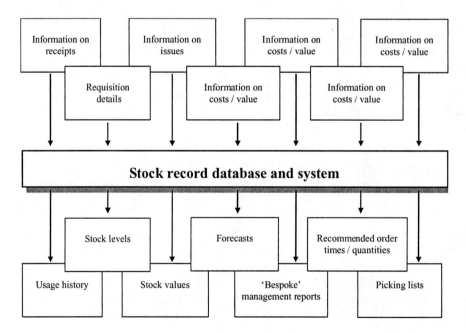

Visual methods aid the control of stock by quantity and, as you will realise, are limited in use. They can be employed successfully only on items for which demand is regular or for which supplies are available at short notice. With predictable items for which there is regular demand and easy supply, it is possible to carry on without any stock records other than the bin card. This requires periodic checks to ensure that supplies are satisfactory.

Control of Inventory by Quantity

When controlling inventory it is essential that every item receives attention. Records are therefore essential. To run a stores function efficiently detailed information on past history and present policy is necessary. Records provide this information and should give a "case history" for every item which can be used to forecast future trends.

The following factors have a marked effect on quantity control:

- *The unit of issue* — This may be in terms of quantity, weight, or numbers and is the smallest unit that is issued. Once this unit has been set for each item, all documents must be made out using that unit. Once exception to this may be the purchasing requisition, which must be understandable to suppliers. If any alterations are necessary it is up to the individual firm to decide whether they should be done by the purchasing department or done before sending the purchase requisition.
- *Probable requirements* — Of necessity this must be an estimate, and to be effective, this needs close liaison with other departments. Future trends have to be adjusted against requirements ascertained from past records.
- *Lead times and availability* — As with probable requirements, past knowledge must be supplemented by close liaison with the purchasing department.
- *Quantity prices and discounts* — Saving of this nature must be compared with storage costs to arrive at a true saving.
- *Cost of ordering* — Because the necessary paperwork and labour are expensive, the frequency of ordering must be considered, particularly on low-value items.
- *Rate of issue* — It is necessary to consider what batches or economic loads will have to be made.
- *High-value items* — Attention must be given to items of high value.

Figure 37. Comparison of stockholding decisions for various stock control processes

Stockholding decision	Stock control process	
	Order level system (Perpetual)	Order interval system (Periodic)
Order quantity	Fixed	Variable
Reorder level	Fixed	Variable
Reorder interval	Variable	Fixed
Buffer stock	Low	High

- *Frequency of deliveries* — Two factors affect this aspect of supply, the size and nature of the item, and the distance the goods have to travel. As you will realise, frequent deliveries over long distances are not very practical and are to be avoided as much as possible.
- *Seasonal fluctuations* — These occur for several reasons which are related to changes in demand, supply, or labour available. These fluctuations occur as a regular basis and cannot always be explained by the obvious, such as the Christmas period or the harvesting period for crops. It is necessary to review historical data to keep in touch with these fluctuations.
- *Stock allocations* — When calculating stock quantities, allowances must be made for any stock allocated for particular uses. Such decisions are reflected in Figure 37.
- *Standard ordering quantities* — You should not confuse this with the unit of issue, although the two may be identical. A standard ordering quantity is one that is set by usual trade conditions. A typical example is the sale of wood screws, bolts, and other small items that are sold in multiples of 100 or a gross.
- *Obsolescence* — Constant checks must be made to minimise the risk of overstocking items which may become obsolescent.

Control of Inventory by Value

When an inventory policy is formulated, attention must be given to the amount of finance available for use in storing materials. It is vital that the capital allowed for this purpose is not exceeded.

The first step is to set a limit against which the main stock account can be compared, this monitors the overall performance. Where the stock value is excessive, action must be taken to lower the total value; the problem is knowing which class of material has caused the error. This can be overcome by splitting the financial limit between the classes of materials and/or storehouses and running separate accounts for each.

It is most important that a commitment record is kept, showing the value of outstanding orders. This can then be compared with the average level of issues to forecast future stock values. Action can then be taken to ensure that the financial limit is not exceeded by deferring future deliveries.

Accurate value control requires regular information, in detail, of the following:

- current balance,
- committed costs, and
- current rate of issue.

All these figures being in monetary terms.

Control by value is exercised on groups of items in monetary terms. Any detail required must be obtained from the stock records.

Minimum Stock Level

The minimum stock level is important because it indicates the amount of stock that is essential for the continued running of the organisation for the period of the lead time for new supplies. As an insurance, it normally will include a margin of safety to allow for extended lead times which may occur due to unforeseen circumstances. For example, it may be the case that the rate of use of an item is 1,000 per month with a lead time of 2 months. The minimum stock level would be 2,000 plus 750 safety margin, making a total of 2,750. You will realise that the setting of these levels demands careful consideration and will have a marked effect on the smooth running of the organisation.

The Maximum Stock Level

This level is set to limit the quantity held in stock to a figure that is within the financial limits laid down as a policy. Consideration must be given to items which are likely to become obsolete and maximum levels may well be lowered to avoid excessive redundancy.

The Reorder Level

This level is set at a quantity which normally should brig in further supplies before stock falls below the minimum level. Occasionally the reorder level is incorporated in the minimum level particularly where the items have a steady supply and demand.

There may be a further level set between the reorder and minimum levels known as the hastening level. This indicates that supplies are approaching the minimum and that action should be taken to check that further supplies have been ordered and will be supplied in time.

Stock control by quantity then becomes a matter of checking stock records whenever a posting is made, comparing balances with stock levels and taking action accordingly.

- **Stock balance at minimum level.** Ensure that further supplies are ordered and progress outstanding quantity.
- **Stock balance at reorder level.** Take action to provide further supplies.
- **Stock balance at hastening level.** Ensure that further supplies are ordered and progress outstanding quantity.
- **Stock balance at maximum level.** Check for any outstanding orders and advise purchasing to delay deliveries.

To make stock control by quantity effective there must be a regular review of stock levels, adjusting those that are ineffective. This does not mean that levels should not be altered between reviews, should this prove necessary. It is also essential that personnel operating these records are trained adequately and made aware of the importance of accuracy in posting and acting on stock levels when balances are made.

Economic Order (or Batch) Quantity

Purchasing in large quantities can give lower prices but leads to higher levels of inventory.

Long production runs spread setup costs and increase efficiencies. However, they can result in stock levels that are too high. Meanwhile, other finished stocks are unavailable, while they await their turn to be produced.

A balance needs to be stuck. Economic order (or batch) quantity theory (EOQ or EBQ) tells us that when total stock holding costs are the same as total stock ordering (or setup) costs, this balance is achieved.

$$EQD = \sqrt{\frac{2FD}{H}}$$

Where F is fixed ordering or set up cost independent of batch size, D is constant demand rate per period, and H is holding cost per item per period.

This theory has shortcomings. It may be difficult to arrive at ordering or setup costs. The formula assumes linearity. Fortunately, the overall result is not affected too much by errors in arriving at these figures. A 10% error, in say, the setup costs, only changes the EOQ by 5%.

A word about setup costs. EOQ theory tends to institutionalise these costs. The greater the setup cost, the greater the economic batch. So we must strive to reduce these costs. Assumptions must be challenged. Methods study techniques simplify and speed up changeovers. Spare change parts can allow cleaning to be carried out within the cycle time. Just-in-Time thinking looks at all ways to eliminate or reduce these costs.

On a positive note, however, EOQ can and does work (e.g., an engineering company purchased castings in batches of 25). After carrying out EOQ analysis it found that the economic order quantity was 40. The purchasing department, armed with this information, negotiated a better price. The new price was fed back into the EOQ equation and a new EOQ of 48 was indicated. The buyer then renegotiated a second price improvement.

Cost of Inventory Investment

There are three costs involved:

- Cost of carrying inventory
- Cost of ordering
- The inventory records show allocated stock. What are the costs of these items?

Cost of Carrying Inventories

These comprise stores operating costs (e.g., labour costs, rent, rates), loss of interest on capital, deterioration and obsolescence, insurance, and cost of inventory control.

Ordering Costs

These comprise the cost of placing the order (e.g., typing, stationery), progress costs, and receipt and inspection costs.

Cost of Running Out of Stock

This comprises of the cost of production "down time," cost of arranging special orders and delivery and the loss of goodwill through lost customers.

Inventory Control and Accounting Methods

Inventory Control Accounts

These accounts are necessary:

- to provide figures for the final accounts,
- to provide the information necessary to run a costing system for materials,
- to provide a means of operating inventory control within the financial limits laid down by the management policy, and
- to give detailed figures for the various classes of goods and for different storehouses or stockyards.

The Main Inventory Account

The main inventory account should be kept by the finance department and shows the total value of stock currently held, this figure being used, after adjustment, for balance sheet purposes. To maintain this figure all receipts are debited to the account and all issues are credited.

You may be confused over the use of the terms *debit* and *credit* when talking about receipts and issues in the main stock account. To understand this clearly you must remember that items in stock, although an asset on the balance sheet, are a liability in the stores account. Another point that you should be clear about is the method of entry. Receipts are added to the existing balance and issues are subtracted. For example:

DATE	RECEIPTS	ISSUES	GOODS RECEIPT OR REQUISITION NO	BALANCE (STOCK IN HAND)
1.1.70	£100		0020	£100
3.1.70	£250		0021	£350
4.1.70		£150	3412	£200
5.1.70		£ 70	3413	£130
5.1.70	£300		0022	£430

Subsidiary Accounts

The main inventory account gives only a general picture of the financial situation and therefore has to be supported by more detailed accounts kept by the stores organisation.

These subsidiary accounts are separated into classifications in the same way as the inventory, giving a means of controlling specific areas of expenditure. An alternative method of control can be obtained by separating the subsidiary accounts according to storehouses, which may well be done in addition to classification accounts.

There are, therefore, three methods of separating subsidiary accounts:

- By *classification of inventory* — using code numbers where these exist
- By *storehouse* — where several are in use
- By *both of these methods*

Remember that the main inventory account is run separately from the subsidiary accounts, thereby giving a means of checking both, as the stock values shown in subsidiary records should equal the total value in the main account. Why are these checks necessary?

Inventory Records

To support the subsidiary accounts that are kept in monetary terms, detailed records showing physical inventory quantities are necessary. The inventory records provide these details and are kept in three forms:

- Showing quantity only
- Showing quantity and unit price
- Showing quantity, unit price, and values of all entries (i.e., receipts, issues, and balance)

The system used depends entirely on the particular requirements of an organisation, and the following points should be considered when deciding:

- The simpler the system, the less risk of errors
- Where a minimum of information is used, reference has to be made to other documents to extend physical balances in monetary terms
- Prices are shown on the inventory record, it can be used as a price list and special attention can be given to expensive items when provisioning
- Where a full record is made, checks can be readily performed on all major transactions, avoiding the necessity of checking entries that represent minor values

Coding of Accounts

All subsidiary accounts will bear a code number to identify the class of material and user department or storehouse, which enables immediate identification to be made on any particular class or location of expense. For example:

Material Code	002	=	Steel
Material Code	003	=	Brass
Material Code	004	=	Copper
Storehouse Code	100	=	Storehouse No A
Storehouse Code	101	=	Storehouse No B
Storehouse Code	102	=	Storehouse No C
Account Code	100/002	=	Value of Steel in Storehouse A
Account Code	101/002	=	Value of Steel in Storehouse B

The whole purpose of having detailed accounts is, therefore, to provide information from which control can be exercised and to be able to provide the earliest possible warning of excess expenditure.

The Integration of Accounts and Material Codes

It is possible to combine the account number with material codes. This is particularly useful where computers are used and can print an analysis of a particular class of goods.

Pricing Issues

It is most important for the successful running of an organisation that material costs are accurately computed, for the following reasons:

- to ensure that all material expense is recovered during the course of a period, usually 12 months; and
- to ensure that jobs that are costed for the purpose of quotation to customers and do not bear unrealistic material costs, making them too low for a reasonable profit margin or high enough to be uncompetitive when selling the finished products.

Before considering pricing methods, you must be quite clear on one point: The purchase price is the net cost incurred to obtain the material delivered to the required location.

Starting with the basic price quoted, adjustments have to be made for the following factors:

Discounts

These are allowances made by suppliers to members of a particular trade or given because large quantities are ordered. The "trade" discounts may vary according to quantity. Discounts are usually quoted as a percentage that has to be deducted from the price list.

Transport

Where the cost of transport is not included in the supplier's price, it must be added on to the supplier's met price; this may have to include movement within the organisation.

Packaging

Care must be taken to ensure that, where a supplier's price does not include packaging, an addition to the price must be made.

No allowance need be made for returnable packaging, unless the full cost is NOT refunded, but accurate records and quick return of packaging is essential.

Insurance

Where "ex works" prices are quoted and goods are insured in transit at a separate charge, an addition to the basic price must be made.

Duties and Taxes

When duties or taxes are payable on goods, these must be included in the total purchase price. Particular care must be taken on import duties and other levels which may be refundable under certain conditions.

Methods of Pricing Issues

Cost Price

Issues are made using the actual purchase price in one of two ways:

- First-in-first-out, referred to as FIFO. As the name implies, each consignment is priced out at the purchase price of that quantity, the price changing when issues are made from a batch having a different purchase price.
- Last-in-first-out, referred to as LIFO. This works in the same way as FIFO but uses the purchase price of the latest consignment as a base. It is rather awkward to work and is very seldom used.

Advantages:

- Very simple to operate, as no calculations are necessary, with the exception of balance totals.
- Balances are related to fact therefore no difficulty will be found in reconciliation of accounts.
- It is very simple to find the total value of goods in stock, by the addition of balances.

Disadvantages:

- When prices change frequently, it requires a great deal of clerical effort to keep stock records and price issues.
- The comparison of job costing is difficult when prices vary on different issues.
- When prices rise or fall there is an equal overvaluation or undervalidation of stock. This may be particularly undesirable when stocks are overvalued, as it becomes necessary to "write off" the excess value.

Standard Price

Issues are made at a fixed price irrespective of actual purchase price or quantity. This standard price is determined by analysis of market prices, future requirements and must be set for a specific period, usually 6 or 12 months. When consignments are received the difference between the purchase price and standard price is credited or debited to a "variance account." The balance of this account at the end of the financial period is reflected in the Profit and Loss Account as an overhead.

Advantages:

- This is an easy method for pricing issues.
- The possibility of error due to changing prices is reduced.
- Issues and receipts are priced at a constant rate and it is not necessary to extend financial balances. When such a balance is required, it can be readily obtained by multiplying the physical balance by the standard cost.

- There is less clerical effort in posting entries on stock records.
- Job comparison, in terms of material use and manufacturing efficiency, is easier.

Disadvantages:

- When material prices rise or fall there is an equivalent under or over-validation of stocks.
- Unless the standard price is set with a close degree of accuracy, there will be a danger of losing the profit necessary for the successful running of the business. It is possible that material costs are being overrecovered, but this may well make the organisation unprofitable due to quotations being uncompetitive.
- Very careful recording must be carried out to ascertain why differences between standard and actual costs occur, so that future standards may become more accurate.

Average Price

An issue price is arrived at by dividing the total purchase price by the total quantity in stock, giving an average price for each item. When a further delivery is received the total purchase price and quantity must be added to the existing stock balance and value (at average cost), and a new average calculated. This exercise must of course be repeated for every new receipt.

Advantages:

- Each item bears an equal proportion of the total purchase price.
- Pricing issues are easier.
- Easy to operate when machine accounting is used.
- Stock balances when calculated into monetary terms are at cost.
- Large or frequent price changes are levelled out.

Disadvantages:

- Calculations are necessary after every receipt.
- Goods returned to stores may be difficult to price.
- The difficulty in comparison of job costs due to varying material costs.
- The balancing of accounts becomes more difficult.

Market Price (or Replacement Price)

All issues are charged at the current market price at the time of issue.

Advantages:

- It provides a good basis for quotations to customers, because the material content is priced at current rates.
- Variations in material costs, with the resulting profit or loss, are shown up in the stores accounts rather than the works account.

Disadvantages:

- A great deal of work is necessary to maintain a record of current prices.
- Stocks are likely to be over- or undervalued.

Selling Price

Issues are priced out at a rate that includes a profit margin, calculated to recover stores costs.

Advantages:

- Stores units become self-supporting because the stores costs are recovered directly from issues and not through overheads.
- Profits or losses that occur tend to be standard throughout the organisation, and this often results in discrepancies being noticed more frequently, which

is very often the case wherein different divisions of a large organisation are critical of the prices charged on stock transfers.
- The balancing of individual storehouse accounts is made easier.

Disadvantages:

- Due to profit being included in stock values, the true value of the stock held requires detailed examination of stock records to arrive at the correct figure.
- For balance-sheet or tax purposes, the cost price is necessary, and this requires calculation.

General Comments

The choice of pricing method is dependent on the nature of the business and the class of material, many organisations using several systems. The following are typical examples of use:

Cost Price

Used for short-run jobs that are typical in jobbing shops, cost price is commonly used for pricing main equipment, machines, or high-value items and bought-out items that require no processing before despatch to a customer.

Standard Price

Standard price is used where large-scale issues are regularly made, as in the mass production industries or large supply organisations such as County Council Stores or the armed services.

Market Price

Market price is used mainly for raw materials where prices fluctuate, particularly in merchantile organisations dealing in such commodities.

Average Price

Average price is a variation on cost price, and selection of this would be a matter of choice in a particular situation.

Selling Price

Selling price is used by supply organisations, primarily to simplify the recovery of stores costs.

When selecting which system to use, keep in mind that inventory values for balance-sheet and tax purposes are required to be at cost or market price, whichever is the LOWER. This requirement is necessary to eliminate any possible inflation of figures, giving an unrealistic appraisal of inventory in the balance sheet.

Price Analysis

The basic question is, *Why analyse prices in such acquisitions rather than relying on commercial competitive market forces to guarantee a good price?* First, price analysis is performed whenever you compare the price of offer A to the price of offer B. Comparing competitive offers with one another is the first comparison base in price analysis. If price is always a factor in sources selection, then, by definition, price analysis is always performed.

Second, "price analysis" is a function that begins well before receipt of offers. Price analysis begins with the purchase request and the independent government cost estimate therein — in terms of questioning that estimate as a potential base for price comparison. Other steps in price analysis include collecting pricing information during market research, selecting price-related factor for ward — also done prior to soliciting, and applying price-related factors to determine evaluated prices for use in the source selection. In short, price analysis is an integral part of the process of soliciting and evaluating offers.

Third, "price analysis" is a necessary enabler in persuading suppliers to submit better prices. Price analysis is vital to detecting both unrealistic and unreasonable initial offers — and equipping buyers with the facts necessary to convince suppliers that their pricing is deficient.

Fourth, private sector buyers question every price — so should government buyers. A primary reason that industry employs buyers is to negotiate price.

Corporate managers regard pricing as among the most important "value-added" functions of industry buyers. In fact, many large firms have such little faith in the competition these days that they are largely abandoning "cut-throat price" competition in favour of single sourcing and/or limited sourcing with heavy emphasis on cost analysis as the basis for price negotiations.

Fifth, buyers cannot afford to ignore available price comparison information. If buyers have information on historical and current market prices but fail to use that information, will their defence be that, "I received two offers, so I ignored the fact that the offered prices were five times higher (or lower) than the price paid last month." This is not a hypothetical consideration. The United States government once awarded a contract to a buy-in price millions of dollars below other offered prices. Contract administration was a nightmare. The true cost of the deliverable (including the government's overhead for contract administration) was far higher than the government would have incurred had the buyer rejected the buy-in price as unrealistic. And, to add insult to injury, the contractor — which lost money on the contract — went to the Congress for extraordinary relief, claiming that the contracting officer knew that its price was unrealistically low and therefore should never have awarded at that price. The Congress paid off that contractor. Hence, buyers cannot afford to ignore information in hand that suggests that a price is unrealistic or unreasonable.

Finally, if the assumption is that downsizing has reduced buying staffs to the point that they have no time for price analysis — that we have to be penny wise and pound foolish, then the time has come to challenge downsizing as having passed the point of diminishing returns in terms of the taxpayer's interests.

Inventory in the Final Accounts

It is necessary at least once a year to arrive at a figure that represents the value of inventory in hand for entry in the profit and loss account; this figure is subsequently entered in the final balance sheet.

The accuracy of inventory valuation is important for the following reasons:

- For taxation purposes, the figure is required to be at cost or market price, whichever is lower.
- Where inventory has appreciated (i.e., increased in value), care must be taken when adding a provision to the cost value. In many instances this is considered unwise, due to the possibility that the situation may change and

the value fall. In addition, appreciating inventory is in effect claiming profit that will not be obtained until a sale is made.

- Under- or overvaluation of inventory does not show the true percentage of working capital that is employed for stockholding purposes.

Calculation of Net Value

Starting with the balance figure shown in the main inventory account, the following adjustments are necessary:

Price adjustment. Depending on the method of pricing issues, with the exception of the cost-price method, there will be a difference between the inventory stock account figure and the actual cost, this difference being shown in the variance account. If the cost-price method is used, it is necessary to calculate the difference between the cost or market price. Using the calculation of the net figure, a decision can be made on what provision should be made for price adjustment. This figure will usually cover the variance that has occurred during the past year and the anticipated variance for the coming year. In nearly every case this provision will result in a deduction form the inventory account figure, as it is inadvisable to appreciate inventory values. Should the inventory value appreciate, no provision adjustment to the main inventory account figure is necessary.

Obsolescence. What is obsolescence? It is the period in which the future use of an item is limited, but there is still a demand for it. When the item is no longer required it becomes obsolete. A typical example is the spares holding for machinery in present use, which is due to be replaced in 1 year's time, or the phasing out of certain piece parts. Although every effort must be made to keep the level of inventory down on obsolescent items, until they finally become obsolete, some stocks must be kept to maintain the necessary service to users. It will be possible to ascertain from the previous years' records the value of obsolete items that occurred, which can be related to the present year's situation, making due allowance for any known changes in requirements. This information can then be used to arrive at a figure, usually expressed as a percentage of the total inventory figure for the year, which can be deducted from the main inventory balance. Obsolescence is not confined to any one class of inventory, but the most difficult to make allowance for, is that caused by a design change or production programme amendment and the provision for this requires careful consideration.

Deterioration. This can be considered in the same manner as obsolescence and is dealt with in the same way. "Shelf life" is one of the factors affecting the setting of levels, but however carefully these are controlled, some deterioration is often inevitable.

Inventory appreciation. Where value has increased with the passage of time, it may be necessary to add provision to the main inventory account figure, although this must be done with extreme care.

Uninvoiced goods. Where goods have been received and entered on the inventory accounts, but no invoices have been received, those items must be shown in detail in the final accounts. If these goods are not shown as a separate item, the main inventory account figure will show an asset that has not yet been debited to the purchase ledger.

The following is the value of inventory for balance sheet purposes, put in a simple form:

- Main inventory account balance
- Plus or minus price adjustment provision
- Minus obsolescence provision
- Minus deterioration provision

You may well find that the last two are grouped together as one provision for obsolescence and deterioration, known by another name as *wastage*. This provision is often used to cover another aspect of loss that occurs, namely pilfering. This is a point to consider with great care, particularly when any discussion takes place, because it has personal implications. It is, however, a significant factor in some organisations, particularly large retail stores that have to make fairly large provision for it. Remember, pilfering is a very sensitive subject, and you should choose your words carefully when it arises.

Identification and Coding of Materials

The Importance of Identification

The wide variety of materials and components moving in and around an enterprise is constantly being referred to, for one purpose or another, by one of the following departments:

- Design and development
- Process planning
- Production control
- Material control
- Production
- Stores and inventory control
- Invoice section
- Cost accounting

In some cases, other departments may be involved, but it should be fairly clear that if every department uses a different language in describing or identifying and item considerable confusion will occur.

This kind of confusion can lead to a number of inefficiencies in a company and result in financial losses and unnecessarily high costs. It is vital, therefore, that a common means of identifying material supplies is devised and implemented firmly throughout the company. The factors that need to be taken into consideration are shown in Figure 38.

Figure 38. Stores coding considerations

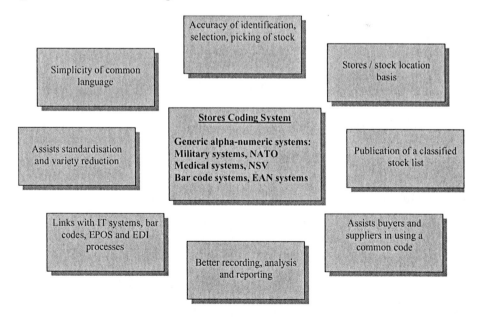

Methods of Identification

We normally refer to or identify most things by a name or description, and in some cases this method is quite satisfactory. Provided that all interested parties use the same name or description, and provided that it is clearly understood how records should be maintained for the items in question, no confusion need arise.

Example: 3" x ½" Bolts and Nuts may also be called

3" x ½" Nuts and Bolts, or

½" x 3" Bolts and Nuts, or

½" x 3" Nuts and Bolts, or

3" x ½" Hex, Rd, Hex. Bolts & Nuts, etc. or

3" x ½" Pins and Nuts, etc. or

3" x ½" Screws and Nuts, etc.

This is a relatively simple example of differences in terminology, which can result in the same item being referred to by a score of different names, so that several stock Cards are in being filed under the different descriptions. This in turn may result in several batches of the same items being ordered or manufactured, so duplicating requirements many times.

Multiply this simple problem by the thousands of items in the inventory, and you can see the difficulties that may result from "identification by Description." Furthermore, the administrative operations of classification, filing or analysis, are complicated by the many items that, though different in themselves, have very similar descriptions. Another problem is that clerical activities become unnecessarily prolonged where there is a continual need to reproduce long, descriptive titles.

Only where there are relatively few items involved, where the descriptions are short and cannot be misused or confused, where the point of reference for filing purposes is quite clear, is identification by description likely to be satisfactory. In other cases, an alternative method must be devised, and the usual approach is to use alphabetical numerical or alpha-numerical coding.

It is clear that some form of coding will be essential in firms where a wide variety of materials is in use. This need would be even greater where sophisticated forms of classification, analysis, or data processing were to be used.

Coding could simply involve allocating a number to each item as it arises, but this method make the identification of items from their codes more and more difficult as the number of items involved increases. This difficulty is reduced by grouping like items together and devising coding systems to indicate the groups into which items are classified as well as identifying the individual items within each group.

The first stage, therefore, in any coding exercise is "classification." This involves grouping items into types or classes. It will be necessary to identify and specify each item and then categorise them within the group or subgroup to which they belong.

Having classified all the items into groups, we can devise a coding system that will be much more helpful in readily identifying items from their codes and that will provide a better basis for analysis of information.

The complete sequence of operations therefore would be:

- *identify* — what the items is, what it does;
- *specify* — its description, dimensions, tolerances, and so on;
- *classify* — to its correct group and subgroup; and
- *code* — by allocating group, subgroup, and item designations.

Benefits of a Coding System of Identification

Having decided that, in the majority of cases, coding is likely to provide the most effective method of identification, we can study this technique in more detail.

In the first place, we should consider the major benefits that may accrue from the use of the technique, so that our subsequent planning of the system will achieve the most advantageous results. The application of a coding system may achieve the following benefits:

- It will identify each item accurately.
- It will become a common means of reference by all functions throughout the organisation.
- It will obviate the need for the repeated use of descriptive titles.
- It will assist in the simplification or rationalisation and subsequent standardisation of materials.
- It provides a better means of recording and analysis.
- It provides a better means of physically controlling stocks.
- It will help to prevent unnecessary duplication of stocks.

- It will provide a better basis for instruction and training or personnel throughout the company.
- It may be used as a stock location reference.

It therefore eliminates many of the problems that may occur when "identification by description is in use.

Methods of Coding

Before deciding which method of coding is to be used, it is important that we consider the many purposes being served and the principal functions that are going to be affected. Frequently, there will be a conflict of interests between the management functions that will use or be affected by the coding system; it is essential that the method we ultimately decide upon gives the greatest overall benefit to the company.

The main purposes and the principal functions interested may be:

- *better identification of the physical materials in the factory* — this will be of the greatest interest to the stores, inspection and production functions;
- *easier reference for recording and analysis purposes* — this will obviously be of concern to the administrative and clerical functions;
- *better means of identifying and classifying for charging the value to jobs* — this will be an objective of the accounting functions;
- *an aid to all activities of materials management and control* — this will be of significant importance to top management; and
- *an aid to applying mechanical or electronic methods of recording and control* — this will be the aim of data processing personnel.

Some systems of coding will be more suitable than others in achieving one or other of the above purposes. We must decide which of the objectives is the most important, in the particular company with which we are concerned. The method of coding must be "tailor made" for that company.

When we have decided the main objectives of our coding system and have obtained agreement from all the functions affected, we must then determine the basis on which materials shall classified and coded.

Methods available include the following:

- *Identification by the nature of the material* — this is the method most commonly used because of its flexibility. Materials are classified into groups and subgroups by virtue of what they are; for example:

Main Group	Sub Group	Item
Steel	Bar	½" Rd Mild
Steel	Strip	4" x ¼" 18/23 Carbon
Fixings & Fastenings	Bolts & Nuts	3" x ½" Hex Rd Hex
Fixings & Fastenings	Rivets	1" x ¼" Pop rivet
Oils & Greases	Lubricant	20/50 Engine oil
Oils & Greases	Coolant	Transformer oil

From the examples above it can be seen that, however wide the variety of materials in use, classification by the nature of the item is flexible enough to cope. This factor is extremely important if we wish ultimately to use a digital significance coding, such as the Brisch system.

- *Identification by end use of the material* — this is the method of classification that works back from a finished product and all materials are ultimately coded according to the finished product, of which they form a part; for example:

Model	Main assembly	Item
Escort	Engine	Cylinder block
Escort	Engine	Cylinder head
Escort	Steering	Steering arm
Escort	Steering	Column
Escort	Transmission	Universal joint
Escort	Transmission	Drive shaft

It can be seen from the above examples that this system of classification is less flexible because materials are used on more than one finished product. Provision must also be made for items common to the range of products (e.g., oil seals, bearings, etc.), and a coding system will be required for such common items.

Consumable items and spares will also require separate coding systems.

There are other bases for the classification of materials that may be used in rather special circumstances, such as:

- identification by sources of supply,
- identification by customer,
- identification by the location of the item, and
- identification by the handling characteristics of the item.

These methods are very limited in their application and are usually inflexible once they have been implemented.

The next consideration in devising our coding system is to determine the whole range of information that the system must be designed to cover, so that every item is individually recognisable from its code number. We may want the code to indicate the following items of information:

- Main-group classification
- Subgroup classification
- Item within subgroup
- Sizes or shape of item
- Colour of item
- Chemical composition of item
- Differences in use of item
- Unit of quantity (e.g., pairs, sets, dozens, rolls, gallons)
- Variations from standard
- Accounting significance

Many systems go no further than coding by group and subgroup and then merely allocating a number to each item within each subgroup; but where there are many items within subgroups, quick identification becomes virtually impossible.

Finally, we must decide whether we are going to use alphabetical, numerical or alpha-numerical coding. Many companies use letters of the alphabet as initial letters for main groups of items but this practice usually results in confusion, as the number of groups increases and initial letters are duplicated for several groups. Furthermore, if it ultimately becomes necessary to mechanise the accounting, recording or control system, it is much more difficult to cater for letters than figures. In general, therefore, it is usually preferable to use numerical coding throughout.

Development of the Coding System

Having decided the main objectives our coding system is required to achieve and having determined the most suitable method of classifying the materials, we must now look at the type of code to apply. First we must consider the main principles to follow in the development of any system of coding.

- The system must be capable of covering all items likely to be used, both at present and in the foreseeable future.
- It must be designed to suit the particular organisation.
- It must allow for expansion without duplication.
- Each item must appear only once in the vocabulary.
- It must be easily understood by all those using it.
- There must be a constant number of symbols or digits in all code references.
- Each group of symbols or digits must signify only one object.
- Descriptions and specifications, upon which coding is based, should be as brief as possible, without affecting accuracy.

Any system of coding should be founded on these fundamental principles, whether it be a system of group coding or a system of digital significance, such as Brisch.

Group Coding

The group coding method is one in which major commodity groups are given specific code references.

Example 1:   01 = Steel
              02 = Oils, greases and fluids
              03 = Fixings and fastenings, and so forth

The subgroup within each major group is then allotted a subgroup code.

>Within Group 01 Steel —
>01 = Bar
>02 = Strip
>03 = Sheet
>04 = Coil

Finally, we must code each item within the subgroup. This may be done by allocating numbers, in sequence, as the item arises, or the item number may be designed to indicate the qualities inherent in the item, such as size, quality, and so forth, by retaining certain series of numbers for certain item classes.

>Within Group 01 Steel, and Subgroup 01 Bar —
>0001 - 0199 reserved for Mild Steel
>0200 - 0399 reserved for 05/08
>0400 - 0599 reserved for 08/13 Carbon Steel, and so forth

Based on this coding system, 05/08 Carbon Steel Bar would have a code number:

>between 01/01/0200 and 01/01/0399,

depending upon the particular item number allocated to the size and length of the material in question.

If the items number 0273 has been allocated to ½" Round in Random lengths, then:

>01/01/0373 - ½" Round 05/08 Carbon Steel Bar, Random length.

Example 2: Similarly, within the next major group, Oils, Greases, and Fluids, the following code may arise:

>02/01/0071 = 20/50 Lubricating Oil,

because 01 has been allocated to the "Lubricant" subgroup, and within that subgroup 0071 has been allotted to 20/50 Oil.

Example 3: Within our third group, "Fixings and Fastening", we may get a code number such as:

03/16/1729 - 4 x 3 Hex Rd Hex Bolts & Nuts 16,

because within main group 03, Fixings and Fastenings, 16 has been allocated to Bolts and Nuts, and within that subgroup 1729 has been allocated to 4" x 3/16" Hex Rd Hex Bolts and Nuts.

As can be seen from the foregoing examples, Group Coding has the following advantages:

- fairly simple to understand,
- can be applied fairly quickly, and
- would cost less to implement.

It major disadvantages, however, are as follows:

- Immediate identification from the code is difficult because the item codes do not represent specific features of the item concerned; they are merely allocated as the item arises.
- Group coding is less flexible than codes using Digital Significance and is more likely to break down when the varieties of groups, subgroups, and items become too great.
- Group coding is of less assistance in the maintenance of standardisation.

Digital Significance Coding

This type of coding system is used where it is important that the description and specification of an item be clearly represented by digits or symbols making up the code number. Each digit has a particular significance and describes a particular factor of the description or specification.

The best known method of digital significance coding is the Brisch system. In this system the code number is made up of a "Surname," which broadly classifies the item concerned, and a "Christian" name, which provides the detailed description of the item.

Example 1:   Surname   Christian Name,
                    112   0120

which, when interpreted, means:

1st figure - 1 = main classification = raw materials
2nd figure - 1 = secondary classification = steel
3rd figure - 2 = type of steel = bar
4th figure - 0 = specification of Steel Bar = Mild Steel
5th figure - 1)
)= diameter of bar in 1/16ths of an inch
        = 3/4"
6th figure - 2)
7th figure - 0 = lengths of material = Random lengths.

Therefore: 112-0120 = 3/4" Mild Steel Bar, Random lengths.

Example 2:   Surname   Christian Name
                    347   4036

which, when interpreted, means:

1st figure - 3 = main classification = piece parts
2nd figure - 4 = secondary classification = fixings & fastenings
3rd figure - 7 = type of fastening = bolts & nuts
4th figure - 4 = length in inches = 4 inches
5th figure - 0)
)= diameter in 1/16ths of an inch = 3/16"
        6th figure - 3)
7th figure - 6 = finish of product = galvanised

The foregoing examples simply indicate the way in which the digits in a Brisch code number may be interpreted to give a description or specification. When designing a coding system of this type, it is necessary first to decide how all items to be included in the system can be divided into 10 or fewer main classifications, so that this factor can be covered by using figures 0 - 9 in the first column.

Each of the main classification must then be divided into 10 or fewer subclassifications — obviously the subclasses under a "Raw Materials" main classification will be different from the subclasses under a "Piece Parts" or "Consumable Materials" main classification. With 10 main classifications and ten subclasses under each, we can get as many as 100 subclasses.

The third figure of the Surname will be used to indicate type of item within each subclass and, with a possible 10 types of item within each of 100 subclasses, we can describe 1,000 types of item by just using the Surname.

Should we require the identification of more than 1,000 types of material, we may need to increase the Surname to four figures.

The Christian name can then be used quite differently for each type of material described by the Surname to provide detailed specifications of the item. The figure may be used individually or in pairs to represent some important factor of the description.

The major advantages of the Brisch system:

- Direct identification of any item from its code number
- Much more flexible for expansion
- As the code must be directly related to the description, it can be used to maintain a standardised range (code numbers not included in the standard range are not ordered or manufactured) — this advantage brings others, namely reductions in design costs, reductions in storage costs, and reductions in tooling costs
- Assists in location of equivalent or alternative materials, when out of stock
- Is ideal when mechanising data processing

The one disadvantage is that it takes a good deal of planning to devise a Brisch system, and the personnel who do that planning need to have more skill than is usual in the planning process and have knowledge about the materials and their descriptions and specifications.

The Stores Vocabulary

When materials have been coded, it is necessary to prepare a code book or manual, showing material descriptions and the codes which will represent these descriptions; this is called a "stores vocabulary." The stores vocabulary has four main purposes:

- It provides the means by which all people, departments, or functions are initially notified of the new codes.
- It provides a permanent record, against which additions or amendments to the materials range are decided.
- It is a ready-reference book for day-to-day working for all departments.
- It provides a sound basis for future training of people concerned with materials.

To be of any permanent use, the stores vocabulary must be properly prepared, designed and presented so that the people using it have confidence in its accuracy and validity.

Stages in Preparing a Stores Vocabulary

Earlier, we determined that the stages leading to the development of an effective coding system were:

        Identity   Specify   Classify   Code

These same stages are inherent in the preparation of a stores vocabulary, but we shall look in more detail at the practical situations in which this work is carried out.

The following show that several departments or functions will be involved in the various stages of development and preparation of the vocabulary.

Preparing a Library of Information

Comprehensive knowledge will be required of all materials, components, and supplies that are in use or will be likely to be used in the foreseeable future. This will mean identifying potential material needs and filing each piece of information for use in later stages.

The department given the responsibility for this task (usually a vocabulary or standards section, or stock control) can make a major contribution to the ultimate effectiveness of the system, if the collection of the information is done with care, and if the filing of the information is done efficiently.

The information may be obtained from design, production, stores, inspection, maintenance, and purchasing departments, from outside suppliers, customers, trade or research associations, or from the British Standards Institute.

It will be necessary at this very important stage to prepare specifications for each item or range of items so that each is filled in an orderly fashion in readiness for subsequent classification and coding. In preparing the specifications, it will be helpful if we adhere, as far as practicable, to the following basic rules:

- Try to make descriptions or specifications simple, clear and specific.
- Develop accurate physical descriptions.
- Determine accurate performance requirements.
- Determine inspections or tests that must be met for acceptability.
- Determine any special marks to be used on materials for identification.
- Indicate where specification will meet several alternative needs.

Consideration of Present Coding Systems

In some cases, several attempts may have been made to codify individual classes of materials, or supplier or customer codes may have been used. We must understand the nature and purpose of these past systems and how they were used so that adequate consideration is given to such requirements in our new classification and coding.

Consultation to Determine Coding System

When all the information has been collected, meetings should be held at which all interested departments are consulted, to determine the coding system most likely to meet the most important requirements. Another purpose of these meetings will be to programme the work to be done and determine the contribution any department may have to make within the programme.

Preparation of Originating Sheets

The next stage is the actual classification and coding exercise, which will be made much easier if the first stage has been done well. In fact, if an excellent job has been made of preparing the library of information, the preparation of originating sheets will virtually be a clerical task, as very few difficulties or queries of classification will arise.

An originating sheet is simply a record of all items in a particular classification of material. All the items are recorded in a logical sequence, and ultimately a code of recorded against each, to provide to the stores vocabulary.

The first originating sheet will show only the main classifications.

ORIGINATING SHEET 1   Main Classification

Material Group	Code
Raw Materials	0
Piece Parts	1
Oils, Greases, Fluids	2
Consumable Stores	3
Tools, Jigs, Fixtures	4
Building Materials	5

An originating sheet will then be prepared for each of the above material groups. For example:

ORIGINATING SHEET 2   Raw Materials — Code 0

Material Group	Code
Steel	0
Cast Iron	1
Copper	2
Brass	3
White Metal	4
Wood	5

This process of preparing originating sheets will be continued in more and more detail as the classifications are broken down further. In the more detailed originating sheets, where descriptions become more extended, drawings may be used to help in showing specification.

ORIGINATING SHEET 346
Salt Glazed Drainage pipes — Tees — Code 573-4...

Diameter A	Diameter B	Measurement C	Code No.
10cm	10cm	1 Metre	573-4441
10cm	10cm	2 Metres	573-4442
10cm	15cm	1 Metre	573-4461
10cm	15cm	2 Metres	573-4462

Finalising the Stores Vocabulary

The preparation of the originating sheets is the process of classification, and when the codes are allocated, we have a stores vocabulary. In some cases, however, it may be necessary to show conversions from old code numbers, in old code number sequence, as an appendix to the new stores vocabulary. In other circumstances it may be only necessary to issue certain parts of the total classification to certain parts of the organisation, with one or two departments getting a complete copy. It is this preparation of the classification and coding, for general use throughout the company, which demands the finalisation of the stores vocabulary in a suitable format, using terminology that is readily understood in the explanatory sections.

Standardisation, Rationalisation, and Variety Reduction

In manufacturing, variety on a theme is common — the basic car or van in a variety of colours, trims, equipment, engines. Thus, variety and marketing promotions and fashion trends encourage the ever-increasing requirement of stock range expansion. The problem is, of course, to balance the fulfilment of variety without overloading stores and stock costs.

One of the most effective ways of managing the range of stock in relation to variety availability is to operate a planned variety reduction programme. This should involve several departments and users in addition to stores and stock controllers. A typical group would include stores staff, production staff, marketing, purchasing, and finance. A variety of reduction programmes will involve a total and regular review of the range of stock within an organisation. The team should analyse its work into various categories. On the basis of such a team in a manufacturing organisation, there will be categories such as the following:

- The range and variety of sales products
- The range and variety of stock, components, and parts to manufacture the sales products

The process of review should be regular and ongoing if it is to be effective, and the programme and the team need to have the direction and executive support of senior management. The review and reduction process is essential to the ongoing production of a viable sales range. In most organisations, and particularly if the organisation has been in existence for some time, a large number of parts, components, and materials will be held in stock. A critical examination of these items will reveal that a number of items, carried as different items, may in fact be the same.

The advantages to be gained from a policy of standardisation and rationalisation, are:

- A reduction in stocks carried
- Reduced inventory costs
- Costs of carrying stack lowered
- More effective purchasing and stores procedures as they can concentrate on fewer items
- Design department can reduce their range of products and adopt a more positive attitude to design
- Quality control can be more effective
- Production methods can be simplified and improved

In order to prepare our store vocabulary, it was necessary to prepare a library of information; we now need this information to assist in deciding those items that will become our standard range. We shall also need to examine carefully each item currently carried in stock and to compare our range of stack items with actual requirements. Then we must:

- identify each item and its purpose or use;
- eliminate from the stock range those items not essentials or duplicated;

- examine critically those items that have similar features (it may be possible to reduce the list even further);
- make a list of items and components that are to be carried as a standard stock range;
- decide size range, standard pack sized, methods of packaging, and so on for the standard stock range (specifications can now be entered against each item in the standard range); and
- arrange for publication of the list of standard items and its issue to all interested departments (e.g., design, production, purchasing, stores, costing).

There will always be a need for certain items not in the standard range to be carried. However, these must be strictly controlled and only allowed in particular circumstances.

A written procedure for obtaining authority to purchase nonstandard items should be issued, as part of the "standards list." Persons authorised to allow the purchase of nonstandard items should be named so that the responsibility for carrying a nonstandard item can be clearly seen.

In a similar manner, a written procedure must be laid down for amendments and changes to be part of the standard list. This will be necessary because lists will need updating to cater for new requirements and to delete items no longer required.

Again we cannot have just anyone altering standard lists, as this would make nonsense of the system. The following must be clearly stated:

- Persons who may request an amendment to the standard range, named by their appointment.
- All interested departments must be consulted on any proposed amendment, and a system for ensuring this must be built into the procedure.
- It must be shown who has the final authority to permit any change in standards.

No change may be made in the standard list unless properly authorised.

The standards list has the following advantages:

- A handbook, a record of all standard stock items is available throughout the enterprise. This will assist all departments, particularly design, production, stock control, stores, and purchasing.

- It is a method of informing everyone of the enterprise's authorised standards.
- It is the means of ensuring that the company's standards policy is carried out.

Specifications

The more widely accepted the specifications we use in adopting our standards, the easier will be our task in obtaining the items concerned. In fact, life is simpler if we can quote a specification, in the confidence that others will know exactly what is required. Consider the problems if there were not National Specifications for items such as bolts and nuts; every manufacturer would use a different thread form. It was to avoid such problems that organisations like the British Standards Institute were set up.

Among specifications in wide use are:

- British Standards Institute (BSI)
- International Standards Organisation (ISO)
- British Pharmaceutical Commission (BPC)
- American Society for Testing Materials (ASTM)
- American Petroleum Institute

Wherever possible, specifications such as these should be used. The benefits are likely to include the following:

- lower costs, because the items will be manufactured on a large scale for several users;
- easier availability of components and items, because they are not specially made; and
- no need to draw up specifications on each occasion that an item is required.

There are instances, however, where the company must issue its own specification; where, for instance, no specification is available. If a company wishes to ensure that its designs and products are not copied, it may also decide to issue its own specifications. All specifications and drawings must be entered on the standards list against each item.

Inventory Reduction

To illustrate the principle of inventory reduction, for example, if a project involves a cost reduction, not only does this result in an ongoing cost saving, but the book value of the components concerned will be reduced when standard costs are next revalued.

This means that any of the components being held as stock (including WIP) at the next annual stock check will have a lower asset value, resulting in the value of assets in the company's accounts being reduced. This reduction will be additional to any changes in asset value caused by changes in stock levels.

Although the aim of any cost reduction project is to increase profits, and the ongoing cost savings will do this, the reduction in book value caused by revaluation will appear in the accounts both as a reduction in assets and as a corresponding reduction in profits. Although this reduction in book value does not itself represent a change in cash flow, the reduction in reported profits represents a reduction in tax liability which does provide a cash flow gain.

Taking an example of a component that used to have a book value of £100.00, which has been reduced to £75.00, the effect will be as follows:

	Old Cost	New Costs
Material	£ 40.00	£30.00
Labour and variable cost	£ 20.00	£15.00
Manufacturing overhead	£ 40.00	£30.00
Book value	£100.00	£75.00
Reduction is asset value	£25.00	
Corresponding reduction in reported profit	£25.00	
Saving in tax liability (resulting from reduced reported profit) (£25.00 @ 35 percent)	£ 8.75	

Stock revaluation results from a change in the standard cost value of components, not from a reduction in stock levels. Thus, for a project that involves a reduction in both the value and quantity of stock, there are four elements to be considered:

- One-off cash flow saving from curtailing the supply process to reduce the quantity of stock

- One-off reduction in tax liability resulting from having a lower quantity of stock at annual stock check
- Ongoing cash flow savings resulting from the reduction in cost of manufacture or purchase
- Reduction in tax liability as a result of stock having a lower book value at annual stock check

However, if a project involves both a major cost reduction and a major reduction in stock levels, care must be taken in deciding how the reduction in stock levels is to be valued. It is necessary to decide whether the cash-flow element (e.g., material, labour, expenses) in the saving from reducing stock quantities is to be valued on the basis of the old method of manufacture or the new method. Two different situations may exist:

- Little risk is perceived in the introduction of the new process, so stocks are allowed to run down before the new process is fully commissioned. In this, case it is the old supply process that is curtailed, and savings would be valued using the old costs.
- Where there is risk of uncertainty regarding the new process, it may be decided to have it fully commissioned before starting to run down stock levels. Full production would be achieved before to use up stocks. In this case, the savings would be valued using the new stocks.

Because the saving comes from curtailing the supply process for both material purchase and manufacture rather than from the sale of the excess stock, the valuation of the cash-flow element of inventory reduction must be based on whether it is the old or new process that will be curtailed. Although this cash-flow saving will occur at the time when the supply process is curtailed, such as by avoiding the purchase of raw material, the reduction in asset value in the company accounts may not be reported until the stock level check at the end of the financial year. By this time, the inventory may have been revalued on the basis of the new cost of manufacture.

The importance of inventory revaluation will be dependant on the magnitude of both the stock reduction and the cost reduction. The way any evaluation is done will depend on the nature of the project, the timing of the changes, and the way the company records changes in inventory levels and book values.

For any project, where there is a reduction in inventory levels or a change in the value of inventory is going to be a major factor, it is essential to investigate in detail how the changes will be costed and what effect any changes in the value of assets will have on the company's balance sheet.

Any reduction in inventory values in a company's accounts will not only produce a cash-flow saving but also a change in asset values that will be reported as a reduction in profits. There is a paradox in that, although inventory reduction is always portrayed as an ideal objective, achieving the reduction may appear to have had exactly the opposite result to that originally intended. Because of this, any project involving a planned change in inventory values must take into consideration the effect on the company's management of having to report to shareholders an apparent failure to meet profit forecasts.

Although high inventory levels are always portrayed as being a symptom of inefficiency, there is no such thing as a *correct* level of inventory. The optimum required level is something that depends on many different factors, such as market requirements, manufacturing facilities, and product design. High inventory levels themselves are not a basic problem, only a symptom of other problems. If the real reason that the inventory is there is not understood, there is a danger that the action taken to reduce stock may not solve the correct problem. It is important to start by identifying and changing the basic reasons why inventory is there; only then should stock levels be reduced. Carrying stock is an integral part of a company's manufacturing operation, and stock is there to help iron out problems in both the supply process and the sales function. The supply problems may be due to the length and uncertainty of the process or to the inflexibility and unreliability of the ordering and scheduling procedures, whereas the sales problems can be caused by fluctuations in sales volume and product mix. The combination of these problems can result in the production process being too long and inflexible to satisfy the market requirements for variations in product specification and delivery.

Holding stock at various stages in the manufacturing process is used to overcome these problems, and there are different reasons for holding different types of inventory. High WIP may be a result of long lead times and uncertainty of supply, as can be caused by the problems of scheduling work in batch manufacturing environments where there is the possibility of scrap and rework if the manufacturing process is unreliable.

It is unrealistic to expect marketing to forecast short-term order input with any accuracy so that manufacturing can plan a uniform throughput. Therefore, to obtain orders, companies may either carry finished or semifinished stocks or change their manufacturing process to provide the flexibility to change quickly output in response to customers' needs.

Changing the manufacturing process to reduce the need for stock, such as WIP, will not in itself bring about a change in stock levels; making a permanent change in stock levels requires a change in the way that the stock is ordered in the material control system. Although large sophisticated material requirements planning (MRP) packages may contain a number of different sets of ordering rules which can be used simultaneously for different components, some MRP packages may have little flexibility for rule changing.

If the change in manufacturing required to reduce stock levels is such that the ordering rules within an MRP package need to be altered, there is a danger that, unless there will be a major saving in inventory value, the change will not be worthwhile. For example, inventory reduction is often portrayed as an objective for investing in Computer Numerically Controlles (CNC) machining centres because the number of operations can be reduced. However, the introduction of a single machine may affect only a relatively small percentage of components, and without a change in ordering rules, all that will happen is that some lead times will be reduced and the components will be put into finished part stores at an earlier date — in effect, increasing the value of inventory.

In evaluating the benefits of inventory reduction, it is important to identify the way in which the supply process will be curtailed to bring about the stock reduction. In reducing brought-in components and the raw material content of WIP, it is likely that material purchases will be reduced for a short time to use up existing stocks. However, in order to reduce WIP, the manufacturing process will be restricted only for a short period of time. As a result, there is a danger that the labour element will not be curtailed because, unlike material purchases, labour cannot easily be turned off and then turned back on again.

It is unlikely that operators' wages will be stopped, so unless specific plans are made that identify how the labour savings will to be implemented, it is possible that Parkinson's Law will operate, with work expanding to use the labour available. As a result, there will be no cash-flow savings in labour costs at all. If the planned labour savings does not occur, the forecast cash-flow element will be reduced, while both the reduction in asset valued and corresponding profit reduction will be increased.

A commonly suggested method of reducing inventory is to have smaller batch sizes by reducing order quantities. This will only be economical if changes are made that will reduce ordering costs, such as batch setup times, thereby reducing the cost penalties of smaller batch sizes. However, consideration must also be given to problems that can arise from an increase in the number of batches.

Review of Other Concepts

Less-standardised approaches, which require less-rigid purchasing methods with more thought about strategy and less thought about firefighting will arise from issues such as sourcing and how to control stock. In order to examine the strategy and draw a considered conclusion, it is necessary to establish typical views with regard to sourcing policy and examine some other concepts.

Managers are presently concerned with the perceived challenge to the West from the Japanese manufacturing industry. Lean Supply, Kanban, Just-in-Time, FMS, robotics, CAD/CAM — a whole new vocabulary has been devised to describe differing aspects of the changes that are taking place. It is necessary therefore to focus attention on the implications for the purchasing function of these developments, the impact on buyer behaviour, collaboration and the effect on industrial sourcing policy in Europe.

From the purchasing viewpoint, Just–in-Time has the following objectives:

- Reductions of raw material stocks
- Improvement of input quality
- Achievement of greater schedule flexibility
- Reduction of bought-in costs through long-term cooperative contracts with suppliers

These objectives require a number of changes in purchasing practise:

- Highly reliable material planning
- Vastly improved supplier quality performance
- Reduced delivery lead times
- Smaller delivery quantities
- Greater increased delivery frequency
- Creation of long-term contracts with suppliers
- Shift form competitive price reduction to long-term cooperative cost reduction programmes with suppliers
- Increase in the level of single sourcing

Criticism of Just-in-Time (JIT) has focused on its reliance on a policy of single sourcing. Such a policy is essential to the implementation of JIT because the technique requires suppliers to make a number of significant changes to their operating procedures. They must, for example, change from a batch to a smooth, continuous form of production to match the change in the buyer's demand pattern. They must achieve enormous improvements in quality control and implement major changes in transport operation. Few suppliers will likely be willing to contemplate making such fundamental and expensive changes without the stability and certainty that long-term, single-sourced contracts provide. Single sourcing is an essential precondition for the successful implementation of JIT. Awareness of this has stimulated warnings about the effects of single sourcing on continuity of supply.

Moreover, the cost benefits of single sourcing are undeniable. On the face of it, the car industry would appear to have confounded in doubters and critics. Appearances can be deceptive, however. Companies adopting JIT may well be storing up a uniquely devastating kind of trouble for the future.

The source of this threat is found in the combination of JIT's requirement of single sourcing with its objective of stock minimisation. Not only does JIT seek to reduce finished goods, work in progress, and bought-in stocks within the organisation itself, it also demands similar reductions from the organisation's suppliers. A mere shifting of inventory, of course, will largely defeat the goals of Just-in-Time. Over the long run, the suppliers will find a way to get manufacturers to pay for it.

With very little, or (ideally) no safety stock in the system, companies using JIT become extraordinarily vulnerable to supply stoppages — certainly, much more vulnerable than companies running a single sourcing policy in conjunction with conventional inventory control policies. The longer the system is in operation, the lower the total stock levels become, the smaller the total number of suppliers, the larger the amount of investment the remaining suppliers are persuaded to make, the more difficult and time-consuming it becomes to resource, and the more vulnerable to collapse the system becomes. The nearer an organisation approaches to the JIT ideal, the more exposed it becomes to the effects of stoppages down its own supply chain.

Why have the Japanese devised and embraced such a potentially unstable system? Their success in the field of manufacturing is unrivalled. The mystery deepens if we consider the conventional responses to the kind of high supply risk situations that JIT creates. In the West, companies typically follow one of two courses of action. First, multisourcing and second, vertical integration.

This description looks like the very antithesis of vertical integration, in which organisations acquire their suppliers and, in this way, secure their sources of supply. The truth is more complex. The Japanese industrial scene is not what it appears to be.

The principal stockholders of Japanese companies are normally other companies. Individuals hold less than 10 per cent of the stock in 97 per cent of the companies listed in the first section of the Tokyo Stock Exchange, which includes the 1005 largest publicly traded companies in Japan. It seems plausible that in many markets these patterns of interlocking directorships improve the allocation of resources. In some respects companies with interlocking directorships can mimic the resource allocation decisions of vertically integrated companies.

We can now see that although the large Japanese corporations are devotees of subcontracting, they have also developed a method of obtaining the benefits of security and supply certainty that accompany Western-style vertical integration without resorting to outright acquisition of their suppliers. This begins to explain the Japanese enthusiasm for single sourcing and their willingness to abolish safety stocks. It is perfectly safe and rational to become dependent on a small number of suppliers if you are directly represented on the boards of those companies and have some control over the way they are run.

The second relevant major difference is frequently dismissed by JIT supporters as being old news and therefore worn out and insignificant. We have known for a considerable time that Japanese industrial relations are positively tranquil, but length of time of that knowledge does not dilute its relevance. Japanese companies face significantly lower risks of supply stoppages caused by strikes.

Another factor negative towards JIT is that, to achieve management effectively and a JIT network, the Japanese tend to focus production of similar items in small factory units of fewer than 300 each. This is fine in Japan, where two thirds of the 240,000 manufacturing corporations have fewer than 30 employees, and where the culture is far different from Europe's. The combination of minimal safety stocks and single sourcing is perfectly rational and desirable for Japanese purchasing techniques without first creating conditions in the European economies comparable to those in Japan appears foolhardy. Single-sourcing per se is not the problem. The European car industry has already convincingly demonstrated the cost advantages of volume concentration on a small number of suppliers, but single sourcing plus a Just-in-Time stockholding policy looks like a recipe for disaster. Within the European industry, the supply sources of the often highly specialised materials and components needed are not numerous. Aerospace, for example, is to some extent unusually vulnerable to supply disruption and the costs effects of a fairly narrow field of market competition. However, a sensible policy of dual sourcing together with good order and market intelligence is an essential part of overall purchasing strategy.

Materials Requirements Planning

It is rarely the case that the demand for an item is smooth and at a constant rate. In manufacturing, it is more likely that the demand for an item will occur in large increments at varying points in time, a characteristic referred to as "lumpy" demand. In such situations the MRP approach has been developed as a means of managing inventory. The MRP system is for controlling inventories of raw materials, work-in-progress, component parts, and subassemblies. A further characteristic is that, as much as possible, production takes place only for actual sales. It has proved to be a very powerful tool in the planning and control of manufacturing industries. You could describe MRP as a system for supplying the number of components required to produce a known quantity of finished assemblies.

The three ingredients of an MRP system are the bill of materials (BOM), the inventory status file, and the master production schedule. These ingredients are fed into a computer system. The system begins with a production plan and schedule and ends with orders being placed and the receipt of those materials.

In comparison to traditional systems, MRP seeks to control inventory by what is occurring or is going to occur, rather than by what has occurred. Thus, the order sizes are linked to needs and the delivery becomes paramount. There may be a tendency to overemphasise expediting incoming deliveries from suppliers. Of course, any halt to production calls the cost-effectiveness of the system into question with a nasty jolt. On the other hand, production plans have been known to change!

In the context of supplier relationships, it is quite possible for customer and supplier organisations to be computer linked, giving access to production schedules, which allows suppliers to increase their own effectiveness by being able to plan and schedule their work. MRP pushes organisations into the realisation of a materials management function, whereby the overall responsibility for the control of materials from the point of leaving the supplier, passing through the organisation, and finally reaching the customers, resides in the hands of one person. This is often cited as a crucial stage in the progression of an organisation towards realising its full performance potential, particularly in the manufacturing industry. Take, for example, a product that has a few components, none of which are manufactured, but that are all bought from various suppliers. The organisation assembles only the bits to make the product, and there is also only one product. (In such a real-life situation, a traditional control system would probably prove quite effective.)

The first item is the bill of materials, which is a schematic listing of all the components that go into making the product in the sequential order of production, or build. The product is "exploded" or "cascaded" into its various assemblies, subassemblies and components at various levels. Some items, such as a nut and bolt, could appear at various different levels. If this were the case, it could be allowed to filter through these levels and accumulate at the bottom. It may be a cheap item, but it could well be crucial to production, and, therefore, it might be subject to a separate traditional system of control, such as reorder level. For example, suppose the master production schedules calls for 150 Product A's to be ready for delivery in week 17. An MRP plan can then be developed. The plan is constructed by combining the information contained in the master production schedule, the bill of materials, and the inventory status file. This latter file shows what materials, components, subassemblies, and so forth are already held in stock, together with their lead time.

This simple example indicates the large number of combinations and calculations facing the computer, where a large number of complex products are produced to meet continually changing demand.

MRP appears quite complex, but to assist you, a summary list of the stages is given, plus a flow chart.

- +Sales forecast — updated with latest actual sales information
- Sales forecast, customer orders, and production policy used to produce master production schedule (MPS)
- MRP programme computes how many of each component and raw materials are needed by exploding end-product requirement into successively lower levels in the product structure
- Net requirements calculated utilising inventory status file (i.e., stocks and current orders deducted)
- Net requirements adjusted by lead times determined
- Purchasing places order
- Goods received

Reported benefits from MRP include the following:

- Reduction in inventory
- Improved customer service
- Quicker responses to changes in demand
- Greater productivity

- Better machine utilisation
- Reduced setup times and changeover costs

MRP is therefore a useful technique in the manufacturing industry for overcoming the problems of inventory management for components which are in dependant and lumpy demand.

Manufacturing Resource Planning

MRPII is an extension of MRP. The first stage of the conversion of MRP into MRPII is the development of a "closed-loop" MRP system. Closed-loop means that the various functions in production planning and control (capacity planning, inventory management, and shop floor control) have all been integrated into a single system. This represents an improvement over MRP because it provides a number of additional features. That is,

- *Priority planning* — "rush" jobs can be moved forward and other jobs pushed back, and the necessary adjustments made to material delivery schedules.
- *Integration of related functions into the system* allows feedback from them, making sure that the production plan is constantly kept up to date — in particular, capacity planning, inventory management, and shop floor control.
- There is *feedback from vendors, the production shop, stores, and so forth* when a problem arises in implementing the production plan that enables adjustments to be made to overcome these problems immediately (i.e., before they become insurmountable).

Tying together these various functions as a closed-loop MRP system represents a considerable improvement over the basic MRP system. However, the final step is essential. This converts the closed-loop MRP system into a full MRPII system, linking the closed-loop MRP system with the financial systems of the organisation.

A closed-loop MRP system + financial system = MRPII. The inclusion of the financial systems in the operation of MRPII gives it two invaluable characteristics, which represent a significant improvement over closed-loop MRP:

- It is an operational and financial system
- It can be used for simulations

MRPII is a company-wide system that is concerned with all aspects of the business and includes purchasing, inventories, production, sales engineering, and cash flow. All departments operate with the same data (i.e., a common database). This recognises the interaction of all business activities; what happens in one area has direct effects elsewhere, and these affects are captured by the system, which adjusts throughout each area. In all areas the data is reduced to the common denominator of financial data, which provide management with the information it needs to manage the business successfully; for example, the values of inventories, work-in-progress, finished goods, and so forth, are known at all times. MRPII is a total management control system.

Another benefit derived from an MRPII system is that it can be used for simulation purposes by taking a "cut' or section across the database and posing "what if" questions. Fore example, we may wish to bring forward a production date, so we pose the question, "What if we work an extra shift?" The system will simulate the consequences for order releases, current order schedules, inventories, work-in-progress, finished product, labour costs, and cost flow. If this is not a viable proposition, then an alternative can be tested, and once this is found, the necessary adjustments can be made throughout the system. The same approach can be used with financial plans, production plant, inventory levels, and so on. It is of course vital that the data within the system is completely accurate, otherwise the results will not be reliable.

MRPII is a computer-based system and simulations utilisation visual display units can be a most helpful aid in planning, as alternative scenarios can be tested during management meetings. The objective of systems such as MRP and MRPII is really quite basic: to give greater control and accountability but also to reduce inventories to a minimum and reduce the length of time between identifying need and fulfilling it to the customer with the ultimate aim of improved cash flow and profitability.

In the next chapter, I examine how to look after the inventory so carefully provisioned — stores management.

Chapter IX

Stores Management

Stores management is a crucial part of the supply chain in terms of location, stock held, storage, and replenishment.

Stores Management Objectives

The stores function is concerned with holding appropriate levels of stocks of the required quality, under the correct storage conditions, for use by other departments.

To realise these objectives, stores management has a number of duties, including:

- receiving, storing, and issuing stock;
- controlling the movement of stock;
- controlling all storage units;
- controlling material handling procedures;

- overseeing quality and quantity control;
- overseeing staff training; and
- implementing clerical administration duties

The Store's Function

The stores have a wide range of functions that must be carried out efficiently and logically to ensure the smooth running of the department, including:

- receiving and maintaining the quality of all incoming materials;
- supplying materials to user departments to ensure continuation of production;
- storing, controlling, and issuing all items in stock quickly and efficiently;
- issuing any tools or spare parts that may be required by the departments;
- ensuring that all health and safety regulations are followed;
- undertaking training of all stores staff; and
- complying with the control of hazardous substance regulations.

The stores provide a service to the company as a whole and to individual user departments. Obligations to particular departments include:

- production departments, to ensure that materials are available as and when needed;
- distribution departments, to ensure that all finished products are marshalled ready for dispatch;
- sales departments, to ensure that stocks for sale are stored and issued correctly; and
- accounts departments, to ensure that information on the value of stock, goods received, and invoice queries are provided promptly.

In turn, the stores rely on other departments. For example, purchasing departments must ensure that all goods required by the organisation are purchased — of the correct quality and at the right price — for timely delivery to the stores.

For any stores management system to function efficiently, considerable time and attention needs to be given to:

- siting of stores,
- construction of buildings,
- stockyards,
- internal layout of stores,
- types of stores, and
- storage equipment.

This chapter deals in turn with each of these critical matters.

The Siting of Stores Buildings and Stockyards

We must usually settle for a site that is less than ideal, but it should be one that, as far as possible, meets the following requirements:

- Clear, level, well-drained land capable of providing foundations suitable for the building or stockyard required.
- Of a size sufficient to accommodate stores buildings, stockyards, access roads, car and lorry parks, and possible future expansion.
- Site convenient for main services (i.e., drainage, water, electricity, and gas).
- Convenient for transport facilities (e.g., motorways, rail points, airports, and docks).
- Away from congested urban areas, where traffic may have difficulties, collecting or delivering.
- Close to user departments or centrally situated to serve a number of units. Planning permission will be required and buildings must conform to local authority specifications.

The site will also have to be within the limits of finance available for purchase, or obtainable on a satisfactory leasing agreement.

The purpose of the building of a stockyard must be borne in mind, and the following matters must be taken into account:

- The size, weight, and handling characteristics of goods and materials. The nature of the goods is very important because it will determine the structure of buildings and the site. Consider particularly explosives, petroleum spirit, and deep-frozen food.
- The location of the user departments and depots to be served from the stores building. Quantities of goods likely to be stored and the rate of turnover.
- Methods of transporting goods to and from the building (e.g., palletisation, containerisation).
- The loading and unloading facilities required, with special regard to maximum weights to be handled and maximum size of containers.
- The traffic volume anticipated. (This will influence the type of handling equipment for which provision will have to be made.)
- Storage methods and equipment required.
- Any security systems needed.
- The number of staff needed for operating the building.

Construction of the Buildings and Stockyards

When deciding upon the construction of the building and stockyard, consider the type of building needed: single story or multistory. Single-story buildings are cheaper, a lighter shell is possible, ventilation and lighting are easier, and materials handling presents fewer problems, whereas multistory buildings make the best use of a restricted site and may be necessary when an existing site must be redeveloped.

Type of Structure

Steel frame or brick pillars; the type of infill must be decided. The load bearing of the framework is the main factor, based on suitable foundations. In a stores, it may be necessary to support additional floors, overhead cranes, and other equipment. The stacking height and free movement of materials are the factors that effect internal construction.

Load Bearing of Floors

The load-bearing capacity of floors must be carefully considered so that it is suitable for the goods to be stocked. Floors will also need to be dust-free and nonslip.

Receiving Bags and Loading Docks

These will need to be of correct size, type, and height to suit vehicles using the stores.

External Doors and Windows

These will need to meet security requirements, at the same time, doors must provide an adequate means of entry and exit, for example, power-driven roller doors with at wicket gate. The larger doors can be raised for vehicles and the wicket gate for personnel.

Draught-proof screens of polythene or other plastic strips help to conserve heat. Internal rubber doors provide the same facility and allow movements of forklift trucks. There must also be doors and screens adequate to prevent the spread of fire. Internal partitions should be of a type that can be easily moved around, to give the greatest flexibility in the use of space.

Heating, Lighting, and Ventilation

In a stores building, much planning should go into heating, lighting, and ventilation. Some form of heating will nearly always be required — the problem is to provide a source of heat that is sufficient, economical, and does not interfere with the storing of materials. Many buildings use fan-heaters for this purpose.

Adequate ventilation must also be provided. Air conditioning may well be required in many conditions. It is important that stock is kept in the best condition, and this may require air conditioning. An air-conditioning specialist should be consulted if it is required.

Natural lighting is the best form and should be provided, if possible. Roof lights are a convenient method of doing this. Fluorescent lighting is effective and cheaper than tungsten lighting.

Welfare Facilities

It is essential to provide for facilities such as a canteen, first-aid post, toilets, and garages. Suitable welfare facilities will be required, and provision must be made for them.

Stockyards

Stockyards provide a means of storing certain classes of materials (e.g., bricks, sand, gravel, timber — any materials that do not deteriorate in the open) more cheaply than is required in an enclosed building. A firm surface area will be required for vehicles and handling equipment, such as cranes and forklift trucks. Such surface areas are usually made of concrete or tarmac. Stacking areas may be made of ash or shale.

Adequate lighting will be required in the stockyard, particularly if work is to be carried out at night. There are several types of tower floodlighting available.

Security fencing and gates will be required for stockyards.

Internal Layout

Before planning the layout of any store so as to provide the most satisfactory base for efficient operations, we must determine all our storage needs very carefully and then decide:

- what is the best that can be done in terms of grouping stocks,
- what can be provided in the way of a building or site for each group,
- exactly what type of service the store will provide, and
- what kind of supporting facilities a particular stores area will require.

A disjointed stores layout plan is likely to result in poor service, inadequate control, costly administration, unnecessary duplication of equipment and facilities, and frequent emergency rearrangements to meet unforeseen circumstances. The factors that will form the basis for our overall planning of storage facilities throughout the company are therefore vitally important and must be carefully considered. The main factors for consideration are as follows:

- What types of service can we reasonably afford?
- What materials must be handled at each location?
- How will materials be constructed?
- What kinds of equipment will be needed at each location?
- What provisions, if any, must be made for overall workflow throughout the company?

Detailed Planning of Layouts

We should have a clear picture of our overall stores requirements, and we can now begin to plan the facilities at each of the designated locations and plan the layout of those facilities to give the greatest possible efficiency.

Whilst satisfying the needs of our overall plan for stores, the layout at each location must be dictated by the particular requirements of individual stores areas. These requirements will be influenced by the following characteristics:

- determination of material needs;
- receipt and inspection of incoming materials and supplies;
- storage, safekeeping, and issue of materials and supplies;
- centralised or decentralised storage of materials and supplies;
- recording and administration of stocks;
- handling and transportation of materials;
- the need for workflow to be considered in the particular location;
- the working space required by each of the functions involved; and
- the type of materials involved and the mix of materials in the particular location, such as raw materials, piece parts, bought-out parts, work-in-progress, tools and patterns, jigs and fixtures, equipment and spares, general stores, packaging materials, and finished products.

The nature of certain materials that require special consideration include:

- those that are valuable or attractive to pilferers;
- fast-moving or slow-moving materials;
- materials requiring special means of storage (e.g., liquids) and freight containers;
- bulky or awkwardly shaped materials;
- dangerous materials;
- identical components that must be stored in two separate areas for different purposes, such as production supplies and supplies of spares;
- the gangways, corridors, or free areas necessary for the lift or travel of overhead cranes or the movement of other materials-handing equipment;
- areas for the receipt or dispatch of internal or external transport;
- the need to assist the administration and the supervision to maintain control efficiently; and
- the need for flexibility, so that the facilities can be adjusted to meet changing circumstances.

Types of Stores

It may well be that, in a small company, all stores facilities must be provided in a single building, and if an efficient service is to be provided, all of the foregoing factors must be considered when planning the layout of that building. The larger the company, however, the more fragmented the stores facilities become, and the more specialised become the activities of each stores location. Whilst this may simplify the layout of individual stores locations, it demands a more detailed consideration of the function or purpose of each.

Some of the more specialised applications that justify individual consideration are:

- centralised goods receiving,
- centralised storage,
- special storage facilities, and
- popularity storage.

In considering these specialised applications, we can examine specific needs as far as layout is concerned (see, e.g., Figure 39).

Figure 39. Warehouse layout (Note: Photograph from Stocklin Logistics Switzerland. Used with permission.)

Centralised Goods Receiving

First, it is essential to recognise that control over the material assets of any organisation is very difficult to achieve or maintain unless control of the material is obtained as soon as it arrives on the premises. If that initial control is lacking, there is a considerable danger that materials will be lost or misused, and their cost may eventually prove an insupportable burden on the company. The first step in the application of this control is to limit the number of points at which materials may be received, if possible, restricting receiving points to one.

It is necessary to consider the "nature of the function being performed," and the activities involved at such a point:

- Receipt of transport of various kinds.
- Unloading and subsequent reloading of materials of various classes.
- Initial checking of goods for damage in transit.
- Recording and documenting goods received.
- Provision of facilities for the technical inspection of those goods requiring it.
- Provisions for goods awaiting distribution to used departments or storehouses.
- Provision for goods awaiting return to suppliers.

The "nature of the function being performed" will tend to decide the general location and pattern of layout, which will then be varied by certain other factors, viz:

- the need for workflow;
- the volumes of work being handled;
- the types of materials;
- the nature of certain materials;
- the working areas needed; and
- the need for flexibility.

Bearing in mind the importance of goods receiving and recognising its purpose in the overall scheme, we can design this department's internal layout to achieve its purpose in the most efficient and economical manner. If the centralised goods receiving department occupies part of a building, the remainder of which is a storehouse, this is a further factor to be considered in our layout.

Centralised Storage

The term *central stores* has four different interpretations, and it is important that we appreciate the meaning and significance of each interpretation before we consider their applications or their overall effect on the layout of storage facilities.

- **Central stores only**. This type of central stores will exist where only one storage point is justified in a factory, and all supplies are provided from that one point. In addition, probably all other storage activities will be carried out at that one location.
- **Central stores supported by substores**. In stores facilities organised in this way, all requirements are controlled and ordered by the central stores where the materials are received and stored. Normally, the substores are located adjacent to the operating departments they are designed to serve, and the stocks held in them are limited to reasonable operating levels. Stocks in the substores are replenished at intervals from the central stores (see, e.g., Figure 40).

Figure 40. Example of central stores organisation

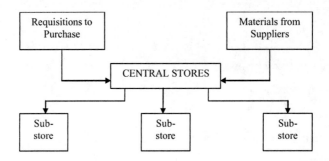

This type of central stores organisation may be used in a large company, where there are many departments to be served within the premises and where many of the materials used are common to all departments.

- **Central stores in addition to departmental stores**. When stores are organised in this way, the departmental stores operate independently, ordering, receiving, and storing those materials that are used only by the department served by that departmental stores. The central stores are responsible only for providing supplies of those items that are common to more than one department. The central stores will order, receive and store common items, and departmental stores will replenish their stocks of such items by requisitioning their requirements for central stores. This type of central stores organisation may be used where the factory departments are widely dispersed geographically, transportation costs make it worthwhile to centralise those items common to all departments, and items can be bought and stored in bulk. Another justification may be that the work of the various departments is so diversified that it would be unreasonable to bring highly specialised materials into a central point merely for them to be distributed to one department.

- **Central stores (main distribution warehouse) and depots**. Sometimes the term *central stores* is applied to a main warehouse in which the finished products of a company are held prior to distribution. From such a stores, the products may be distributed to substores or depots that are located at strategic geographic points from which the best service can be provided to customers. Such depots may operate with or without the control of the central warehouse, but as with all centralisation, a central stores tends to ensure closer management control over distribution priorities, whilst a depot reduces the transportation problem within its own area, in addition to providing quicker service.

Both centralisation and decentralisation have their advantages, and there is an unfortunate tendency to rush to obtain the advantages claimed for centralisation without giving any consideration to its disadvantages or to the equally strong claims of decentralisation in certain circumstances.

Advantages of Centralised Stores

- Allows closer management control
- Justifies the use of more advanced control methods and techniques
- Creates economies in storage space because quantities held in stock can be proportionately smaller (e.g., five separate stores may need to hold 20 each of a particular item: If centralised, it would not necessarily mean that 100 of the item need be held).
- May justify the use of better storage, handling, and transportation facilities
- Better facilities may be provided for receipt, inspection, and testing of materials
- Stocks will be turned over with greater regularity, thus avoiding depreciation or obsolescence
- Allows for more specialisation by stores personnel
- Reduces the number of orders placed for the purchase of particular materials, thus facilitating quantity buying

Disadvantages of Centralised Stores

- Involves extra handling and transportation costs
- Requires a much stronger organisation or inefficiencies may arise
- Will involve more documentation if it involves distribution through substores
- Greater dangers of shortages and loss arise if the central store is badly managed
- Bad management of any kind will have more serious repercussions and be more costly

- Central stores personnel may be less concerned with local needs in the factory and so deal less efficiently with them

If one is considering the claims of decentralisation, the advantages and disadvantages tend to be the reverse of those for centralisation.

Special Storage Facilites

In listing the factors to be considered in the detailed planning of layouts, the following were mentioned:

- The nature of the functions being performed
- The need for workflow
- The volumes of materials to be handled
- The working areas necessary for each function being performed and for the volumes of materials

These factors are considered again when considering the requirements for effective layout in a central goods receiving department; *the nature of the materials* has special relevance when considering the layout of facilities specifically for the storage of supplies.

Whether a company or its stores function is large or small, whether or not it justifies central goods receiving, and whether it uses a centralised or decentralised stores organisation, there will invariably be some materials that require special consideration as far as storage is concerned.

Materials that may be better controlled if held in different storehouses include:

- raw materials (e.g., ferrous or nonferrous metals, in bars, strips, coils, sheets);
- component parts (e.g., piece parts or bought-out parts stored for final use);
- engineering supplies (e.g., tools, jugs, fixture patterns, equipment, spares);
- general stores (e.g., consumable materials, small handtools, protective clothing, packaging); and
- finished goods.

Materials that may be stored more suitably in stockyards include:

- raw materials (e.g., ingots, billets and slabs of ferrous metals, timber);
- solid fuels (e.g., coal, coke); and
- building materials (e.g., bricks, sand, gravel, stoneware).

Materials that require special consideration, either because they are dangerous or because there must be special means of dispensing or controlling them, include:

- **Oils**. (i.e., fuel oils may need to be stored in containers, above or near to the boilers or furnaces that use them. Lubricating oils may be stored in reservoirs above or below special purpose or automatic machinery);
- **Petrol**. (i.e., petrol may be stored in underground tanks in or near a company garage or maintenance shop, but it must be in an accessible position for all vehicles requiring supplies);
- **Dangerous goods**. (i.e., goods such as explosives or highly inflammable materials, which may have to be located at safe distances from normal working areas, need specially constructed buildings with protective earth mounds or baffle walls);
- **Solid fuels**. (i.e., some solid fuels may weather badly or may be subject to spontaneous combustion so that protective measures may be necessary to avoid physical or chemical changes taking place);
- **Valuable or attractive goods**. (i.e., goods that are especially prone to pilferage and require special protection);
- **"Clean" goods**. (i.e., goods that must be stored in a manner that prevents their becoming contaminated with other materials); and
- **Specially "bonded" materials**. (i.e., materials that must be segregated from other, similar materials because they are "free issue" materials that are a customer's property; approved or tested materials that must be segregated from nonapproved materials; materials that are subject to a tax or duty that has not yet been paid; or components designated as spares for customers and that must be held separately from production supplies).

Finally, materials requiring special consideration so that they can be made immediately available to user departments in order to avoid unnecessary handling may occur in the following:

- **Work-in-progress stores**. It may be necessary to provide work-in-progress quarantine areas in appropriate locations in the factory if it is impossible to maintain a balanced flow of production from machine to machine or department to department in the factory; it is inadvisable or impossible to allow the work-in-progress to remain scattered around production departments, but where it is undesirable to bring large volumes of materials back into stores for short periods of time, these "stores" will provide control and safekeeping of materials and components but may not be the responsibility of the stores manager. However, they will influence the planning of storage facilities throughout the company.
- **Open access stores**. Where items of relatively low value are being used on a continuous basis at a rapid rate, and where the handling and control costs are disproportionate to their value, we may decide to make them freely available to the user departments from an open access store within the department. Similarly, where sets of components have been kitmarshalled for subsequent assembly departments, the sets may be transferred to open access stores ahead of the assembly production programme.
- **Popularity storage**. Rate of usage is the final factor to be considered under the general heading of "nature of the material." Some materials are fast moving (i.e., they are used quickly and regularly); other materials are slow moving (i.e., whilst their usage may be regular or intermittent, they tend to stay in stores for long periods of time). This popularity of certain materials will affect not only the ordering policies or stock levels, but also will need to be considered when planning the layout and location of supplies. Fast-moving materials are less likely to deteriorate, but they should be as near to the issue point as possible to reduce the distance travelled by personnel responsible for issue, whereas slow-moving materials can be stored further from the point of issue but are likely to be more prone to deterioration.

Planning Storage Equipment

There are a number of basic questions should be considered when planning storage equipment, including:

- Are we making the most economical use of the space available?
- Are we achieving the greatest overall benefits for the storage costs incurred?

- Are we paying the most economical prices for the most suitable equipment?
- Will the equipment help to provide the most efficient service?
- Will the equipment assist in the handling and controlling of stocks?
- Will it help to provide the right conditions in which to hold stock?
- Will it present any dangers to premises or personnel?
- Will it provide the right degree of security for the stocks?
- Does it give us flexibility in use?

Considering these questions would enable us to arrive at a general policy for selection of stores equipment, but this does not mean that we can then proceed to purchase a standard range of equipment to meet all needs effectively.

A very wide range of storage equipment is already available and is being continually expanded, and in most cases it has been designed to meet the widest range of "standard" needs without necessarily meeting any particular need with complete satisfaction. One danger of such standard equipment is that it appears to be less expensive in the short term, whereas in the long term it may turn out to be more costly and probably involve some insurmountable space, flexibility, or manoevrability problems.

This does not mean that all our storage equipment must be special purpose or custom built; what it does mean, however, is that we must give the fullest consideration to our equipment needs if we are to get the best possible results at the most economic cost. First we must look at the materials that have to be stored, and the locations at which they will be held, to determine the types of equipment necessary, based on factors such as:

- the nature of the material (e.g., size, weight, shape);
- the volume to be held;
- the degree of protection required from pilfering, from dirt and from atmospheric conditions;
- the problems of handling the material;
- the needs for physical or administrative control over quantities, flow, and so forth;
- the nature of the building being used;
- the location of the stocks in relation to their point of use, and the space available;
- the handling methods or facilities available or necessary;

- whether materials are received, stored, and issued in unit quantities; and
- the rapidity of stocks turnover of individual materials.

Considering these factors will outline certain requirements that must be met in selecting the equipment that will satisfy our needs. The requirements include:

- strength, to support weight;
- durability, to withstand constant wear;
- ease of operation, to assist efficiency;
- flexibility, suitability for a variety of uses;
- protection provided, against, for example, dirt or misappropriation;
- adaptability, for different locations;
- safety, for premises, materials, and personnel;
- manoeuvrability, for swift rearrangement of storage areas where necessary;
- cost, giving the greatest value for money spent;
- dimensions, to fit the space or headroom available, or to contain the volume required; and
- suitability, to the method of handling or type of material held.

Careful consideration of the basic principles of effective storage, together with clear recognition of the practical requirements to be satisfied, will enable us to determine the best methods to adopt, and the most suitable equipment to use. Any efforts we exert in this direction will help to provide maximum flexibility, and fullest utilisation, both now and in the future, within the economic and space limitations imposed upon us, thus avoiding:

- uneconomic use of space,
- unnecessarily high storage costs,
- unnecessarily high costs of equipment,
- inefficiency in providing a service,
- difficulty in controlling stocks,
- detrimental effects on the condition of stocks,

- dangers to premises and personnel,
- lack of security for stocks, and
- lack of flexibility in use.

Handling Equipment

Goods Movement Theory

The first thing to remember about the movement, handling, or transportation of materials is that it adds to the cost without adding in any way to the value—it is important to remember that basic principle when planning the primary activities involved, so that unnecessary movement is eliminated.

Even then we cannot assume that, whatever handling methods we employ, we shall achieve the best results at the lowest cost; we must plan them carefully, considering the following principles:

- Major handling or movement should be restricted as far as possible by siting incoming and outgoing materials correctly prior to any operation and using the most helpful methods for "holding" the materials at any point.
- Try to plan the work on a "flow" principle, which will involve correct routing of materials; correct movement of personnel involved in the activities; proper designation of working areas and working groups; suitable arrangements being made for obtaining and disposing of containers; and proper routing of documentation.

Frequently these factors are determined prior to considering materials handling, and unnecessarily expensive handling methods have to be adopted as a result, whereas if they had been considered with the handling problems in mind, the handling methods could have been much simpler and the whole operation much less expensive.

- Eliminate wasteful methods wherever possible by employing unit loads to eliminate handling and perhaps counting individual items; using pallets where frequent movement is involved; using the force of gravity wherever possible to add movement.

- Where mechanised methods of handling are necessary, select the most appropriate equipment, carefully consider what degree of flexibility is required from the equipment purchased; decide whether some form of standard equipment can be used; consider whether the volume of work involved justifies special-purpose equipment; consider whether some conveyor system should be employed in place of handling.
- In the event that the "first choice" equipment breaks down, decide whether alternative methods of handling the layout adopted allow the alternative methods to operate.
- The methods adopted should be designed in the interests of safety, first of personnel, then of property.
- Equipment should be designed and installed for safe and efficient operation, and where operators are required, they should be properly trained for the job.
- The environment in which the materials are handled will affect the choice of certain equipment (see the Layout Considerations section in this chapter).
- We must compare the overall "benefits" of alternative methods with the "costs" of employing those methods.

Investment Justification

The investment and running costs of different handling methods can easily be computed, and these costs must be set against potential benefits of each of the alternative methods, which may include:

- savings in time and labour,
- reductions in damage or breakages,
- increases in output or turnover,
- more efficient use of space, and
- reductions in risk to life or property.

The majority of these benefits can also be quantified in terms of money, and cost comparisons between a number of alternative methods will show the type of handling that will more readily justify investments and give the greatest profit.

Example:

METHOD A	Cost per Annum
Depreciation on equipment	Nil
Labour cost	£6,000
Space cost	£1,000
Potential cost of damage goods	£200
Potential profit on turnover in this area before handling costs	£18,000

METHOD B	Cost per Annum
Depreciation on equipment	£1,000
Labour cost	£4,000
Space cost	£2,000
Potential cost of damage goods	£500
Potential profit on turnover in this area before handling costs	£19,500

METHOD C	Cost per Annum
Depreciation on equipment	£5,000
Labour cost	£2,000
Space cost	£3,000
Potential cost of damage goods	£700
Potential profit on turnover in this area before handling costs	£20,500

Method B is more profitable to employ, although it is not so highly mechanised as Method C, nor does it achieve the same level of output or turnover. However, Method B maximises profit on the operation.

Reduction in overall costs of operations is the same as profit in circumstances where profit cannot be measured as return in excess of costs on output or sales.

Layout Considerations

Layout, of course, is one of the fundamental principles to be considered in planning materials handling, but it is a factor that deserves more detailed consideration, because space utilisation is an inherent problem in all materials movement.

The planning of the layout and the best use of space must be accomplished along with the determination of the best possible handling method, not fitted in somehow after equipment has been purchased. The main considerations will be as follows:

- The use of the "flow" principle as far as possible in the siting of incoming materials, the holding areas for materials, obtaining or disposing of containers, the routing of materials through the process, designation of working areas, correct movement of the people involved, implementation of alternative methods in case of breakdown, and the siting of outgoing materials.
- Maximising the use of the space available in relation to the type of equipment under consideration by the holding or storage of materials at the right levels to assist operations and avoiding the storage of fresh air.
- The provision of adequate room to manoeuvre by the provision of adequate gangways, providing sufficient headroom or clearance for conveyors or overhead handling, access to and from all points for equipment and personnel, and the provision of suitable surfaces for floor-operating equipment.

Again, these factors should be considered BEFORE methods or equipment are selected, otherwise the best possible choice cannot be made to give flexibility, adaptability, and, ultimately, profitability in the handling of materials.

Types of Handling Equipment

Apart from the normal methods of handling, such as lifting, carrying, pushing, or shovelling — all of which may be quite adequate in some circumstances — there is a wide variety of mechanical methods that fall into four categories:

- Industrial trucks
- Cranes and hoists
- Conveyors
- Pumps — pipelines — feeder systems

Industrial Trucks (Manual)

This range of equipment is designed to provide simple mechanical assistance in the operations of lifting, moving, or transporting loads that are too heavy to manhandle or that can be handled more economically in bulk lots. Manual industrial trucks include such equipment as the following:

- Sack trucks
- Platform trucks (manually operated)
- Platform lift trucks (manually operated)
- Drum lifts
- Cylinder trucks
- Pallet trucks (manually operated)
- Carboy tippers
- Lifts or mobile ladders (manually operated)
- Special purpose trucks and trolleys

Industrial Trucks (Power Driven)

Examples of power-driven trucks are shown in Figure 41. Power-driven trucks have been designed for a wide variety of applications. Their purpose is to handle loads that cannot be manhandled even with the assistance of the simple mechanical aids, or to transport loads over longer distances at greater speed. Power-driven industrial trucks include such equipment as the following:

- The fixed-platform power-driven truck
- Power-driven platform lift trucks, such as a 4-directional truck
- Tractors and trailers

As the volume of materials to be handled has increased, the problems of double-handling have demanded new methods of storage which, in turn, have led to the need for new ways of handling. As a result we have the various types of pallet and stillage and a wide range of forklift trucks to handle them. Stocklin Logistics Switzerland has an excellent Web site for viewing such a range (*www.sld.ch*). Before dealing with the applications of such trucks, we must consider the following factors:

- *Pedestrian or driver operated* — This will depend upon the loads to be carried, the space available, and the distances to be travelled.
- *Petrol, LP gas, diesel, or electric driven* — Consider whether for internal or external use, economy of running, economy of maintenance, capital cost, and mechanical reliability and availability.
- *Solid or cushion tyres* — This will depend upon the loads to be carried, the nature of the application, and the surfaces upon which it is required to operate.

Standard or special forklift trucks designed to cope with a wide variety of applications include:

- normal or high lift,
- reach trucks — with forward movement of the forks,
- straddle trucks
- lifting attachments for special purposes (e.g., ram - for coils, clamps - for drums),
- side-loading trucks, and
- electrical stackers (see Figure 42).

Another development in the field of power-driven industrial trucks is the automatic or robot system, the main purpose of which has been to reduce the manpower requirements in warehouses or stores for collecting or distributing large volumes of many items of stock.

The robot trucks are loaded at and controlled from a central point and are directed electrically along prewired gangways to the points within the warehouse where the goods are to be unloaded and stored. Similarly, goods from stock can be loaded on the trucks, which are automatically directed to a central point for issue, packing, or despatch Such a system is expensive to install and demands careful planning of storage locations for fast- and slow-moving items and the balance between them; "traffic jams" of robot trucks would cancel out the benefits that the system was installed to obtain.

Figure 41. Special trucks (Note: Illustration from Stocklin Logistic Switzerland. Used with permission.)

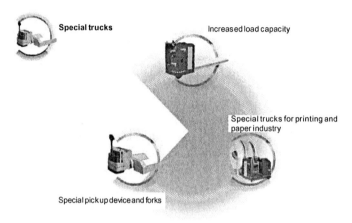

Figure 42. Electrical stackers (Note: Illustration from Stocklin Logistic Switzerland. Used with permission.)

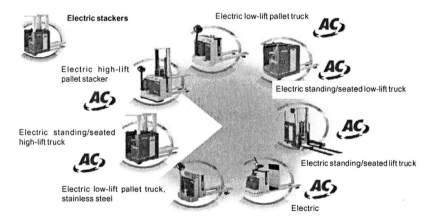

Figure 43. Hubwagon (Note: Illustration from Stocklin Logistic Switzerland. Used with permission.)

Cranes and Hoists

There are certain circumstances in which cranes or hoists are preferable to other forms of materials handling equipment. These circumstances can include:

- where heavy materials must be lifted for loading on to trucks or other vehicles for transportation,
- where heavy materials need to be lifted and moved only a short distance for further processing,
- where awkward loads are involved which cannot be handled or industrial trucks,
- where the movement involved is between two or more constant points, and
- where insufficient space is available on the floor to allow materials movement.

The following are examples of the various types designed to meet the problem:

- *Pull-lifts* — A hand-operated chain-block at a fixed point to lift heavy materials for loading on vehicles or machines.
- *Electric hoists* — An electrically operated version of the Pull-lift for basically the same purpose.
- *Monorail* — A single overhead rail from which a pul-lift or electric hoist is suspended on rollers, to allow loads to be moved to any point over which the monorail passes.
- *Swinglift jib* — A swinging arm on which a pul-lift or electric hoist is attached to allow loads to be moved to any point within the arc of the job.

- *Mobile or rolling gantry* — a steel structure which straddles the working area and is mounted on rollers and rails. A Pul-lift or Electric Hoist is suspended on rollers from the gantry, which then allows manual movement from side to side as well as along the length of the working area.
- *Overhead cranes* — A power-driven vehicle mounted on a fixed gantry running the whole length of the working area. The lifiting apparatus can be power driven from side to side across the working area as well as along the length of the gantry. The lifting is also electrically powered and can be controlled either from an overhead cavin attached to the vehicle or form ground level by hanging controls.
- *Jib crane* — A lifting arm that is fixed at one point; both the arm and the lifting apparatus are power driven and usually controlled from a cabin that rotates with the arm. Jib cranes are usually used for lifting heavy loads to considerable heights.
- *Mobile crane* — A jib crane mounted on a manually operated or motorised vehicle; usually used for lifting and transporting occasional awkward loads over reasonable distance, or where an overhead crane cannot be erected.

Conveyors

Where a continuous flow of goods or materials passes between two or more fixed points and the cost and utilisation of space can adequately be justified, a conveyor may be installed. Usually, the expense that a firm is prepared to incur in installing conveyors will be in direct relation to the volume of goods or materials involved.

The type of conveyor selected must obviously depend upon the type of materials to be handled, but wherever possible one should use gravity to drive the conveyor and thus avoid the cost of power and driving plant.

Within the general classification of conveyors, therefore, we include the following:

- Slides and chutes, for parcels and cartoons
- Gravity roller conveyors, used for many purposes from the movement of hot-rolled steel bar or strip, to the movement of packing cases

There are also the power-driven conveyors, chain-driven from electric motors:

- *"Live-roller" conveyors* — In which some of the rolls in each section of track are driven by chain as with the wheel of a bicycle; or there is the tow-line principle in which cog wheels, driven by electric motors, tow an endless length of conveyor.
- *Overhead conveyors* — For carrying materials or goods suspended above the working areas in which they are to be used or through process areas such as paint dipping or heat treatment.
- *"Subfloor tow conveyor"* — An endless chain below floor level onto which carts or trucks are hooked and towed to the point at which the materials they contain are required.

Another conveyor system is the pulley-driven conveyor, an endless belt moved by power driven pulleys or rollers positioned at one or both ends of the conveyor system. Such a conveyor can be either:

- *a belt conveyor* — mainly used for transporting small items that must be "contained" by the conveyor itself, such as small components, solid fuel, ashes; or
- *a slat conveyor* — where the "containing" ability of the belt conveyor is not necessary but where a flat surface is desirable.

Pumps, Pipelines and Feeder Systems

In circumstances where the materials to be supplied are large quantities in gaseous or liquid form or are solids in powder or fine-grain form, it may be advantageous to handle or transport them via pipelines or feeder systems. In this way the materials are enclosed in pipes or ducts, giving the following advantages:

- easier control of material movement,
- less likelihood of waste,
- protection from contamination is facilitated,
- flow of materials is more easily regulated, and
- sometimes provide the easiest method of connecting the storage unit with the user location.

Where the storage unit can be located above the user unit, it may be possible to use gravity feed, which saves the costs of providing power. Examples of gravity feed are:

- fuel oil from tanks above furnaces,
- lubricating oil from reservoirs above machines, and
- grain from silos to road transport.

In other circumstances it may be necessary to introduce pumping units to "push" materials along the pipelines or vacuum units to "suck" the materials along. This method of handling is now being applied to moving solids that can suitable be suspended in a liquid "transporter" (e.g., coal suspended in water or ore-bearing earth suspended in a suitable fluid).

Pipelines and feeder systems have a wide variety of uses that can prove more profitable or less costly than more conventional forms of handling, but the same benefit-to-cost analysis must be applied, and invariably the main factor justifying their use is the volume of materials to be handled.

Security

Stock is often a company's greatest asset. Bearing this in mind, compare the level of security afforded to the collection of one week's wages usually devoted to safeguarding the stores!

The security of stores buildings and stockyards is a natural base from which to start discussing security. Particular factors to consider include the following:

- A strongly built store, with security fencing in cases where the store is not part of the main premises. In case of stockyards, adequate security fencing is an essential requisite. Security lighting may also be considered in some locations.

- Doors and windows are weak points, and therefore doors should be kept to a minimum. Proper locks and bolts should be provided for all doors. In the case of large doors necessary for vehicle access, it is good practice to have a small "wicket" door for everyday use. Windows, if they open, should also have locks and have wire mesh or bars for protection against forced entry.

- Burglar alarms of various types and their installation.
- Security patrols should of course include stores on their irregular patrols. The local police will usually have a crime-prevention officer who will advise on security matters.

Keys are a weak point in any security system, and therefore should only be issued to authorised personnel. Limit the number of days keys are available to individuals and record the name of the authorised person receiving the key. Duplicate or master keys should be kept in a secure place in the charge of a responsible person. Access to stores should be limited to authorised personnel under the control of the stores officer. Particular care must be taken to see that people such as drivers, maintenance fitters, and the like do not get into the stores.

Out-of-hours issues are a problem for security because, quite often, stores staff are not available. The best solution is preparation through avoiding the need for out-of-hours issues, by planning and issuing requirements in advance. If it is essential to make an emergency issue, a named official should be made responsible for the security of the stores.

In any stores, there are items attractive to a potential thief. Secure areas within the stores should be provided for these items. Scrap and redundant materials are often a security risk, because they are often segregated from the main stores. This also applies to returns, awaiting despatch to suppliers.

Fire is always a hazard and the installation of firefighting equipment is a necessity. This must be maintained at regular intervals. The local fire brigade should be consulted on fire precautions.

Safety and Safe Methods of Working

It makes good sense to have safe methods of working in order to avoid personal injury and to safeguard the company's interests.

In cases where personnel are injured at work, the manager responsible may well face prosecution under legislation if he or she has failed to ensure that safe working conditions and practices are maintained. The particular points to which the stores manager must pay attention are as follows:

- Good layout of the stores, providing for clearly designated gangways, marked with white lines or similar methods. These gangways must be kept free from obstructions at all times. Areas for receipt of goods, inspection, returns to stores, scrap, and redundant stock, as well as storage areas should be properly designated.

- Stores must be kept clean and tidy; what is generally called good housekeeping is an essential element in providing safe conditions of work. Many accidents are caused by persons tripping and falling over obstacles and the like. Piles of inflammable rubbish, such as empty packaging, are also a real hazard.

- Cleanliness must be enforced by management. This can be aided by the sealing of concrete floors and the provision of sheets and dust covers where required.

- All rubbish and arisings must be segregated and proper facilities provided for temporary storage until removal. This removal must be on a regular basis, because old containers, paper, cardboard, wood, wool, and so forth soon accumulates in any stores.

- Storage equipment must be properly used and goods stored in it correctly. Particular care must be taken to ensure that the weight limits and capacity of all equipment is known, and not exceeded. In a similar way, the load-bearing capacity of floors and maximum storage heights must be known.

- Lighting is an important factor in safety, and all working areas must be adequately lit. The actual lighting required will depend upon particular circumstances. For example, very good lighting will be needed where the selection of small items is carried out. All passages and alleyways must be lighted to prevent accidents.

- Provision of handrails is required where gangways are above ground level or where the worker may experience difficulty in walking.

- The stores manager must ensure that all equipment under his or her control is properly guarded. Forklift trucks will need overhead guards to prevent loads injuring the driver in the case of accidents.

- Nonslip surfaces should be provided on ramps and sloping paths.

- Loading and unloading docks and wells are areas of particular danger in a store. Removable handrails will be required, as will curbs or stops to prevent forklift trucks running over the edge of the dock.

- Warning and informative notices are an essential aid to safe methods of working. Many will be familiar to you, such as "Petroleum Spirit," "No Smoking," "Exit," and so on. These are available as "standards" from suppliers. Other signs to suit your own particular requirements are available and can be made to your specification. Some signs must be displayed, and colour is a useful method of conveying warnings or information. Danger

- signs and fire equipment are red and caution signs are yellow (forklift trucks are normally yellow).
- Protective clothing and equipment must be provided and worn in appropriate situations. It is the responsibility of management to ensure that safety helmets, goggles, gloves, overalls, safety shoes, and boots are provided, and, what is more difficult, management must make sure that the equipment is used properly.
- The organisation will have a safety officer that the stores manager must consult on safety matters. Instructions regarding the safety of equipment and practices should be issued in writing by management to all personnel working in the stores. It is important that people such as crane drivers, forklift truck operators, and slingers are aware of safety regulations.

Remember, it is the responsibility of management to provide safe working conditions. Legislation moves quickly, and the need to keep up to date is paramount.

Food for Thought

Most materials will deteriorate in store, in the course of time. The following steps need to be taken to prevent deterioration:

- **Suppliers' deliveries**. Packaging must be suitable for product and on arrival should be thoroughly checked. Most suppliers want their goods to arrive fit for use. An example is sterile goods in hospitals.
- **Order of issue**. Rate of deterioration varies. The longer a product remains in stores, the more the risk of deterioration. Stock rotation, first-in-first-out, and shelf life are all important considerations. An example is photographic materials.
- **Heating and lighting**. Damp is the supervisor's worst enemy. Correct and adequate heating is essential. An example is textiles. For some specific products, light-sensitivity can also be an issue. Examples are drugs and dressings.
- **Stock preservation**. Some stock needs to be preserved against premature deterioration. Packaging, apart form its basic function of protecting goods in transit, also assists in preservation. Stores may also add packaging as protection for goods in store, including dustproofing, waterproofing, vapourproofing/sealing, rigid packing for efficient stacking, and packing in

small boxes to keep items tidy. Examples include canned goods that need to be stable, stationery that needs to be dustproof, and electronic equipment that needs to be water- and vapourproof.

- **Specific protective measures**. If store is adequately heated and ventilated, then the majority of items will require no special treatment; but some materials are special and present their own problems. These could include cement, timber, textiles, crops, metal, and machinery and equipment. All detailed protective measures need careful and constant watching.

The stores-issuing section is a key activity and the objectives should include the following:

- All requests must be authorised and issued in accordance with agreed-upon procedures.
- Appropriate documentation raised and subsequently, posted.
- Stores systems must be updated.
- Issues to be made promptly and in accordance with agreed standards of service.
- Staff employed on issuing must be trained and effective.
- Where possible, with customer's agreement, issues should be preplanned to even workload.
- Stores location system and layout of racking should ensure that fast-moving items are located to ensure efficiency.
- Staff must be aware of the necessity of the security of goods when awaiting collection/delivery.

Many organisations produce a written manual, detailing the stores' policies and procedures. There are advantages and disadvantages to having a manual:

Advantages:

- Provides, in written and accessible form, a record of all standing instructions/procedures.
- Assists with training, particularly new staff.
- Assists with standardisation of procedures and paperwork.
- Ensures stores is easier to audit.

- Can be used as a basis for performance measurement.
- Defining the duties of staff and supervision becomes easier as well as standardisation of staff behaviour.

Disadvantages:

- Can be very time-consuming to produce and therefore can be costly.
- Needs regular updating to be effective.
- Sometimes not read by all staff, and therefore not followed.
- Can stifle individual initiative and creativity.

There is no right answer here, but logic suggests the advantages outweigh the disadvantages.

Case Studies

The Problem

Some years ago, Iceland UK installed an automated sortation system fed by a pick-by-light pick-to-belt system into one if its frozen food depots. However, changes in the patterns of business have taken place, and this has resulted in a belief that the system was no longer able fully to meet Iceland's needs. Also, reliability has become more of a problem and support for the control system difficult. As a result of these problems, Iceland decided to call in consultants to advise them on how best to proceed. Because of their experience of retail warehousing and distribution, and particularly of warehouse automation, Iceland chose *The Logistics Business* to undertake the investigation.

The first step taken by *The Logistics Business* was to spend time with all the people directly involved in the use and operation of the system to understand the problems and any further changes in the business that might affect performance. As is often the case, they found they were usually hearing about symptoms and therefore followed up with a structured investigation to understand the causes of the problems. By combining the information gathered with their experience of other warehouse operations, they were able to match symptoms and causes and hence consentrate on solutions.

The Solution

The Logistics Business concluded that the sortation system could meet the needs of the business if certain steps were taken. These included changes to the way product was zoned and picked, changes to the strategy adopted for use of the sortation output lanes, and adoption of new picking methods, not involving the pick-by-light. They also recommended changes to workload balancing and to the frequency of store deliveries. Estimates were made for the cost of improvements to the control system, which were shown to be favourable in comparison with the cost of other proposed changes.

The Success

- Iceland was given clearly documented options to use as the basis for decision making.
- Discussions on the future of the sortation system were no longer based solely on opinion but upon clearly presented factual information.
- This demonstrated how success with automated systems is not dependant on the equipment alone. Performance is greatly influenced by the strategy adopted for operation of the system and by day to day management skills.

The Problem

Barclays National Records Centre (BNRC) UK holds some 2 million boxes of documents of varying types and moves up to 7,000 of these boxes per day. Growth in recent years has been very great, as more activities have been centralised, and this had put pressure on people, systems, and equipment. The starting point was a thorough review of activities using a unique Health Check. By involving employees at all levels, this allowed a focus on the issues most likely to bring immediate benefits. In particular, more thinking about internal customer service and the need of service level as a means of measuring performance. Then moved on to address specific areas where changes to layouts, equipment and systems could improve performance.

The Solution

In some areas, *The Logistics Business* recommended the use of barcode identification as well as the introduction of radio data terminals. Specifications were prepared for new software to manage some expanding part, so the business and *The Logistics Business* then managed the writing of this software and its implementation. In one area of the business, where particularly high growth was expected throughout, *The Logistics Business* designed new mechanical handling systems and managed the introduction of a carton conveyor.

The Success

- Managers and other staff are more focused on giving good service to their internal customers.
- Continued growth in handling requirements has been accommodated whilst service levels have been maintained or improved.
- BNRC has been more able to fulfil its role as an extension of the activities of the banks branches.
- New technologies have been introduced into areas that had previously operated using very conventional methods.

The Problem

The question facing Boots plc UK when it came to consider the refurbishment of one of its larger warehouses in Nottingham was whether or not to replace the existing equipment on a like-for-like basis or to seek another solution. The main consideration was how to maximise the use of space in their existing 35,000 square metres. Although Boots has its own in-house project team, this was already heavily committed, so it was decided that on this occasion outside help would be sought. *The Logistics Business* was chosen for this task. They worked very closely with Boots' team. Problem definition was not merely a question of data analysis. Whatever solution was arrived at, it would have to last for at least 20 years and Boots, in common with most major retailers, did not know what their business would be like over that time. Consequently, the solution would have to be flexible and capable of adapting to a range of situations. A number of options were explored, ranging form straight replacement to more novel satellite and shuttle systems. They took responsibility for preparing the detailed presentations of the options and put these forward to the team for evaluation. They then developed the chosen option and prepared detailed invitations to tender. Following receipt of tenders, they formed part of the evaluation team that made the final choice of supplier.

The Solution

The solution chosen is automated. Aisle-changing stacker cranes fed by conveyors and shuttle cars form the basis of the solution, and as a result of recommendations made, overall storage capacity has been increased. A major factor affecting the refurbishment was minimisation of disruption to the existing warehouse operations. Designing an implementation method whereby operations could continue whilst installation was carried out was a major challenge where the experience of *The Logistics Business* brought some particular benefits. The contract for the refurbishment, worth some £7 million, went ahead smoothly and on time. The project is rated as highly successful.

The Success

- The Boots team has benefited from the wider experience of *The Logistics Business* to add to its own in depth knowledge of the Boots business.
- Options have been evaluated objectively with unanimous agreement that the most appropriate solution has been adopted.
- The refurbishment has gone ahead with minimum disruption.
- Storage capacity has been increased and flexibility maintained.

In the next chapter I will overview transport and distribution of those items we have now successfully stores managed!

Chapter X

Transport

Shipping, transport, and distribution in terms of supply chain management can be grouped under one heading: Logistics. Logistics planning involves not only the transportation side of distribution but also provides the "place element" in the marketing mix by helping to ensure that products arrive in sufficient quantities and in saleable condition at points from which the consumer can most easily buy them. Thus, logistics management includes forecasting demand and then matching supply to meet that demand through procurement of materials, production scheduling, inventory management, order processing, warehousing, and transportation. In international systems, the logistics planning function comprises a number of subsystems that have central points-of-reach territory. There is a further subsystem for the management of local logistics (i.e., the transport and distribution systems used by the importer to move products to customers in the market concerned).

Logistics, as well as being essential for moving goods to their destinations, is also a key marketing activity. As such it requires marketing management's attention. Logistics contributes to a major portion of costs, particularly in international business. Logistic planning also plays a major role in creating a good relationship with customers, ensuring that sales opportunities are not lost because of stock outs (which allows competitors to eat away at the company's market share). In assessing the real cost of transportation, you should be concerned with factors relating to reliability, time, and price. Decisions in choosing methods of transport and distribution therefore will be based on "trade-offs" between these factors. Transportation costs are often peculiar in that they frequently bear little relation to distance. Competition and volume are the key factors in cargo pricing. For example, the rate of goods transported from the Far East to the East Coast of the United States costs less than the transport rate of goods going the other way. Costs from the United States to South America are frequently lower than costs of transport among South American countries. All transport costs have increased, however, largely due to increased security operations.

Introduction

The problems with planning transportation can be enormous, and considerable costs can be concealed (e.g., the costs of out-of-stock positions that cause a business loss, or delays over insurance claims). Transport is clearly a critical function within the overall logistics discipline. This chapter looks at the component parts of transport consisting of the following:

- Fleet management
- Vehicle replacement
- Vehicle scheduling
- Maintenance and security
- Containers
- Loading equipment
- Road vehicle design
- Haulage
- Rail freight
- Air freight

In the 21st century and the post-9/11 world, costs and shipping times have increased primarily due to increased security checks.

Fleet Management

The main duties of the fleet manager are composed of the efficient operation of his or her fleet and, in addition, the attainment of any further objectives laid down by top management. The fleet manager will do this by first achieving maximum utilisation of the vehicles he or she operates, by setting and maintaining correct weight/distance standards, and keeping within budgets and making sure vehicles are properly maintained.

There are probably more laws, legislation, and statutory regulations concerning road transport than any other activity. For example, in the United Kingdom, the fleet manager will need to be aware of the following:

- The Highways Acts
- Road Traffic Acts
- Transport Act
- Vehicles and Driving Licenses Act
- Heavy Commercial Vehicles (Control and Regulations) Act
- Motor Vehicles (Construction and Use) Regulations
- Goods Vehicles (Plating and Testing) Regulations

Note the foregoing is by no means exhaustive and the fleet manager must ensure that he or she is aware of all present and relevant legislation, regardless of the operating country.

A host of matters arise from this legislation that impose duties upon fleet managers. Among these matters, some of the more important are to ensure that:

- vehicles are not overloaded,
- vehicles are not loaded in such a way that the load is unsafe,
- vehicles are properly maintained to the standard required by law,
- vehicles are correctly tested and plated, as stated in the regulations,
- drivers do not exceed permitted hours of work,
- a record of work is kept by all drivers, and
- drivers must hold a current driving license of the appropriate class for the vehicle to be driven.

An important aspect of every manager's job is to manage the function. This means setting standards, measuring actual performance, and, combining the two, enabling him or her to correct any deviations. Budgetary control is a convenient and effective method of control. This can be equally well applied to fleet management. It is these costs that provide the fleet manager with the information that he or she needs to control his or her department.

Other information required is mileage: average operated per day and average mileage maintained per day; tonnage or volume equivalent carried. The following indicators will be needed to measure performance:

- Total operating costs per period (usually 1 month)
- Cost per hour
- Cost per mile
- Cost per ton (or volume equivalent)
- Cost per day operated
- Cost per day maintained
- Cost per depot
- Cost per vehicle
- Cost per vehicle class

You will see from this list that the manager can establish the cost and efficiency of the department and its individual depots, where applicable. He or she can also check the performance of types of vehicles, or even an individual vehicle, if required.

Vehicle Replacement

Anyone who owns a car knows how quickly they need to be replaced and the problems involved with financing the purchase of a new model. This is, of course, a much greater problem for a fleet manager, who has to maintain a definite number of vehicles on the road to keep the goods moving. The first necessity is to establish a clear policy on replacement, based not only on the need to replace vehicles at the end of their economic life, but upon such factors as the following:

- Long-term strategic planning (e.g., What goods shall we be transporting in the future, and where shall we be sending them?)

- Capital resources available
- Any legal requirements at home or overseas, or any impending legal requirements
- Economic loads, unionisation, containerisation
- Design and construction of vehicles
- Vehicle maintenance needs
- Vehicle depreciation

Having decided that we must renew our fleet according to a planned policy, and having decided which vehicles we need for our replacement programme, we come to the question raised earlier: How do we finance the purchase of new vehicles? Some of the methods available to companies are as follows:

- **Outright purchase**. This is simple if the capital is available at a reasonable price (remember, the price of borrowing money is the interest paid). Capital allowances are available that can be set against the purchase.
- **Hire purchase**. This is often favoured because it avoids the need to find large sums of capital. At the same time, a tax allowance is given as if it were an outright purchase. Hire purchase rates are the price of borrowing the money and must be studied before entering into an agreement. Note that the purchaser does not obtain ownership until the last instalment is paid.
- **Lease**. This method avoids the need to provide working capital, and because the vehicles are on lease, the operator does not have to worry about depreciation. However, there are problems to be considered. One important point is that the vehicles will never belong to you. Leases are usually for a fixed number of years, and you are obliged to have a vehicle for that period of time. Lease charges will need to be studied, and you will also have to take into account operating and repair charges, which are often additional to the basic charge.
- **Contract hire**. Details of the contract must be studied carefully, to ensure exactly who is responsible for insurance, maintenance, supplying replacement vehicles, and so forth. The basis of charging and the rates of charge also require careful investigation.

Choosing the Right Policy

As has been indicated, choosing the right policy is not a straightforward decision — many factors have to be taken into account. A detailed analysis of quotations for each method will have to be made; remember that it is not only the immediate replacement cost that has to be taken into account but also the cost of operating over a number of years. An analysis must also be made between the various methods of replacement, and such matters as tax allowances and inflation must be taken into account. This will give the true cost of each method and, together with the company's objectives, strategies, and financial recourses, will enable the selection of the right policy.

Vehicle Scheduling

The objective of scheduling is to achieve optimum vehicle utilisation by operating vehicles at maximum load and at minimum cost. In carrying out this objective, the fleet manager will wish to ensure that the fleet is used efficiently and that vehicles are available when they are required. Similarly, the manager needs to ensure that the most suitable vehicle for particular loads and journeys are used.

Constraints

In scheduling and routing vehicles, the fleet manager must regard a number of constraints imposed by legislation, the organisation's resources, and the needs of the customer. Among these are as follows:

- The legal permitted driving hours
- The need for drivers to have days off
- Speed restrictions
- The maintenance and servicing requirements of vehicles, which involve vehicles being off the road
- The number of vehicles the fleet manager has at his or her disposal at any one time
- The types of vehicles the fleet manager has available, because this will govern the capacity that is available
- Depot locations, and the number of depots the fleet manager operates
- The types of traffic involved; when schedules are prepared, parcel traffic will be different from heavy haulage
- The number of calls to be made and their distance from each other

- The time involved in loading or unloading at each call
- Whether an urban area or a rural area is involved
- Any special requirements of the trade involved or of customers
- Such matters as public holidays, industrial holidays of customers, and local holidays; not forgetting early closing days, if in the retail trade
- The type of roads available (e.g., motorways, dual carriage ways)
- Temporary restrictions caused by road works, building operations, and similar work
- Certain loads may require special routes, to avoid obstructions, or bridges with weight limits and the like

How to Choose the Route

Whilst there are a number of (expensive) software packages available, this is a considerable problem because there aren't packages that can process every route scenario. There are many factors to consider. Often, there are several ways of selecting vehicle routes and loads for vehicles. These include:

- **Pigeon-hole method**. This is probably the simplest method and is widely used for this reason. Delivery points are grouped together into geographical areas that have been adopted on the loading deck, usually in special bays. When the goods for each area are known, a detailed schedule is worked out and a vehicle allocated. This method is most suitable where the number of areas and delivery points are limited.
- **String diagrams**. Another simple method is the use of string diagrams to select the best routes. A good map is required, showing transport depots and customer delivery points. The map will, of course, be to a known scale enabling distances to be read easily. A pin is fastened to each depot location and also at each delivery point. A piece of string is fastened to a depot and taken to each delivery point in the sequence that appears to be the best route. In this way, it is possible to show a number of alternative routes, and the distances involved can be measured. The best route or routes can then be selected. In practice, the maps will be mounted on board and coloured strings will be used to show alternative routes more clearly. An ancient practice I agree, but one that is still in use in smaller organisations around the world.

- **Distance saving.** This means selection of the optimum routes by first selecting the worst route. This would normally be by making an individual call each time to one customer, we would next try linking the two nearest delivery points together and see what the savings would be. The next nearest point would then be linked up, and this would continue until an acceptable route emerged.
- **Travelling sales representatives.** Visiting each customer by the shortest route and returning to the depot. It has a limited use in practice.
- **Linear programming.** This is an operational research technique developed to show how limited resources can be used to their optimum. As the title suggests, linear is proportional, and assumes that if for instance we have more time we can produce more goods. The basic method used in linear programming is to locate an extreme point of a feasible region; examine each boundary edge intersecting at this point to see if an overlap along any edge would increase the value of the objective function. If this is so, move along the edge to the adjacent extreme point. Repeat until the value of the objective function no longer increases.

For example, we assume that an organisation has depots and stock as follows:

Depots	Stock
Anytown	30
Hightown	32
Northborough	22
Westborough	26

Customer orders are as follows:

Customer	Order Quantity
Smith	34
Brown	40
Jones	36

The transport costs from each depot to each customer will be assumed in this case to be as follows:

Customer	Anytown	Hightown	Northborough	Westborough
Smith	16	18	12	6
Brown	12	22	10	20
Jones	6	16	14	18

We are now in a position to select the best routes, for there are a number of alternative solutions available. One solution may be for stock to be allocated as follows:

Customer	Qty	Depot Route	Qty	Depot Route
Smith	8	Northborough (1)	26	Westborough (2)
Brown	26	Anytown	14	Northborough (4)
Jones	4	Anytown	32	Hightown (6)

The cost of doing it this way are as follows:

Delivery Route	Cost/Item	Qty	Cost
1	12	8	96
2	6	26	156
3	12	26	312
4	10	14	140
5	6	4	24
6	16	32	512
		Total Cost	1,240

This gives us only the cost of using one method. We need to repeat this exercise for each possible method and by a process of elimination discover the most economic route. This appears to present a system of "trial and error," but linear programming is a planned method of trying all alternatives until the best solution is found.

In our example, the allocations and costs are as follows:

Customers	Depots: Anytown		Hightown		Northborough		Westborough	
Smith		16		18	8	12	26	6
Brown	26	12		22	14	10		20
Jones	4	6	32	16		14		18

An alternative is for Smith to take one from the Anytown depot; however, if we do this, we must reallocate issues from other depots. The whole exercise must then be calculated to see what the difference in cost in the revised method is, against the original, such as in the following:

Customers	Depots: Anytown		Hightown		Northborough		Westborough	
Smith	+1	16		18	8-1	12		6
Brown	26-1	12		22	7=1	10		20
Jones	4	6	32	16		14		18

In cost terms we have the following:

- Cost of Anytown to Smith 16, less Smith to Northborough 12 — an increase of 4.
- Northborough to Brown 10, less Anytown to Brown 12 — a decrease of 2.
- In this case, a net increase of 2 in cost is repeated for each unused route.

Supervisors should monitor and evaluate the effectiveness of their own distribution planning by measuring their performance against targets set by themselves or by their line managers. They should analyse any variances between the planned and actual performance, to assess whether these have been caused by deficiencies in their planning (e.g., setting unrealistic schedules or failing to take account of external changes). This will then enable supervisors to improve their planning in the future.

Maintenance and Security

Maintenance and security are two factors that all transport managers must give considerable attention. Road safety is constantly receiving attention from legislators and the press, and rightly so. Road vehicles carry the majority of goods in transit, and therefore, security is a major function of transport management.

Facilities for Maintenance

A high degree of maintenance of required to keep a modern transport fleet on the road and maintained properly, according to legislation. Accordingly, any organisation operating vehicles must consider how it is going to maintain and service its vehicles. Methods available include the following:

- **Organisation's garage and workshops.** This requires properly equipped premises with all necessary facilities to service and repair vehicles. It also means employing qualified fitters, vehicle electricians, and other staff. This method is convenient, as there is complete control over maintenance programmes. Repairs can be carried out to suit the operating schedules and it is very flexible. On the other hand, it is expensive to maintain these facilities and is therefore uneconomic for many operators with small fleets.

- **Contact maintenance**. This is the method that must be adopted if circumstances do not justify having one's own workshop facilities. Most commercial garages will be willing to enter into a contract for the servicing and maintenance of vehicle fleets. The types of contracts available are too numerous to be dealt with here and need to be considered in detail. However, the contract may cover regularly planned maintenance or simply servicing when required. Vehicle manufacturers often have schemes whereby contract maintenance and servicing is carried out through their agents.

Quality Control

Quality control is a major aspect of vehicle servicing and maintenance because there is little point in arranging for maintenance if it does not meet the required standard. A mixture of road transport publications mixed with a little common sense suggests the following:

- Positive checks should be made at predetermined intervals of time or mileage on items that affect the safety of the vehicles.
- Staff carrying out service and repair of vehicles must be aware of the significance of defects.
- Any vehicle inspector or other staff whose duty it is to inspect vehicles must have authority to rectify defects and to take unsafe vehicles off the road.
- Written records must be kept showing when and by whom inspections are carried out, the results of the inspections, when and by whom remedial work is done, and details of the work.
- Under-vehicle inspection facilities should be provided.
- A system must be provided whereby drivers can report defects in writing. The clearance of the defect should also be recorded.
- The mechanical condition of hired vehicles and trailers is the direct responsibility of the user (the employer of the driver). Documents that are required to ensure an effective system of maintenance are service sheets for the predetermined time/mileage checks, inspection check lists, drivers defect report, vehicles history record, job cards, and planning sheets.

- Proper planning maintenance is essential if the vehicles are to be kept on the road and there are a number of aids to the planning needed.

Security

One has only to think of the wide variety of goods moved by road to realise how desirable many of these loads are to thieves and terrorists. Insurance companies as well as operators of fleets are concerned about effective security. In fact, insurance companies often require certain precautions to be taken by the operator as a condition of providing insurance.

Security is an attitude of mind that must be cultivated to ensure that everyone is aware of the problem and the elementary safeguards necessary. The advice of the insurance companies is always available, and so is that of the police.

There are some common sense actions possible:

- Recruitment of staff. References should be checked over the last 5 years and any gaps investigated. Beware of telephone numbers for references, it may be an accomplice. If a driver is engaged do not let she or he take out a vehicle until you have their income tax details.
- Alarms and immobilisers should be fitted; models that provide protection without the driver getting out of the vehicle are available. The devices should be checked frequently.
- Drivers hauling valuable loads should be instructed not to get out of their cabs if stopped by the police, but instead offer to go to the nearest police station. As an anti-hijack measure, bolts should be fitted inside the doors.
- Vehicles should not be left unattended, especially at night.
- Keys should never be left in the vehicle. Numbers should be removed from security locks, starter and ignition keys, or switches. If a key is lost, change all locks and switches.
- Drivers should be asked to change their routine by not visiting the same cafés at regular times.
- When a vehicle is sold, remove the company name.
- Suggest a cash bonus, payable if the drivers observe security rules.

Security is also important for the long-term future of the business, because if an organisation gets a reputation for bad security, customers may withdraw their trade.

Containers, Unitisation and Palletisation

It is advantageous if consignors can load goods at their premises, so that those goods can be transported and delivered to the consignee without the necessity of unpacking and handling individual items in transit. The aforementioned aids enable this to be done, as they are all methods of providing a "unit" from one mode of transport to another. There is, therefore, no interference with the load in transit.

Containers

A container is now a major piece of transport equipment, and because its purpose is to ensure that a load is transported without interference to the consignor, it is important that it can be moved across national boundaries. It would be a major problem if containers were of different sizes and aptness in various countries, therefore the International Standards Organisation (ISO) has made recommendations for freight containers that are generally accepted by national and international standards (see, for example, ISO 17712:2003).

The ISO suggests that general-purpose freight containers are of a rectangular shape, weatherproof for transporting and storing a number of unit loads, packages, or bulk materials; they confine and protect the contents from loss or damage and can be separated from the means of transport, handled as unit loads, and transhipped without rehandling the contents. A freight container is an article of transport equipment that:

- is of a permanent character and accordingly strong enough for repeated use,
- is specially designed to facilitate the carriage of goods by one or more modes of transport, without intermediate reloading,
- is fitted with devices permitting its ready handling, particularly its transfer from one mode of transport to another,
- is so designed as to be easy to fill and empty, and
- has an internal volume of 1 square metre or more.

The freight container does not include vehicles or conventional packaging.

Standard container sizes are based upon a module of 2.4 m x 2.4 m and will take the loads varying from 10 to 30 long tons.

Types of Containers

It is important to remember than an ISO standard, although valuable, is not going to meet all requirements, and many organisations will wish to design their own containers to suit their needs. Floors may be required to be strong enough for forklift trucks to enter when loading or unloading. Sides and posts may be required to be suitable for use with special lifting devices. Many types of containers are available, including:

- high-capacity boxes,
- demountable tanks (for bulk liquids),
- ordinary boxes,
- insulated containers, and
- curtain-sided containers.

Organisations despatching by these methods may own their containers, which will be painted in their colours and hence have advertising value. Alternatively, they may be hire such containers.

Continental Operation

If companies are regularly sending goods across Europe, for example, it will be an advantage to have Transport Internationaux Routier (TIR) registration, which enables containers to cross customs frontiers easily. A point worth noting is that for European tax purposes, the container is not part of the unladen weight of the vehicle.

Unitisation

Unitisation comprises assembling a number of small packages into one large package, or "unit load," which makes handling much easier and, when loading or unloading, will:

- reduce the amount of labour required,
- enable mechanical handling to be used,
- reduce vehicle turn round time,
- make loading and stowage easier,
- allow safer working practice to be used,
- reduce damage and pilferage, and
- permit marking and labelling of consignments to be simplified.

Unitisation, therefore, reduces handling and transportation costs.

In the case of air freight, these advantages are very important, because speed is the main reason for using this method of transport. Unitisation means that a much speedier method of loading is possible compared to handling loose items of cargo. The customer can share in the reduced costs because airlines offer special rates for bulk unitisation cargos. Security measures (inspection, scanning, verifying source of the units) are, however, an increasing problem since the terrorist attacks such as that which occurred on September 11, 2001, and elsewhere.

Standard Packaging

Many organisations have a range of standard packs that take certain quantities of each product. Therefore, when an order is received, it is known at once which standard "outer" pack will be suitable. This not only takes advantage of unitisation principles but means that the air or shipping space can be booked right away.

Palletisation

I will not describe in this section pallets and their construction but rather palletisation, used to facilitate transport loading.

As with unitisation, the advantages gained from palletisation can be summed up as the reduction in handling and transportation costs, and the particular advantages are also similar:

- Enables mechanical handling to be used
- Reduces road vehicle turn round time

- Makes loading and stowage easier
- Reduces damage and pilferage

The possible cost savings by using pallets are considerable, because goods can be picked up by forklift truck and taken aboard ship or into container and stowed. At this point it is worthwhile reminding ourselves of what a pallet is. It is quite simply a device on the deck of which a quantity of goods can be assembled to form a unit load for the purpose of transporting it, or of handling or stacking it with the assistance of mechanical appliances. This device is normally made up of two decks separated by bearers, or of a single deck supported by feet; its overall height is reduced to a minimum compatible with handling by fork lift trucks and pallet trucks; it may or may not have a superstructure.

Ownership and Return of Pallets

The ownership and return of pallets represents a considerable problem because everyone using pallets has their own, and the cost of having them returned can be considerable. One solution is to use low cost, nonreturnable (LCNR) pallets. The pallet has to be strong enough to support loads and to withstand forklift trucks moving them, but to have a low cost. In practice, LCNRs are usually reenforced with plastic. Another solution is to use a "pallet pool," where all users contribute to the pool and use pallets accordingly. The drawbacks that pallets have when compared with containers are as follows:

- The pallet offers only limited protection to goods.
- A reasonable amount of labour is required to handle pallets.
- The pallet loads cannot be transported under bond, as they cannot be sealed.
- A single pallet load is not an economic unit of transport.

In addition, there has been a failure among countries to agree on a standard for pallets. For example, the United States and Europe have different standards.

Mechanical Aids to Loading and Off-Loading

The time spent loading and unloading vehicles can be considerable and can therefore be costly in terms of vehicle time. Any aid to make this operation more efficient will reduce these costs and speed a vehicle's turnaround time.

Equipment that is suitable for most purposes is available, but the problem is to select the equipment most suitable for particular circumstances. To decide on the correct equipment, one must consider the following:

- Weights of materials to be handled
- Quantities of materials to be handled
- Nature of goods involved
- Handling characteristics of the goods
- Frequency of loading
- Customers needs

Although in many cases vehicles are unloaded or loaded by equipment mounted on the loading bays, circumstances often require the ability of the vehicle itself to load and off-load. The following are examples of equipment used in both circumstances.

Equipment for Loading and Unloading Bays

Automatic dock levellers, or elevating platforms, are extremely helpful on loading bays because vehicle platforms vary by height. These levellers enable forklift trucks, barrows, and the like to be driven from the dock directly into the vehicle. Dock levellers may be built into the bay or be portable or power driven.

Forklift trucks are widely used, and a wide range of models are available with an even wider range of fittings and adoptions (e.g., fittings for handling drums, coils, clamps for certain loads, crane hooks). Pallet loads are intended for forklift truck movement and palletisation is therefore advantageous.

Cranes also have a wide range of uses in loading and unloading — particularly where large and heavy loads need to be moves — but cranes are unable to deal with large volumes. Installing cranes is costly and the amount of goods traffic unloaded must justify the high capital cost involved. Cranes do, however, have freedom of movement within a certain area. The following are the main types of cranes available:

- **Fixed jib**. This crane has a single mast in a fixed position, therefore its operation area is limited.
- **Gantry type**. This crane comprises load-bearing girders supported at each end and running on rails that gives the gantry its means of movement. On the girders is a trolley that houses the lifting mechanism that provides the traverse movement, therefore permitting traverse movement in all directions. Control is located in a suspended cabin or is maintained by a remote-control switch.
- **Wheeled type**. These cranes are mounted on road wheels and are useful and mobile pieces of apparatus. Several types are available for purchase or hire.
- **Rail-mounted cranes**. The use of these cranes is limited to areas where rails are laid.
- **Pully blocks and hoists**. Although these are types of cranes, they are smaller than most and can usually be fixed where required for a particular job. Awkward and cumbersome loads can be unloaded with these cranes. There are many types available, varying from traditional rape-blocks to the pul-lift types using a roller chain.
- **Telphers**. Telphers are another type of crane that is useful for particular operations. They are cab-operated and run over a certain area on a mono, or single, overhead rail. Movement is, therefore, restricted to one direction. When fitted with grabs, they are often used for loading loose materials such as sand, gravel, or coal.

Other loading equipment include the following:

- **Pneumatic tubes** are another means of handling loose materials in powder form and are often used for flour, sand, and similar materials. The tubes are laid from the loading bay to where the material is produced, and the material is sucked along the tube.
- **Pipelines** are needed where liquids are involved.
- **Conveyors** are also widely used in loading and off-loading materials and are particularly suited to high-volume loads, as movement is continuous and comparatively cheap. Conveyors may operate by gravity or by power. They may also be fixed or moveable. A fixed conveyor takes up considerable

space and, for unloading purposes, portable conveyors are often found to be more useful. Conveyors are vulnerable to damage, and therefore care must be taken when handling them. Conveyors are available to suit a wide range of materials (e.g., flat belt, toughened belt, slatted, filler, and so on).

In many circumstances, such as vehicles delivering to retail shops or scattered depots, handling aids are unlikely to be available at the site of unloading or loading. Therefore, we have to consider aids that are available for use on vehicles.

Loading and Unloading Equipment Available on Vehicles

Tail lifts are provided on a wide range of vehicles. Lifts are also available for the side of the vehicle, so loads can be transferred to the pavement easily. A tail lift is the "tail" of the vehicle that forms a platform on which goods can be lowered to ground level by power. The vehicle must have a chassis and framework strong enough to support the mechanism.

Rollers are provided in the floor of the vehicle, allowing loads to be moved easily inside the vehicle. These rollers may be retracted below the floor to prevent the load from moving. Cranes are also available for mounting onto vehicles, though a specially strengthened floor and chassis is required. Various types are available to suit particular purposes. Tankers are normally fitted with pumps that permits them to discharge their loads into the customers' tanks or wherever required. Vehicle equipment suppliers are normally happy to advise the most economically advantageous solution.

Road Vehicle Design and Road Planning

Because goods vehicles are costly to buy and maintain, it is essential that the fleet is operated efficiently; this includes ensuring that the vehicles are those most suitable for their intended purpose.

In deciding the type of vehicle for a particular use, must consider the following factors:

- The goods or materials to be carried
- The goods we may wish to transport in the future
- Our distribution area
- Number of journeys made
- Potential changes in distribution patterns
- The expected life of vehicles
- Any relevant government legislation
- Any advantages offered in terms of cost, customer relations, or turnaround time in using special purpose vehicles, or particular design modifications
- What our competitors or independent haulers are likely to do

One of the first decisions to be taken is whether to use a standard vehicle available from vehicle manufacturers or to have the vehicle, at least as far as the vehicle's body is concerned, specially made.

Standard Vehicle Bodies

Manufacturers of road haulage vehicles have a large range of these available "off the shelf." Therefore, a study of what is available will be well worthwhile, because a standard vehicle body will be much cheaper than a specially designed one. Indeed, in the light-van class (and most other vehicles up to about 6 tons), it is doubtful if it is worth having a custom-designed van body. Manufacturers also have available a number of engine sizes and various axle ratios.

Custom-Built Vehicles

The main reasons for choosing to have a vehicle body built to your own specifications include the following:

- To obtain more economic distribution because vehicles can be designed to carry greater loads.
- Vehicles can be designed to facilitate materials handling.
- Vehicles can be designed to suit your routes.
- A specially designed body may minimise damage to goods.

Disadvantages to buying a custom-built vehicle include potentially lower resale value, flexibility of operations may be reduced, and, if the nature of your goods change, new vehicles may be needed.

Motor Vehicle (Construction and Use) Regulations

These regulations apply to commercial vehicles and trailers and must be observed by all operators. Therefore, anyone considering designing their own vehicle body should understand them.

The items covered include the following:

- maximum weight in relation to wheelbase,
- length and width of chassis,
- brakes,
- tyres,
- lighting equipment, and
- mirrors

There is a choice of vehicle bodies available; the most common types include the following:

- The *bon van,* widely used where goods need protecting during transit, often used for clothing, foodstuffs, and general parcels traffic.
- The main general-purpose vehicle is the *platform truck*, which comes in two basic forms: (a) the flat platform, which has no sides, can carry most goods, which are protected by tarpaulin and ropes; and (b) a platform with sides, which is often used for loose material such as coal, sand, soil, and the like. It may be fitted with tipping gear to facilitate unloading.
- *Swap* or *demountable bodies* are an attempt to combine the advantages of the bon van with the flexibility of the platform vehicle. The bon van in this case is a separate unit, which is lifted on or off of the platform vehicle, as required. This gives the effect of a dual-purpose vehicle, for when the bon body is not mounted, a flat platform vehicle is available. The bodies can be built to suit the needs of the operator.

- *Articulated vehicles* are used extensively for the transport of goods, and the variety available is considerable. Basically, however, they are either flat platform or bon type and consist of a separate towing unit and vehicle body. The towing, or tractor, unit comprises the cab and power unit, to which can be coupled various bodies. Therefore, a towing unit can take a load to a customer, detach the body, couple up another body, and return with it to its depot. This greatly assists loading and unloading; more important, probably, is the quicker turnaround time that can be achieved by this method of operation.
- Many other types of vehicles are available and if money is no object — almost anything can be built on a chassis. However, the most commonly used categories are special containers, or skips, used by scrap dealers for collecting swarf or similar materials, tankers for liquids (from milk to oil), special vehicles for ready mixed concrete, and refrigerated units.

Road Planning

The economic use of the vehicle is the objective, and this is likely to be better achieved if the vehicle is designed to suit particular needs. If it is decided to go ahead with custom-built vehicles, to facilitate economic loading, the manufacturers of the vehicles should be consulted.

Factors to be considered in deciding size and type of body include the following:

- nature and weight of loads;
- method of packing, size of pallets, unitisation and use of containers; and
- nature of the goods and method of distribution.

A study of these factors will enable decisions to be made on the following matters:

- type of body and of chassis required;
- which loads will require a bon van, or platform vehicle, and so forth; and
- methods of loading (e.g., rear loading, side loading).

Accessibility is an important feature when planning vehicles. Those delivery goods to High Street shops will have different requirements than the lorry delivering heavy machinery. Among matters to be taken into account are the platform height of the vehicle and the need for rear doors, roller shutters, side doors, or curtain sides.

Methods of Construction

A vehicle must be suitable for its purpose, but at the same time have durability, strength and lightness. A wide variety or materials are available in the construction of vehicle bodies, all with advantages and disadvantages. Among these are steel and its alloys, strong but liable to corrosion (aluminium alloys are not liable to corrosion). If damaged, all metal panels can be beaten out. Plastic, which is durable, including glass fibre, cannot be repaired so easily if damaged. Often in large vans, roof lights are put in to assist loading. The purpose and use of the vehicle will enable the most suitable combination of materials for body construction to be decided.

It is less expensive to fit loading aids at the time of manufacture. In addition, other interior fittings may also be considered desirable and should be considered at the construction stage. Such items may include tie rails, shoving bars, rubbing rails, and damage bags. The cab is an important part of any vehicle, but this is not strictly within the scope of body construction. However, we shall achieve our objective more easily if strain on the driver is minimised; therefore, comfort and safety is important. Such items as seats, air conditioning, radio, and so on must be considered. Good instrumentation and warning systems are also an essential aid to good driving

The legislation relating to the safe carriage of goods in general should be checked. Legislation covers the mechanical condition of vehicles, safe driving, securing of loads of sheeting and roping, and the use of shoring bars and webbing restraints similar to car seatbelts. The carriage of dangerous goods is usually covered by separate regulations regarding the design and construction of petrol tankers, for example, and the labelling of such vehicles to indicate the nature of their contents to other road users and the emergency services that may be called out to deal with any incident.

Distribution and Marshalling

The pattern of distribution must be studied and such factors as the following taken into account.

- Urban and rural routes
- Delivery of goods to a large number of individual customers
- Bulk deliveries
- Number of special loads (such as heavy machinery)
- Collections
- Vehicles needed for each load

Suitable arrangements must be made for marshalling goods for distribution, including the following:

- planning of loads according to geographical location, and the need to make up a full load;
- planning loading so that goods are in order of delivery; and
- a separate marshalling area will be required with, perhaps, separate "pens" for each route.

There will usually be partial loads or parcels that will not justify sending a vehicle but that will usually involve public haulers.

Road Haulage

The advantages of road transport are as follows:

- **Flexibility.** HGVs can go almost anywhere and can carry almost anything.
- **Door-to-door delivery.** (from consignee to consignor)
- **Speedy delivery**
- Capital investment in movement of goods can be low, as one vehicle can often carry a variety of goods over many routes
- Special or elaborate packing is not usually needed

If a company decides to distribute goods by road, they may choose to send them either by a public haulier or to purchase or hire a fleet and operate it themselves. The advantages of using a public haulier include the following:

- As the organisation does not operate any vehicles of its own, it has no responsibilities or problems in the area of transport when a load or consignment is available.
- A particular type of vehicle can be used to suit particular needs.
- All costs are known in advance (the rates charged), the most competitive charges selected, and plans made accordingly.
- Transport facilities, such as garages, workshops, and so on, do not have to be provided.

Charges for sending goods by the public hauler are based upon weight of consignment and the distance carried. Full loads and specials are also charged on a similar basis.

General Parcels Traffic

Often called "smalls," most haulers issue a set scale, depending on country, of charges for small parcels. There would, for instance, be a set of charges for parcels collected in the Birmingham area and delivered in the United Kingdom and a further list of charges for traffic between North Wales and Scotland, and so on. These scales are subject to various modifications according to particular circumstances. For example, there will be extras for collections and perhaps a reduction if parcels are delivered to a depot only. There are minimum charges levied by most carriers. Also, if vehicles are detained for a long time, extra charges may be incurred. Where an organisation deals with large volumes of parcels, such as a mail order, special contract arrangements can be made with the hauler. A typical contract agreement would be based on the number of parcels despatched over a period, the delivery areas, and the availability of vehicles and result in a flat rate scale for all parcels delivered anywhere in a single country.

Contract Hire

Organisations often feel that for reasons for operating convenience and prestige it is necessary to run their own fleet. A method of doing so, without laying out large sums in capital expenditure for purchase, is to hire a fleet of vehicles. Some of the advantages offered include the following:

- The organisation has complete control of operating the vehicles, and in respect of the drivers.
- Considerable flexibility because the vehicles are under the organisation's control.
- Vehicles are normally painted in the hiring organisation's livery, and so advertising and prestige are gained.
- The hirer is usually responsible for servicing and maintenance, licenses, and other charges.
- The agreement will usually provide for replacement vehicles if any are off the road for any length of time.
- Costs are known in advance and can therefore be allowed for in budgets.

Disadvantages of contract hire include the following:

- Costs may be incurred, as the vehicles are limited to carrying goods for the hirer, and return loads may be difficult to obtain. This means that vehicles may sometimes by running empty.
- Charges will continue, regardless of the use made of the vehicles.
- Transport facilities, such as garages, offices, and loading and routing staff will have to be provided and will be a cost upon the organisation, in addition to hire charges.
- At the end of the contract period, the vehicles will revert to the company from whom they were hired.

Basis of Charges

In each case there will be a detailed contract between the hiring company and the hire company, which must be negotiated to suit each particular circumstance. Typical agreements might include the following:

- **Heavy haulage.** A fixed annual charge plus a charge per mile, or a high annual charge but the mileage charge operating after a specified mileage. Period of hire might be for 5 years.
- **Light vans.** A fixed annual charge up to a specified mileage, and a mileage charge when this is exceeded. Again, the hire period may be for 5 years.

The agreement must be studied carefully to make sure that it meets your requirements and that the costs you intend to be covered are in fact covered. The following are points to check:

- the charges do cover maintenance and license charges,
- if replacement is provided if a vehicle is off the road,
- if any advance charges are required,
- insurance cover is adequate for your requirements,
- the conditions under which replacement vehicles are supplied, and
- if mileage charges are reasonable.

Own Fleet

Many organisations prefer to own and operate their own vehicles because this gives maximum control and flexibility, and may well be cheaper than other methods. Advantages are the organisation has complete control over vehicles and drivers, which gives maximum flexibility in operation. Similarly the vehicles can be used to project image by its livery and for advertising particular products. An organisation operating its own fleet will have to provide a transport management function, and the necessary supporting organisation. Workshop and garage facilities for maintenance and facilities for storing and issuing fuel are required along with facilities for drivers and mates. The following are disadvantages of owning a fleet:

- Provision of capital sums to acquire and replace vehicles
- Difficulty in assessing exact costs of providing own fleet because some costs will be hidden in general overheads (wages and salaries department, etc)
- Vehicles are licensed for your use only, and cannot be used for anyone else (i.e., hired out)
- Charges are incurred whether vehicles are used or not
- Problem of unbalanced loads; vehicles may run empty due to difficulty in obtaining return loads
- Tendency to use vehicles without regard to cost, "as they belong to the organisation anyway"

Operating Costs of Own Fleet

All the charges that are involved in the organisation of a transport undertaking, and the costs that are incurred in either the movement of passengers of goods are covered by the term *operating costs*, and for the sake of convenience, these are divided into standing charges, and running costs.

Standing Charges

Immediately a business is commenced and vehicles obtained, certain expenses will be incurred whether or not the vehicles are operated on the road; such charges are not related to the number of miles run of the number of hours worked.

These charges are as follows:

- Interest on capital
- Depreciation on cost price of vehicle, less residual value, and cost of tyres
- Revenue licences; annual cost
- Road-service licence and certificate of fitness, certainly within Europe
- Licence; annual cost
- Insurance
- General administrative charges
- Garage expenses
- Wages

Each one of these components that together form the standing charges of an undertaking will now be considered separately.

Interest on Capital

It has been contended that operators should include in their standing charges a sum equal to that which they would receive if the capital had been invested in government or other high-class securities instead of being invested in vehicles;

that the interest on capital should therefore be an element in standing charges. There seems no logical reason why this should be done, for it is not the general practice for trading organisations to allow interest on fixed assets in assessing costs of production. This should be absorbed by the item allowed for profit. It may be found, therefore, that some operators will allow for interest on capital, while other operators ignore this item completely and rely on the percentage of profit added to cost.

Depreciation

Depreciation is due wear and tear, depreciation in value due to fall in market price, and obsolescence due to the constant improvement in design. Wear and tear is the common cause of depreciation in value, and for this reason there are those who contend that the charge under this heading should be included in running charges; but even if a vehicle remained stationary all the time it would depreciate in market value and in the end become obsolete; therefore, inclusion of depreciation in standing charges is the general practice.

The cost of tyres must be deducted from the purchase price of the vehicle. As several sets of tyres will be fitted to the vehicle during the course of its useful life, it is thought proper that these should form an element of the running costs. Finally, in estimating the amount to be written off for depreciation, the operator must assess the value that is expected to be obtained from the vehicle upon sale at the end of its useful life. Many operators sell, and buy new vehicles, rather than arrange for extensive refits that would make the vehicle mechanically should for several more years. This value on sale, or scrap value, must be allowed in providing for depreciation. The charge for depreciation is therefore based on cost of vehicle, less cost of tyres, less residual value. The resultant sum is the amount to be provided for depreciation, before distribution of profits, during the expected life of the vehicle.

Insurance

Adequate insurance against all risks is necessary in any business, while third party risk insurance on vehicles is made compulsory by law. Further insurance must be taken out according to the nature of the business and the work undertaken. For the purpose of costing, insurance is included as a standing charge, for it is incurred whether the vehicles are on the road or in the garage. They may be reduced on the vehicle if it is taken out of commission for the considerable time.

Licences

Licences cover both the revenue licence and also the licences that are necessary by virtue of the provisions of the Road Traffic legislation. The charges paid for these licences are fixed, but the cost of the revenue licence varies with the unladen weight of a goods vehicle or the seating capacity of a passenger service vehicle. This item must therefore be allocated in accordance with the amount paid for each vehicle. With licences at a fixed rate per annum, the cost is divided proportionately among all vehicles of the fleet.

General Administrative Charges

General administrative charges include the salaries of office staff and managers' and directors' fees; rents, rates, taxes, lighting, and heating of offices; postage, telephones, and stationery; timekeepers and watchmen; garage and depot staff; and other essential expenses that are incurred for the benefit of the business as a whole and that cannot be allocated to any particular vehicle. These items can only be included among the standing charges and as such are assessed on a time basis. Such charges could be allocated to a vehicle in accordance with mileage run, but it would be very difficult to allocate the item precisely.

Garage Expenses

The wages of garage and depot staff may be included under garage expenses instead of under general administration charges, together with all other expenses relating to the upkeep of the garage, such as rents, trades, taxes, lighting, heating, and so on. It may be noted that the repair shop is usually treated separately in order that its cost may be allocated over the repairs to the vehicles. Day-to-day maintenance may be detailed to carry out duties in the garage, and the proportion of wages for time so spent should be allocated to garage expenses.

Wages

This item covers the wages of drivers and of statutory attendants or mates in the case of goods vehicles. With road haulers, drivers usually have charge of one vehicle, and their wages can therefore be charged to that vehicle, but where the driver's time is spent on two or more vehicles, then the time must be ascertained and the wage split up accordingly. Drivers are also entitled to an annual holiday, and this must be allowed for in making up costs either by charging it up against the driver's own vehicle, or spreading the item over the whole fleet. Wages must be included with the running costs.

The previous items form the total cost of standing charges. With road haulers, it is usual to find the standing cost for each vehicle, and it is essential to divide some of the items in accordance with the varying tonnage of the vehicle.

Running Costs

Under this heading are included the following charges:

- Petrol or other fuel lubricants used
- Maintenance and repairs; cost, or a fixed weekly sum
- Sundries; cost

Fuel

The quantity issued to each vehicle must be ascertained and charged to that vehicle, and the mileage for each vehicle must be obtained for each unit of fuel consumed and also for lubricating oil.

Tyres

The wear on tyres in accordance with the mileage and the charge under this item must be assessed accordingly; the manufacturer's assessment of life must be taken until the operator has sufficient experience upon which to base his own calculations. Some operators include this item under maintenance.

Maintenance and Repairs

The cost under maintenance and repair varies from week to week and in accordance with the life of the vehicle. Experience should be the guiding factor in this connection. A weekly sum should be charged to each vehicle, based on usage, to cover any items used in maintenance and repair of the vehicle.

Sundries

There are many small expenses that cannot conveniently be included under any of the previous sections and must be charged out to each vehicle or allocated proportionately among all vehicles.

Rail Freight

Railways have certain advantages when arranging for the movement of goods. Among these are:

- a reliable and speedy service between main cities;
- collection and delivery to customers, if required; and
- the possibility of special contracts for the movement of large regular consignments.

On the other hand, problems using railways may include:

- good and secure packaging requirements,
- lengthy delivery times if customers are not on the main line,
- danger of pilferage, and
- consistency of timetabling.

There are a number of services offered by most rail organisations:

Ordinary Goods Service

These are single consignments that may be delivered or collected from the station. Alternatively, the railways collect goods for despatch and delivery to consignee.

Passenger Express Parcels Service

Here goods are carried on normal passenger services. This is intended for parcel traffic, and parcels may be handed in at any station. It is also possible to arrange for parcels to be collected and delivered by the railway.

Freight Sundries

Freight sundries are a door-to-door service and is collected from the consignor and deliver to the consignee by road. There is a weight limit of on consignments.

Priority, Express Passenger Service

This service gives priority from station to station. Parcels can be despatched on stated trains by request. Special charges apply to this service.

Use of Containers by Rail

Containers offer many advantages in the despatch of goods; there are many types of various sizes available. This means that a container is available to suit many types of goods. Containers can be loaded by the consignor, transported by road to the railway, and afterwards, taken by road to the consignee.

Special Arrangements for Large, Regular Consignments

Examples of the type of goods are minerals such as iron ore, coal, oil, cement, and even motor cars, which are moved to distributors in this way. Anyone who has travelled by rail, will have seen trains made up of oil tankers or car transporters; these are company trains operated to suit the needs of particular companies. To take advantage of this service, it is better if the companies have their own rail sidings connected to the main line rail system.

Rail Charges

At one time railways operated an inflexible, rather complicated rate-charging system. This has now been abandoned. Many customers today are very large organisations placing substantial amounts of business, and making individual contracts. Examples include:

- mail order or other organisations with a large amount of parcel traffic, which may arrange a special price per parcel irrespective of distance or parcel weight;
- large organisations operating "company trains" (e.g., motor-car manufacturers, cement manufacturers, and similar bodies with "bulk" contracts), will negotiate special contract prices; and
- freightliners, which also negotiate individual rates with customers for hire or lease of containers as well as for the transport by freightliner from "door to door."

Air Freight

Modern travel means air transport. We now travel by air as a matter of course for holidays and for business. Air freight is now as important as passenger travel and is as convenient when wishing to send goods from one place to another.

There are disadvantages of air freight when compared to other methods of transport, including:

- a higher cost of transport;
- restriction in size and weight of materials to be sent by air;
- prohibition of certain items;
- possible delays and diversions due to weather; and
- security delays.

We must consider against these the advantages of despatching by air:

- Speed of delivery
- Reduction in standard of packing is possible
- Lower insurance rates may be obtained
- Greater security of goods
- Marketing flexibility is obtained

When one considers the advantages and disadvantages of air freight, it becomes clear that in the following circumstances, air freight is fully justified.

- Where goods are urgently required (e.g., medical supplies or a part required for plant that is broken down)
- The nature of the goods make it imperative that they are delivered quickly (e.g., daily newspapers, fresh flowers)
- Where the value is high compared with weight or size (e.g., precious stones, modern transistorised electronic equipment)

Regulation of Air Freight

Regulations are carried out by an international body that represents various member countries who have international airline, known as the International Air Transport Association (IATA). This organisation fixes rates and makes regulations that are observed by all airlines. The following are among the more important:

- **The Cabotage Principle**. This states that all air freight within a country's boundaries must be carried by that country's airlines. This prevents foreign competition on domestic routes.
- **Determination of cargo rates**. Air cargo is always calculated per kilogramme gross weight, or if bulky material, per volume equivalent. IATA determines air-freight rates based on the above calculations and from airport to airport.
- **Minimum charges**. These apply for small consignments irrespective of actual weight or volume. They take precedence over charges that would be make if the general cargo rate were applied.
- **General cargo rate**. This applies to all goods not in a specific rate grouping. These consist of minimum charges (m) usual rate (n) and quantity rate (q) at various brake points.
- **Specific commodity rate**. This applies to specifically designated commodities carried between two specified points, for consignments at fixed minimum rates. It is lower than the general freight rate.
- **Class rates**. These apply to specifically designated classes of goods for carriage between points in a specified area or areas.
- **Special bulk unitisation charges**. Where goods are shipped in IATA registered and standardised containers, special rates are available. Most

routes use pallets and containers, and freight comprises will be pleased to discuss the method of transport with customers.

- **Documentation**. The most important document is the consignment note or airway bill. This note is a standardised IATA document and is in two forms: one for use on domestic routes and one for use on international routes. The consignor prepares a number of copies, one of which he or she retains, a copy goes to the airline, and a copy accompanies the goods. It is evidence of a contract and a receipt for the goods. Unlike the bill of lading used when goods are sent by sea, it is not a negotiable instrument (that is to say, ownership cannot be changed by endorsing the bill), nor is it required in order to obtain the goods.

- **Declaration of value**. The value of the consignment must always be stated, although the statement "no value declared" is allowed. Valuation charges are made on a weight or volume basis, below this value, no charge is made.

- **Valuable items**. Where valuable items are to be sent by air, quantity rates do not apply.

- **Hazardous goods**. Certain items are classed as hazardous, and will not be accepted for air freight. Among these are explosives, compressed gases, and inflammable liquids.

- **Other matters dealt with by the IATA**. These include uniform labelling of consignments, making advance arrangements when necessary, tracing consignments, arranging transfers, and so forth.

Other Documentation Required

In order to prepare the IATA airway bill, and generally to make the necessary arrangements for despatch by air, the following are needed:

- Export license (if applicable)
- Commercial invoices (several copies)
- Packing lists
- Certificate of origin
- Instruction for despatch goods form, or a similar method of giving despatch instructions

If receiving goods by air, the following documents will usually be required:

- Import licence (if applicable)
- Commercial invoices
- Packing lists
- Certificate of origin
- Customs declaration forms

Food for Thought

Trading organisations, when deciding on whether to own and operate their own vehicles or to use the services of contractors, should employ classic make-or-buy purchasing decision techniques. In the particular case of transport, organisations should be aware of the marketing techniques employed by contractors (such as emphasising the immediate cash-flow benefits from the sale of the existing vehicle fleet, which may have the effect of turning the whole exercise into a very expensive form of borrowing for short-term gain). The future prospects for door-to-door parcels delivery services in most countries are stimulated by the globalisation of business and the growth of mail-order retailing. Other factors include the legal environment (e.g., the abandonment of state-run monopolies) and the provision of the necessary transport infrastructure. The objectives of the supervisor when making decision about the day-to-day allocation of vehicles to routes and loads should be to satisfy customer's requirements at the lowest overall cost. These should be related to performance targets and budgets but should include long-term as well as short-term goads. (As an example, many organisations try to ensure that the same driver delivers to each customer daily so as to build up good working and marketing relationships between them.)

The current trend in the fast moving consumer goods (FMCG) sector towards large, centralised supply points can be explained by the drive for cost-effectiveness and the increased efficiency of road transport, which enables 24-hour delivery to be achieved throughout a country from a single supply point, subject, of course, to security constraints.

Case Study

The Problem

Vacuum Generators, who were a division of Fisons Instruments, manufacture a range of specialised scientific equipment. With users throughout Europe demanding rapid delivery of components, Vacuum Generators decided that their sales growth depended largely on the level of customer service provided. Market research showed that no single supplier had a particular competitive edge but that guaranteed delivery times could significantly improve a supplier's market share. The question was, Could distribution be improved to provide a quicker guaranteed service whilst, at the same time, reducing costs?

When *The Logistics Business* examined the distribution network, it became clear that there was considerable scope for reducing stocks and cutting lead times by eliminating the locally held stock and shipping directly from Vacuum Generators' warehouse in Hastings. However, this had been tried in the past and discounted by Vacuum Generators on the basis that it was too expensive to ship the many small, low-value items that customers required. Therefore, in order to confirm the view and assess the overall viability of a new strategy, they needed to put together a detailed analysis of all goods ordered and shipped over a 6-month period. With efforts concentrated on Germany (by far the largest market), every order despatched was analysed and compared with alternative shipment methods.

The Solution

It became apparent that there were significant benefits to be gained from holding the stock centrally and shipping to customers' "on demand" using one of the global parcel carriers, such as DHL or TNT. What is more, when the costs were analysed, it proved to be cheaper to deliver overnight than on a 2- to 3-day delivery service. This was because for overnight delivery airfreight is used, and this favours the lightweight packages that made up most of the Vacuum Generator's deliveries. Hence, it was decided to offer customers a guaranteed 2- to 3-day delivery service but to use the overnight service of the carriers, thus being confident of achieving high standards of performance.

The Success

- Delivery times have been reduced from more than a week to less than 3 days

- Service performance has greatly improved
- Overall delivery costs have been reduced
- Stock is now held at one location and total inventory is lower

Details of other cases and service provided by The Logistics Business Organisation can be obtained from their Web site (*Info@logistics.co.uk. http://www.logistics/co.uk*).

In the next chapter, I consider physical distribution of goods.

Chapter XI

Physical Distribution

We have, so far, looked at the operation of stores and stockyards, transport operation, and the various samples of legislation with which the stores manager must comply. We need now to consider the methods of achieving effective planning and control of the distribution of goods, to customers, stores and warehouses. Without effective distribution, the supply chain is doomed

Distribution

The development of distribution facilities and techniques is increasingly evident in the attention given to this area of company activities, taking into account the need to coordinate:

- *transport* — vehicles and routes;
- *warehousing* — central and local;
- *production* — batch size and lead time;
- *customer service* — appropriate level; and
- *finance* — capital investment.

In practice, the optimum distribution system may result from "trade-off" agreements within the organisation, combining individual cost advantages and disadvantages to obtain an overall cost benefit to the organisation and a satisfactory customer-service level. Distribution can be a source of competitive advantage

It is interesting to note that organisationally, the concept of a totally coordinated distribution system at senior management or director level, is complementary to the development of a "linked" system of procurement of supplies, storage and inventory control, production control to obtain the benefits of a total supplies system and access to the early stages of design and development in choice of materials.

Distribution Planning

A number of factors must be considered in planning a distribution system, the first and most important being the needs of the customer. However, it would clearly be impossible to send a vehicle every time a customer required an item, and we have therefore to balance the customers needs against the cost of providing that service. There are a number of distribution channels by which a product or service reaches a customer, and these are illustrated in Figure 44. Customers' needs are varied, and we must decide the type of transport organisation and distribution system best suited for a particular customer. In many trades, a weekly delivery is required; this is not difficult to plan but it is as well to remember that people expect a delivery of a particular day, and this should be taken not of and adhered to if possible. In many cases weekly deliveries must be on specified days. There are trades where daily deliveries are required. Suppliers of drugs and medical supplies are such a case; fresh foods such as bread and cakes are another.

In some cases, goods are sent out when a full load is made up, but this is unusual because most businesses are based upon a regular delivery service. This is true of deliveries made from central stores to substores and depots. Special loads of the type we see taking machinery to a plant with police escort are, or course, "one-offs" and need very careful planning.

Loads

The type of load and the quantity and/or volume are important factors that must be taken into account when planning the distribution system. The nature of the

Figure 44. Channels of distribution

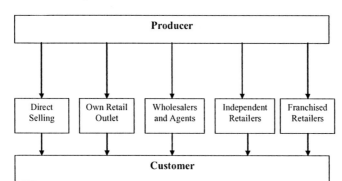

goods must also be considered. Perishable goods must be delivered right away and will require particular methods of handling. Petroleum spirit and other inflammable or toxic substances will be subject to special regulations. Corrosive loads will also need special precautions. If any of these goods with special handling problems are to be carried, arrangements must be made when distribution is being planned.

Organisation Required

The aforementioned factors, together with the volume of traffic involved, will give the basis for deciding the type of organisation best suited for the purpose. A decision must be made on centralising or having a decentralised method of operating. Where the work is mainly of a local character, it is probably sensible to operate on a decentralised basis. This means vehicles operating from a depot in each area where there are customers or stores, each depot having it own manager and organisation. This method has the advantage of direct control by local management and it is flexible. However, where an organisation has a number of vehicle depots, it may be costly because a number of vehicles must be carried at each depot, some of which may be underutilised. Where a company is operating on a national basis, it is more likely that a national centralised system will be adopted. This will make maximum utilisation of transport easier, because central planning is possible. It also makes it uneconomical to use management aids, such as computers, for vehicle scheduling and loading. Support services such as an organisation's own workshops are also possible with centralisation.

We must also consider the method of operating and the type of service, for this will also influence the organisation of the transport service. The organisation that provides a delivery service to each customer will need more detailed planning than a company who does not provide this service. Many large organisations find it economical to have depots or collection centres at each regional location. This enables them to use large vehicles that, when fully loaded, are more economical to operate than small vehicles involved in the same traffic. This method is often known as "trunking" and is popular where the volume of traffic justifies it, as a large vehicle can take a load from one depot to another and return with a load. It is, of course, also necessary to provide a local service, either by own transport or by using local haulier on a subcontract basis. A local management organisation will be needed. If the job is subcontracted, this can be avoided; but you will have lost direct control of delivery to your customers.

Where the traffic is only serving factories or depots within an organisation or group, the local factories or depots may collect form a central depot in the region at regular times. There are often localities that have to be served that present special problems.

Warehouses and Depots

The provision of warehouses and depots will obviously affect the planning of a distribution system. This first point to consider is if warehouses are necessary. Two factors have, in recent years, altered the basis of providing warehouses. The first is the provision of a modern motorway system, which makes it possible to supply a very wide area from a central warehouse. The second factor is the recent development of large vehicles, which make it economical to move large loads via the motorway network.

Nevertheless, there may well be a case for warehouses to be provided, based upon the following:

- *Types of goods being transported*; perishable goods may require local storage where goods are regional (only sold in some areas)
- *Cost of vehicle operation*; it may be that vehicle mileage is sufficiently reduced by providing a local warehouse to make it an economical proposition; better vehicle utilisation may also be possible
- *Disaster relief*
- *Customer's needs*; if customers can be better served by having a local warehouse, or they request such a service, then there are reasonable grounds for providing such a facility

Among factors that should be considered are the:

- *cost of order processing,*
- *stockholding costs,*
- *lead time* for the customer,
- *time taken to process orders,* and
- *in-country delivery*

The Management of the Function

This will depend upon the needs of the organisation, and there is no general pattern. The needs of the company, the nature of the traffic and the customer, and the market must all be studied. It is common, however, to have a distribution manager, but in some companies, this function may come under the marketing director's or logistics director's responsibility.

Logistics and Delivery Planning

In its original meaning, *logistics* referred to the means of moving and quartering troops and of supplying their needs. Today it is also used as a general term for planning the movement of all kinds of materials. It is the means of deciding the best way of doing this that we are now to consider.

The objective of planning a delivery service is to organise the types of vehicles and the routes to be used in order to achieve the highest mileage at the highest loading. If this can be done, the transport cost per load or item will be the lowest possible. This is important because, as noted earlier, transport adds to the cost but not to the value of goods.

Now, having our objective clearly in mind, we can plan to reach it. Planning decisions, however, must be based on realistic facts established by research and investigation. This investigation must include the following:

- Operating costs of transport vehicles
- The distribution and location of customers and collection points
- Loads to be carried, size and weight, and also the nature of the goods

Copyright © 2006, Idea Group Inc. Copying or distributing in print or electronic forms without written permission of Idea Group Inc. is prohibited.

- Individual customers methods of ordering and their requirements (if collections are to be made, these too must be taken into account)
- The number of vehicles available, their type and size
- Maintenance and planned servicing requirements

As a result, the actual planning of deliveries can be made and routes decided on the basis of where customers are and the goods required, customers' particular requirements, and the vehicles available.

A Goods Loading Bank

Generally, it is found that operators of parcels services maintain loading banks; but a small loading bank will often be of advantage to the general carrier, for there are occasions when good have to be off-loaded from a vehicle, upon which repairs must be effected, and the use of a loading bank will then make transference easier. It is not unusual for one vehicle to be backed against another for transfer of goods to be carried out, and although this may be effective for certain loads, it has disadvantages. Again, where goods have been collected and sent to a distant point and it is found that delivery cannot be performed immediately, as, for example, during a holiday, it may be an advantage for an operator to off-load and store the goods temporarily, thus releasing the carrying vehicle for further service.

The first point to be considered before constructing a loading bank is the flow of traffic, and this must be considered in relation to the services given by the operator. It is possible that several vehicles will be engaged each day between main towns, so that the time goods remain on hand before being placed on the on-carrying vehicle is very small. On the other hand, the services of the operator may extend over a large rural area, where a vehicle operates over a certain route of alternative days, twice weekly, or even five-times-a-week service. In such cases, parcels must remain on hand and be stored temporarily, and the size of the bank must provide for this temporary storage. One operator may deal with many more packages than another, and yet the need for a large loading bank may not be so great. Other operators, again, accept goods in bulk from rail and arrange for delivery to outlying districts on receipt of instructions from suppliers; the size of the loading bank must therefore be extended to cope with the temporary storage necessary, or an upper-story must be added to the building for this purpose. The question of the flow of traffic, or the speed with which it can be cleared, must receive first consideration in determining the size of a loading bank.

Siting, Construction, and Layout of Depots

The quantity of traffic to be handled, and the speed with which it is to be cleared, must, therefore affect the size of the depot. In deciding upon the site for a depot, several factors must be borne in mind. The depot must be situated near the principle sources of traffic in order to eliminate empty running as much as possible, for this is entirely unremunerative; it must be so placed that easy entrance and exit is available for all types of vehicle likely to be used — a side road, for instance, would be better for this purpose than a main road; the ground space should allow for further development and for a marshalling yard in addition to the space occupied by buildings. It must also be decided whether vehicles are to be under cover during the night, or left in the open, as this affects the amount of covered space required.

Upon deciding these points, one may then consider the layout of the premises that must conform, to an extent, to the shape of the plot. Within the depot must be placed the loading bank, or banks, for the transfer of goods and, in a separate part of the buildings, the repair shops, stores, rest room, and so on. The size of the repair shops will be considered in relation to the work to be carried out, for it may be day-to-day maintenance only, or the repair shops may cater for all repairs, chassis, engine and transmission, and body.

Once site and layout have been determined, the operator can then make plans for construction and, apart from this having a pleasing appearance, the main points to be considered in connection with it are lighting, heating and ventilation, and the provision of the essential services. Buildings must conform to local byelaws, and so all plans will need to be passed by the local authority. There are very few operators of goods transport vehicles that have depot facilities that compare with the operators of road passenger transport. To look over any goods operator's building that is situated near by him and passenger garage, and this difference will be very apparent. The buildings may, however be adequate for the goods operator's business. If possible, inspect a large goods depot, and also a passenger operator's garage, and from them consider the question of siting, layout, and construction. A loading bank may be single-sided or double-sided, or a number of bays may be constructed in order to make the maximum use of the space available. The advantage of a double-sided bay is that reception of goods can be more easily controlled where a large number of vehicles are engaged; the work of sorting is performed without interruption and goods stacked in the delivery section. The height of a loading bank must be similar to the platform height of the vehicles, in order to avoid the use of labour unnecessarily in off-loading. Bays containing large unit loads using powered mobile storage are quite common.

Receiving and Despatching Goods at Depots and Warehouses

Normally, it is to be expected that collecting vehicles will return to the depot in the evening after making collection rounds, and delivering vehicles leave on their rounds in the morning, so that a large amount of the sorting work and reloading is done in the late afternoon and the balance in the following morning. There will be some movement of goods awaiting suppliers' instructions for delivery; sorting will be carried out during the day. The question of the amount of labour to be engaged on sorting and checking must be conditioned by the flow of traffic, some early and some late turns being essential. In order to facilitate sorting, the delivery section of the bank must bear indication boards, plainly visible, showing the various sections of the bank allocated to various delivery points, and as the work of off-loading proceeds, the goods are immediately transferred to the section of the bank appropriate to the destination. Within each section of the bay allocated to traffic for delivery, there may or may not be further sorting required. If goods are to be placed on a trunking vehicle, no further sorting is necessary; but where delivery is to be performed, goods must be placed on the vehicle in such a manner that the driver does not have to search the vehicle for a particular parcel. Goods must be so loaded that the first deliveries are at the rear of the vehicle; the last goods to be delivered must be the first to be loaded. This involves sorting out the goods in the order in which delivery is to be carried out, either by first examining and sorting out the consignment notes, if these are available, or by reading the labels on the goods in the stack and making out a delivery sheet or loading list.

Lock-Up

Some of the goods dealt with will be of high value and so need special care; other goods may not be deliberable due to insufficient address or the refusal of the consignee to accept delivery. All such goods must be removed from the loading banks and transferred to a lockup until such time as the manner of disposal has been decided upon.

Supervision

Much of the successful working of a depot depends upon the manager in charge. He or she will receive their instructions from the depot manager and ensure that they are carried out. He or she will supervise the checkers and sorters under their control to ensure that the work that he or she allocated to them is properly done. The safety of goods whilst lying on hand in the depot are also the manager's responsibility, and he or she must take all steps available to reduce damage to goods by handling and loss through pilferage. The manager must keep the key of the lockup in his or her possession, and no unauthorised person must have access to it. The order in which waiting vehicles must be off-loaded and the manner of loading vehicles is under the manager's control. He or she must be experienced in the handling of the various classes of goods dealt with and the use of the various appliances that are available for the movement of goods, and he or she must also be satisfied that traffic is securely stowed on vehicles before they leave the depot.

Checking of Goods

The object of checking goods are, first, to see that they agree with the details on the collection or delivery sheets or on the consignment notes that may be either prepared by the sender or in the carrier's office; second, to ensure that only goods covered by consignment notes or load waybills are placed on forwarding vehicles; and, third, that the goods are in apparent sound condition, properly packed and labelled. When vehicles enter the depot after making collections, the drivers will report to the manager, who will allocate a discharging standard instruct a checker and sorters to deal with each vehicle. The driver of each vehicle will hand all their consignment notes to the checker, who, as the unloading of the vehicle proceeds, will mark off the note that the package or packages have been inspected and is or are in order for forwarding. Should the checker find any package apparently inadequately addressed, or not properly packed, or suspect that a package contains damaged goods, he or she should place it on one side. The checker will then obtain instructions from the foreman in charge, or from the office, as to the action to be taken. In many cases, it will be necessary to communicate with the sender to clear up any point of doubt. If no consignment note is obtained from the sender, a note must be taken of the goods, and this note must be handed to the office so that the necessary documents can be prepared. The fleet number of the in-carrying vehicle may be placed on the consignment note as a record for future use, if required. When the off-loading of a vehicle has been completed, all consignment notes should be handed into the office for inspection and to enable the loads for the outgoing vehicles to be made up.

The work of checking outgoing vehicles is similar. The consignment notes making up the load will be received from the office, and the checker will see that these are placed in delivery order. The checker will then supervise the actual stowing of the goods on the vehicle and again he or she may put the fleet number of the out-carrying vehicle on the consignment note. In many undertakings, a waybill is prepared, especially for use on trunk journeys, to which the consignment notes are attached. When loading is complete, the checker should initial the waybill or loading sheet.

Incoming vehicles from other depots must be checked as carefully as other vehicles when off-loading. The waybill should be handed to the checker for marking off, and any discrepancy between the waybill and the goods received should be noted on the waybill. We must never of course be satisfied with the method of delivery and routing we are using; one method of ensuring that we are still operating efficiently is to review operations. Here it will mean taking each vehicle, the routes used, and recording such factors as:

- total mileage per trip;
- mileage to each delivery point and between delivery points;
- the number of deliveries or collections;
- time leaving and returning to depot;
- time at each collection or delivery point; and
- details of loads, such as weights, handling problems, and other relevant information.

As a result of the analysis of this information, improved operations can be developed. Points to look for include such indicators as routes that always take longer than expected; holdups when loading or unloading at the depot or at customers premises — in fact, anything that is not normal!

Budgetary Control in Distribution

The master budget of a business is the method by which the performance desired is achieved. It is a method of management control as it is a method of determining standards in each area of performance, measuring actual performance, and comparing results. A company budget is normally based upon the sales forecast, which, after any adjustments for stocks and capacity, becomes the production programme. The cost of meeting this programme is calculated and becomes the production budget. The production budget is in turn broken down into its component parts, such as materials budget, plant budget, and labour budget.

In a similar way, the sales forecast is translated into the sales budget. In order to achieve this level of performance, it is necessary for each department to operate at a certain level. This will only be possible at a certain cost, which will become that department's budget. The distribution budget will be one of the departmental budgets, which combined with all others will become the overall budget. The objectives of this overall budget are to:

- control the performance at each level of the business and to ensure that company objectives are attained,
- coordinate the various activities in pursuit of the common objective, and
- allow "management by exception" and therefore allow management to concentrate upon areas of deviation from standards.

The Budget Period

For convenience, the budgetary period is usually 1 year, broken down into 12 month "mini-budgets." As the period of control is monthly, if the actual expenditure exceeds, or is less than budgeted, action can be taken quickly, certainly within a short time of the monthly figure being produced.

The Distribution Budget

The factors contributing to this budget will be as follows:

- Warehouse rent and rates
- Warehouse wages and labour charges
- Warehouse salaries
- Warehouse heating and lighting
- Warehouse maintenance
- Drivers wages and other related costs
- Vehicle costs
- Garage and workshop costs
- Fuel costs (petrol and diesel oil) and lubricants
- Any incidental charges

Care must be taken to ensure that the budgeted figures are realistic, are based on known facts, and anticipate increases in costs during the budget period.

Cost Centres

The distribution budget will be broken down into cost centres. This is to enable standards to be fixed for each depot, garage, or stores — whichever breakdown of operations is most convenient to control the department effectively. In this manner the cost of operating a depot or stores can be known each month, and compared with the budget. Action can be taken where there is a difference between the two figures. This is the real meaning of "management by exception"; the management needs only to look at those instances where the actual figure is different from the budget. The majority of cases where the figures are the same need not be looked at any further. In a similar way stocks can be controlled by valuation. A cost centre can be a particular stores or warehouse, and if required can be further broken down into material classifications. This it is possible to see the value of stock in a warehouse and also the value of say steel, or types in that location. Thus, if labour charges or fuel costs are high at a certain garage, they can be investigated and corrected.

It is the manager's responsibility to make sure that products reach customers. This distribution activity is as much part of the company's marketing mix as are product, pricing, and promotion decisions. In fact, in some markets, the impact of the distribution element on sales can exceed that of the other mix elements. Seen in this light, the means whereby the product reaches the customer assumes a vital importance in marketing strategy. The implications of this view of distribution's marketing role are therefore far-reaching and can involve a considerable reappraisal of attitudes as well as of the means of distribution used. Moreover, as the average European company spends 15% of its sales revenue on distribution-related activities, it is not difficult to contemplate the benefits of such a reappraisal.

Although place is a convenient shorthand description used to define of the quartet of "P's" that go to make up the marketing mix, it represents the means whereby the needs of the market and the offering of the company are physically matched. As such it provides the addition of time-and place utility to the product. Without this added value the product is worthless. Without effective planning and control there may be no products to physically distribute. There is in essence a chain and this is shown in Figure 45. Again, each link should be reviewed and assessed in order to develop the full strength of the chain.

Figure 45. Transport and distribution links in the chain

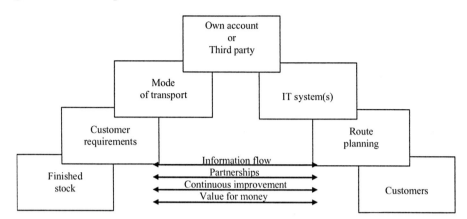

Food for Thought

Forklift trucks are often taken for granted. A daily check should be undertaken and cover the following:

- Levels of hydraulic and engine oils, fuel, battery and coolant, where applicable
- No leaking from any of the above or from lift cylinders
- All controls are functioning correctly (i.e., handbrake, hand and foot controls, hydraulic lines, steering)
- Cab, safety frame, wheels, and tyres are satisfactory

Forklift trucks can be multipurpose, but there are different types and should be used properly:

- **Counterbalance**. The most popular type of truck for lifting or stacking operations where the load is carried on forks projecting forward of the front wheels and that can move vertically only.
- **Reach**. Here the forks are accommodated within the wheelbase while goods are in transit but projected forward when lifting the load so no heavy counterbalancing is required and the truck can turn easily in confined spaces.

- **Side-loading.** Similar to the reach truck, but the mast and forks are projected from the side; is particularly useful when lengths of material such as piping and timber are to be carried and/or stocked alongside aisles in the stores

The use of materials handling equipment may frequently be abused. Examples of GOOD use include the following:

- **Narrow aisle forklift trucks.** Quick in operation, can reach greater heights than conventional trucks so useful when ready access to all levels is required
- **Overhead travelling crane with fork attachment.** Can complement the normal crane by handling pallets in loading and/or unloading circumstances
- **Pallet conveyors.** Moving pallet loads along permanent routes by hand; when powered, can cover long distances with minimum manpower, with possible stopping points to allow such operations as weighing, collating, and strapping
- **Pedestrian stacker.** Manually operated but can lift moderate loads to a limited height but, although very manoeuvrable, can only move as fast as the operator walks
- **Chutes.** Used for moving goods from upper to lower levels and particularly useful for loose materials, robust packages, and items not liable to damage

It would not be the first time an organisation ran out of space, perhaps because there is a lack of capital to build or extend storage, no further space on site, seasonal fluctuations in sales patterns requiring additional stocks, or simply temporary stock increases to cover exceptional circumstances. When you discuss the terms for hiring temporary accommodation, consider the following questions:

- Is a complete building, or only part, required?
- Is this a purely temporary arrangement, or is there any possibility for a long-term hire?
- What is the period of letting at first and length of notice required for termination?
- Who is responsible for heating and lighting?
- Who is responsible for insurance to cover buildings and/or stock?

- Is there agreement about the responsibility for general maintenance?
- Is there adequate access for type of transport that could be used for deliveries and/or dispatch?

You would be surprised how many people forget transport access!

In recent years, growth — both internal and through acquisition — resulted in sales trebling. This has been accommodated through the use of a number of short term fixes and support from a variety of third-party distributors. To reduce costs and improve control, the company was keen to develop a new distribution strategy.

Case Study

The Logistics Business was invited to undertake a programme of data analysis (difficult in this case due to the rate of change reflected in the raw data collected) and develop plans for the future.

Data dumps were taken from the client's computer systems to provide details of all sales orders over a 2-month period. From this it was determined that both peak and average activity levels could be assessed and projected into the future based on the general business forecasts. Part of the project involved helping to develop a distribution strategy to cover all of Scottish Power's stores in both Scotland and England. From the data collected it was possible to model distribution patterns through the country and find a solution to make best use of the existing infrastructure. From this and other data it was possible to develop a statement of the business requirement.

The Solution

Solutions included plans for extending and greatly improving the performance of one distribution centre and layouts for a completely new distribution centre. Both warehouses were designed around a mix of narrow-aisle trucks with separate picking and replenishment aisles, and gravity conveyor-based pick faces for both pallets and cartons, block stack, and shelving. Product lines were then assigned to particular picking and storage areas depending on throughput, physical size, stock volume, and product type. Recommendations for computerised warehouse management were also made.

The Success

By basing the analysis on raw data, it was possible to ensure far greater accuracy in the analysis. The analysis of products using a number of different measures enabled products with different characteristics to be grouped and optimised around those specific characteristics. At the end of the project, Scottish Power had a clear set of costed plans for a distribution network to meet the future needs of the business.

United Parcel Service

A greatly admired organisation worldwide, United Parcel Service (UPS) is well capable of handling major or minor distribution operations anywhere in the world. The main characteristics of their service are that shipments are consolidated when they clear customs, and thus there is less paperwork to process. Logically, therefore, you can save time and improve efficiency while reducing brokerage fees and the chances for errors. Goods can bypass distribution centres and be delivered directly to stores or customers, reducing distribution-centre handling and storage costs. Inventory-ownership time can be reduced, and the result is faster delivery and more consistent service for stores and customers. Tracking through online interface provides shipment visibility 24/7. Access to online shipping information lets you to see the status of your UPS shipments in transit to final delivery. Origin labelling eliminates reprocessing of packages and reduces the risk of error, loss, and damage. UPS has a comprehensive Web site with relevant, nonhyped, case studies (*www.ups.com*).

Modelling Systems

Although there is considerable pressure to improve the operation of supply chains, their inherent complexity can make modeling a supply chain a difficult task. This difficulty is compounded when the need to model the effects of product and process design changes are also considered. Yet, there could be considerable benefits in designing supply chains, taking into account the operation of the supply chain as well as the design of the product and the design of the manufacturing processes. This book does not seek to provide an academic development methodology for systems modeling. It is a too specialized theoretical subject for the practical nature of this book. However, there is a proposed methodology called "Product Chain Decision Model" (PCDM), presented in a brilliant paper by Blackhurst, Wu, and O'Grady (2005).

Radio Frequency Identification

Radio frequency identification (RFID) is viewed as the most transformative technology to emerge since the bar code. It promises significant improvements in quality of information and real-time tracking across the supply chain. RFID enables organisations to more readily identify and track unique product information and allow greater control, accuracy and flexibility in managing goods as they move through the supply chain. With a strategic approach, RFID can help organisations transform supply chain processes, meet compliance requirements, and, gain long-term competitive advantage (Jabjiniak & Gilbert, 2004).

In the final chapter, I will examine and consider e-business in the 21st century.

Chapter XII

E-Business

In this chapter, I examine electronic data interchange and the phenomenon of e-business with a focus on e-procurement.

A Definition of Electronic Data Interchange

The broadest definition of electronic data interchange (EDI) is the exchange of information between two difference computer systems. During the 1980s, the introduction of information technology (IT) into companies has enabled significant change within business (e.g., change in working practices, change in organisational structure, change to business strategies), thus bringing improved efficiency, management control, and customer service and with them, a bottom line of greatest importance, perhaps, in the 21st century.

Technologies such the PC, local area networks (LANs), and more widely based corporate networks have been adopted, and within an organisation, this has enabled the application (e.g., a material requirements planning system) to be brought closer to the end user and has facilitated the sharing of information among applications across common databases. This implementation of technology has brought with it real business benefits to the organisation.

There is, however, a further dimension to the implementation of IT, and this is the electronic exchange of information between the applications of different organisations: electronic data interchange. The business requirement for EDI is clear: Whatever the business, organisations must be able to trade in order to survive. To achieve this, documents such as orders, delivery instructions, and invoices must be interchanged and processed. Furthermore, because market conditions can change rapidly, these communications must be fast and accurate, with administrative processes minimised to ensure that, at all times, market opportunities are exploited and profits are maximised. In other words, the organisation needs to communicate effectively with all of its trading partners, whatever their function in the supply chain, whatever their size, and wherever they are. EDI services allow the exchange of trading data, such as orders and invoices, directly from one computer system to another, regardless of its make, size, or location and without the need for manual intervention. As such, the consequential benefits to be obtained from the use of EDI are very significant. In the ordering process alone, the speed of moving information means that the supply chain can work together to ensure the right stock is in the right place, to ensure that the order is delivered on time, to ensure that the market opportunity has been captured, and to minimise working capital in the process. In short, EDI gives competitive advantage in competitive markets.

The winners of the 21st century will be those organisations that not only implement but also exploit IT and particularly EDI more creatively, more efficiently, and more successfully than their competitors. They will be companies that form much closer working relationships with their trading partners, customers and suppliers, and EDI will be a key enabler in this process.

The Fundamentals of EDI

There are many different ways in which two businesses can communicate with one another: face to face meetings; paper transactions; telephone conversations; the telex or the fax; and, more recently, electronic mail. In each of these cases, an "operator" is required within each organisation for the communication to be completed — in essence, they are all forms of person-to-person communications. In addition to personal communications, IT has allowed organisations to

Figure 46. Basic EDI network (From High Level EDI Overview, by M. Parfett, 1998a. Used with permission.)

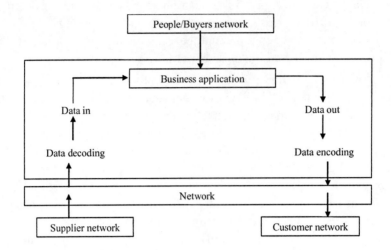

offer trading partners access to their computer systems (including airline reservation systems and insurance quotation systems) by a variety of communication methods,. Whilst one "operator" becomes the computer system, it is still, in essence, interrogated by a person at the other end; hence, we have person-to-computer communications.

EDI takes this one step further: a dialogue between two computer applications without the need for any personal intervention. EDI transactions are designed to be generated by a computer application, not a person. Likewise, an EDI transaction coming into a company is not designed to be printed and read but rather to be entered directly into a computer application. The basic functions are shown in Figure 46.

EDI has two main components:

- **Data standards**. If organisations exchange commercial data such as orders and invoices with trading partners, a formal, explicit definition of the document is necessary that enables the sender to know what information to send and in what order and that enables the computer receiving the transactions to know exactly what the information contained within the transaction and, therefore, know how to process it. As EDI has developed over the years in different parts of the globe, there are have been many different data standards available. The standard to choose depends on the standard used by the trading community. In an industry sector in which there is no accepted standard established, the choice will depend on the business requirements of the sector.

- **Communication.** There are many different ways in which data can be exchanged between computers without the need for manual rekeying. Computer diskettes or magnetic tape, for example, can be used to exchange data, but they still rely on some kind of courier service to relay them between trading partners — which obviously has time-delay implications. Discounting these options, the choices are point-to-point connections or leased lines between organisations; packet-switching services usually offered by the public telephone service providers (commonly known as the PTTs) or value-added network service providers (VANs). Whilst all three options are used in the United Kingdom, most of the interorganisation EDI is conducted using the services of VANs. The main reason for this with respect to communications is that the EDI services deal with different trading partners' different computer protocols and provide store and forward facilities so that a data exchange does not have to be scheduled for when both partners have their computer systems available for the task.

Why Use EDI?

External and Internal Pressures

External and internal triggers, working independently or together, drive EDI. The major pressure driving organisations into EDI is external, that is, pressure from major customers. Some are building EDI capability into conditions of contract, others are imposing financial penalties for each paper document submitted. The other external driver is competition. Needing to match or stay ahead of the competition — particularly in servicing customers — leads to the introduction of EDI.

Internal pressures are much more diverse. Organisations seeking to reduce the cost of purchase are attracted to the cost savings EDI delivers. Inventory reduction programmes, support for Just-in-Time (JIT) programmes, order-cycle and lead-time reductions, and the need for greater productivity are all supported by EDI.

EDI Benefits

EDI offers substantial benefits for improving the efficiency and effectiveness of the purchasing and supply chain functions. Most organisations focus on the cost saving aspects of EDI. These include:

- stationery,
- postage,
- mail handling,
- data entry and correction, and
- inventory reductions.

The speed of EDI transactions also beneficial. Reduced-purchase and delivery-cycle times contribute to reduced lead times with a subsequent reduction in inventory. The information exchanged in the EDI chain is, in some instances, part of a legal process. Purchase orders, invoices, and some freight documents have legal as well as business purposes. If nothing else, EDI eliminates the battle of the forms. However, the electronic environment is perceived as highly uncertain because of the increase in information available. The need to manage uncertainty is axiomatic (Golicic, Davis, McCarthy, & Mentzer, 2002).

Supply chain operations involve vast quantities of information, and efficiency in supply chains demands efficient means of handling this information. Information technology has been, and is, used extensively in certain sectors of the supply chain: inventory control, logistics manufacturing planning, distribution, purchasing, and sales order processing are commonplace. In some organisations, these functionally based systems have been integrated to reflect more accurately internal supply chain operations. With EDI, it can be seen that this integration expands across organisations, continuing the trend of directing IT investments to facilitate greater degrees of integration. EDI will significantly improve the efficiency of information across the supply chain, bringing great benefits to purchasing and logistics operations. By creating a link between business processes in different organisations (or disparate parts of the same company) EDI will result in significant changes. Not since the introduction of Just-in-Time has a concept been devised that will have such far-reaching implications, and for once, the West leads Japan.

Electronic Procurement

This section explores the business issues affecting the level of implementation of e-procurement in organisations. It uses empirical research into 750 organisations to suggest that issues of leadership and waste management are of greater importance than development of e-procurement capability to secure competitive advantage. Those who have developed e-procurement capability have done so strategically but have yet to enjoy significant cost and time savings. The research also identified the management implications of effective e-procurement.

Context

Business issues can be categorised into the drive for competitiveness, critical factors that emerge from that drive, and power relationships. Arguably, all these issues affect one of the biggest strategic opportunities in business history — namely, e-procurement. The drive for competitiveness is influenced, for example, by general instability of the U.S. economy, the tragic events of September 11, 2001, and subsequent terrorist attacks worldwide, perpetual local wars in eastern Europe and the Middle East, the pace of technological change, fluctuating oil and fuel prices, and globalisation per se. Allied to this instability is the desire for product/service improvements, cost reduction, and the efforts by major purchasers to push risk as far down the supply chain as they can. Critical factors emerge from the drive for competitiveness. These include the need for a strategic approach to business, utilising new technologies, meeting the logistics demands of the 21st century and ensuring the workforce updates its skills in a timely manner. Anecdotal evidence suggests that partnerships and trust now take a back seat to the old-style adversarial relationships. All this occurs as organisations (often encouraged by national government) implement or consider implementing e-procurement, whether it is buyer managed, supplier managed, or third-party managed. Potentially, e-procurement provides opportunities for coherent procurement, improving buyer supplier relationships, and eliminating time-zone obstacles. E-procurement in the aerospace industry, for example, has greatly improved efficiency (Cullen, Martin, & Simpson, 2002). E-procurement strategy is a field for empirical measurement beyond the basic monitoring of processes. Previous research has shown that the benefits from more effectively organising supply chain resources, strategy, structure, responsibilities, approaches, and policies are far greater than the possible savings from a simple departmental cost/efficiency focus. However, the status accorded the procurement function in an organisation frequently is determined by the image the function projects inside and outside the organisation. Support throughout the organisation will determine the status of procurement and the role it plays. Unfortunately, most nonprocurement personnel have a very simplistic view of the function. They understandably demonstrate little regard for internal procurement performance measures, which they view at best as tactical and at worst as how many lunches procurement staff are bought.

In the more enlightened organisations, the linkage between e- procurement strategy and organisational performance was established when organisations began to realise the impact the procurement function had on their competitive position, and they gradually shifted the role of procurement from tactical to strategic. Clearly, if procurement is to sustain this move from a tactical to a strategic role, there must be a shift in focus by from efficiency to effectiveness. Procurement staff must think in terms of the potential strategic implications of their actions and routinely interact with other functional managers to develop coherent and integrated strategies. What follows in the literature survey is an overview of procurement and e-procurement with a focus on small and medium size enterprises and their pursuit of competitive advantage.

Literature Overview

Local economies in United Kingdom contain a significant percentage of small- and medium-sized enterprises (SMEs) — in many cases as much as 80% or 90% (CBI, 2000). Although these SMEs are viewed with interest as suppliers by customer firms who have coherent supplier development programmes, purchasing within the smaller firms receives little attention. There is a limited amount of analysis of purchasing in SMEs, although there is broad anecdotal agreement on a number of points. In particular there appears to be scope for improving purchasing and a need to improve and develop credible methodologies for purchasing. Over the past 3 decades, managers in major industrial customers have clearly tried to improve their purchasing image (Buvik, 2001). This has progressed from a clerical function in the 1960s, through a commercial activity of the 1980s, to a strategic activity in the 1990s (Kraljic, 1993; Spekman, Kamuaff, & Salmond, 1994). Some purchasers have clearly made significant progress resulting in the competitive advantage of an organisation (Heller, 1999). Others have not made such moves; examples are Marks and Spencer, J. Sainsburys, ICI, Nissan, Shell, Rover, BMW, and Daewoo (Carr, Leong, & Sheu, 2000). It is important, however, to ascertain whether SMEs have kept pace or been helped to advance (in terms of purchasing expertise) by major purchasers as the drive for competitive advantage continues. There is, however, some doubt SMEs are capable of the strategic thinking necessary to develop competitive advantage strategies (Jennar & Johnson, 2002).

There are some fundamental issues associated with pursuit of competitive advantage (Davies & Ellis, 2000). These include instability through changes of ownership (Emiliani, 2000), changes in strategic direction (Gunasekaren, Forker, & Kobu, 2000), the speed of technological change (Curkovic, Vickery, & Droge, 2000b), globalisation of sources of supply for state-of-the-art products (Quayle, 1998c; Rugman, 2001). This constant drive for product/service improvement results in a tension between incremental approaches and radical innovation (Perrings & Ansuategi, 2000). Similarly, a desire for instant achievement of cost reduction results in risk exposure being pushed down the supply chain (Lummus & Vokurka, 1999). This leads to an increase in contractual liabilities and can intimidate the small firm against supplying to a major purchaser (Alderman & Thomson, 1998; Ringwald & Brookes, 1999). The recipe for competitive advantage of value-added, rareness, organisational structure, and imitation cost barriers is difficult to achieve, even though the recipe is fundamental (Gowen & Tallon, 2003).

As well as fundamental issues, critical factors emerge from the pursuit of competitive advantage. There is a need for a board-level priority to be given to purchasing and, indeed, the whole supply chain (Tikkanen, 1998). Effective purchasing needs resources and capital — a growing concern particularly for organisations, as it can lead to risk adverse behaviour (Wrennall, 2000). The emphasis placed on specification purchasing (particularly those that are over precise) may stifle innovation where suppliers are not offered early participation in the design process (Tanner, 1998). Critically, smaller organisations are often the minority partner within the supply chain (Min & Galle, 2001). To counter this, both purchasers and suppliers (whatever their size) may need to focus on a fair and reasonable relationship — a non-"cheating" relationship (Harland, Lamming, & Cousins, 1999; McIvor, Humphreys, & McAleer, 1997). Globalisation and mobile markets introduce new logistics challenges. The benefits of local sourcing need to be considered, and perhaps offset, by the risks of losing control of product knowledge. Consequently, the creation of future sources of supply may establish sources of competition (Tan et al., 2002; Taninecz, 2000).

Another critical factor in e-procurement is what it actually means for purchasers and suppliers (Oakes & Lee, 1999). E-procurement is currently one of the most discussed topics in supply management with the potential to dramatically change the way purchasing is carried out (Essig & Arnold, 2001); indeed, a revolution through e-purchasing (Telgen, 1998). E-procurement is well defined and can take the form of e-mro, Web-based ERP, e-sourcing, e-tendering, e-reverse auctioning, and e-informing (De Boer, Harink, & Hejboer, 2002). Strategically, e-procurement should create value for the firm (Essig & Arnold, 2001). E-procurement is also seen as ideal for hypercompetition conditions (Knudsen, 2002; Sheng, 2002; Sweeney, 2002). E-procurement is nevertheless merely a means for becoming more productive and efficient — not a tool to mistreat suppliers (Leonard & Spring, 2002; Reynolds, 2000). Evidence suggests, however, that with only 2% of European business-to-business transactions occurring on the Internet (despite 25% signing up to all e-marketplace), little is being e-purchased, and buyers are having difficulty in making e-procurement decisions (Gardiner, 2001; Snijders, Tazelaar, & Batenburg, 2002). Similarly, suppliers remain wary (Caldwell, Harland, Powell, Woerndl, & Zheng, 2002; Gardiner, 2001). CIPS evidence supports this view, with 77% of businesses yet to develop e-supply strategies (CIPS, 2001).

An inability to integrate e-procurement with overall business strategy is another problem (Harink & Van Rooijen, 2002). Despite the apparent low take up of e-procurement, there are many benefits claimed (Yeo & Ning, 2002). These include reduced supply chain management costs, reduced inventory, increased supply chain flexibility, reduced delivery times, increased supply chain visibility, and reduced purchasing costs (Reynolds, 2000). However, a blanket impact of e-procurement will not suffice (Caldwell et al., 2002). Part of the low take-up problem is how these benefits might be achieved along with capital outlay, implementation costs, and change management implications (Arbin, 2002; Clarus Corporation, 2001; Emiliani & Stec, 2002; Mullane, Peters, & Bullington, 2001; Wymbs 2000). Similarly, time organisational culture, supplier relationships, and users are barriers to e-procurement implementation (van Hooft, & Stegwee, 2001; Wagner, Fillis, & Johansson, 2002).

Most published case studies reveal that organisations that adopt e-procurement solutions are already involved in supplier relationships at a distance, such as mail-order or telephone-based sales and services (see, e.g., Axelsson & Larsson, 2002). These organisations also tend to have a good understanding of computer-based systems before they embark on e-procurement solutions, and they usually do not opt for radical changes to their purchasing and customer supply systems – indeed, paper-based systems are often maintained in parallel (Sriram & Bannerjee, 1994). Usually, they modify and extend existing computer-based systems such as EDI, or they extend e-business options but retain older noncomputing systems (St. Piere, Parks, & Waxman, 1999). Nevertheless, the pace of business change, once the process of adopting e-procurement solutions has begun, can be very fast (see, e.g., Croom, 2001; Fraser, Fraser, & McDonald, 1999; Winser & Tan, 2000).

None of these authors focus on the business case for e-procurement introduction. The implications are that the cost of change is undertaken without the benefits being clear (Min & Galle, 2003; Murphy, 1996; Porter, 2001; Ritchie, Brindley, & Peet, 1999; Wilcox, 1999). Thinking strategically about e-procurement, its success is based on reach, affiliation, and richness (Poirer & Bauer, 2002; Quayle, 2002c; Wrennall, 2000). Reach is access and connection; affiliation is about whose interests new business represents (i.e., existing or new customers); richness is about depth and detail of information. What is more important, there appears to be a need to identify critical success factors and a need for a consistent effort to achieve them (Jeffcoate, Chappell, & Feindt, 2002; Kinder, 2002; Osmonbekov, Bello, & Gilliland, 2002; Quayle, 2003).

Fundamentally, therefore, e-procurement systems and strategies need to be effective. The research provides evidence of the deployment of e-procurement in organisations and the business issues, which must be faced in today's business environment. Overall, the literature and reality suggest the need to examine customer relationships, supplier relationships, people management, and administration in order to establish the managerial implications of e-procurement. In today's market, where organisations are driven to improve their bottom lines by finding new ways to reduce costs and gain efficiencies, an optimised purchasing system is critical. E-procurement is theoretically at least, a complete solution that brings ultimate control to the entire purchasing process — delivering rapid, dramatic, and quantifiable return on investment (ROI). This comprehensive solution eliminates the bottlenecks, unregulated maverick spending, and time-consuming paper trails associated with typical procurement processes.

With this centralised e-procurement solution, employees are empowered to manage their own purchasing, governed by the organisations business rules. Inefficient, manual tasks like requisition approvals are automated and streamlined. This means that procurement managers are able to take on more important tasks like analysing trends, strategic sourcing, and negotiating contracts — so one can buy smarter, saving both time and money. In effect, this is control and insight to improve the bottom line (see also Biomni, 2001).

E-procurement should give leverage with suppliers, improved visibility of spending, and reduce purchasing-cycle time. The aim of the research was therefore:

- to explore the degree to which e-procurement is deployed in European organisations;
- to understand the current business issues and priority currently accorded to e-procurement;
- to establish what cost savings had been achieved by those using e-procurement;
- to trade electronically, facilitating an increase in overall business; and
- to identify potential paths for extending e-procurement activity in organisations.

Deploying random, multistage stratified sampling, questionnaires were mailed to the chief executives of 750 European organisations, with a turnover of less than

32 million euros trading for at least 7 years, employing fewer than 200 people, ensuring a wide geographical and industrial spread. The research aims were sought/achieved under the broad headings of customer relationships, supplier relationships, people management, and administration. Specifically, the research sought an insight into customer relationships in terms of:

- increased supply market opportunities,
- supplier development activity,
- changes in relationships,
- changes in pricing practices,
- customer expectations,
- changes to product portfolios,
- face-to-face contact, and
- and whether business had increased, resulting from being able to trade electronically.

Furthermore, the research sought an insight supplier relationships in terms of:

- changes to contractual practices,
- the supplier base,
- legal issues arising, and
- changes to face-to-face contact.

Insight into people management included:

- changes in working hours,
- locations, skills, and business processes, and
- organisational structures.

In terms of administration, research involved:

- use of external support,
- introduction of procedures,

- reductions in costs, and
- increased sales.

With a 28% response rate, the findings of the questionnaire may be considered an indication of the current 21st century trends.

Breakdown of the Survey by Industry

Table 1 gives the percentage and number of companies included in the survey, by sector ($N = 750$).

Table 2 gives the percentage breakdown of those companies that responded, by sector ($n = 210$, or 28%).

Table 1. Survey sectors

Sector	Percentage	Number of Companies
Manufacturing	38	285
High Tech	20	150
Electrical and Engineering	15	112
Packaging and Distribution	10	75
Finance Associated	8	60
Service/Utility	4	30
Construction	3	22
Agriculture	2	16

Table 2. Survey sectors responding

Sector	Percentage	Number of Companies
Manufacturing	36	76
High Tech	28	59
Electrical and Engineering	20	43
Packaging and Distribution	5	10
Finance Associated	4	8
Service/Utility	3	6
Construction	3	6
Agriculture	1	2

Copyright © 2006, Idea Group Inc. Copying or distributing in print or electronic forms without written permission of Idea Group Inc. is prohibited.

Results and Analysis

The replies to the questionnaire were analysed and the results are presented in the following sections. Three kinds of response were required from the questions. Some statements simply required an indication of agreement. In these cases, the percentage of companies indicating agreement is shown.

The second type of question asked for a score (from 1-5 where 1 is highest and 5 is lowest) to indicate the importance given to an area. In this case, the average scores of those answering the question are presented. The third type of question asked for company views. The research set out to establish the main issues faced by organisations, the awareness of and progress toward e-procurement and the development issues wherever they are located in the supply chain. The analysis gives the overall picture regarding these priorities and adoption of e-procurement.

Priorities Attached to Issues at Site

Figures 48 to 50 show the importance attached to issues at site. The sum of the responses for each question is divided by the number of answers to give the average score. Nonanswers are ignored.

Nothing too surprising here, but the ratings in Figure 48 perhaps indicates significant influence of generally accepted buzz words and "consultancy speak." They also reflect a narrow view of business survival. The medium priority issues are given in Figure 49. These are issues one would expect to see, although perhaps customer management and time-to-market may have a higher priority in the 21st century.

The issues of the lowest priority are given in Figure 50.

Figure 48. Highest priorities at site

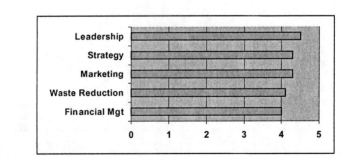

Figure 49. Medium priorities at site

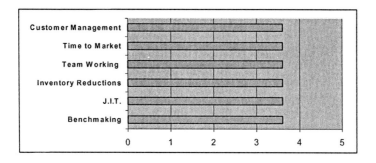

Figure 50. Lowest priorities at site

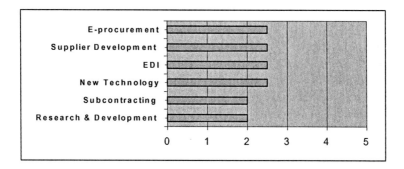

These low-priority issues are particularly disappointing, both in themselves as low priorities and as they are issues relating to innovation. Note also that the responding organisations considered supplier development as a low priority both in terms of being developed and developing their suppliers.

Supplier Development

Of the 28% that responded to the survey, 30% have a supplier development programme. Conversely, less than 10% are part of a supplier development programme initiated by their customers. The survey results do show disparity by sector in terms of companies having a supplier development programme. Figure 51 gives the sector breakdown.

Given an overall average of 30%, it appears that construction (30%), high technology (30%), and agriculture (10%) organisations have considerable scope

Figure 51. Supplier development programmes by sector

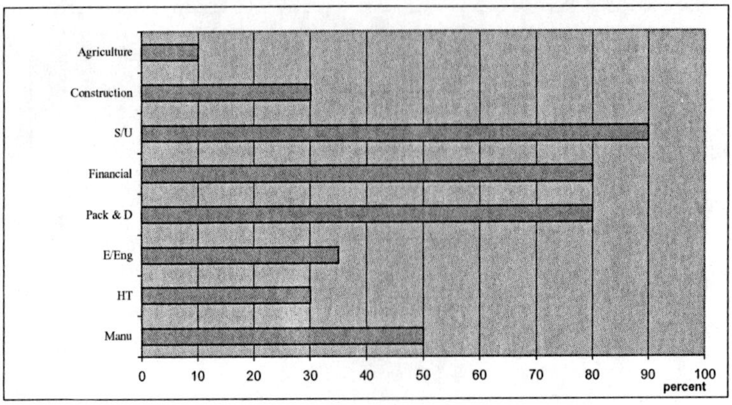

[Bar chart showing percentages by sector: Agriculture ~10, Construction ~30, S/U ~90, Financial ~80, Pack & D ~80, E/Eng ~35, HT ~30, Manu ~50]

for implementing supplier development programmes. Some 52% of the companies have a separate purchasing function, which is on average five buyers. However, 48% have a designated employee (often the owner manager) whose duties include purchasing. Table 3 provides an overview of e-procurement implementation.

On average, 10% of all procurement activities is carried out electronically. This is an encouraging overview and leads to establishing why companies had decided to implement e-procurement. The reasons given are in Table 4.

Table 3. E-procurement status

POSITION	PERCENTAGE
In process of implementing	30
Implemented	59
Plan to implement	4
Considering	5
No plans	1
Tried and Abandoned!!	1

Table 4. Reasons for implementation

DRIVER	PERCENTAGE
Supplier driven	3
Customer driven	8
Own strategy	89

Table 5. Customer relationships

STATUS	PERCENTAGE
Improved a lot	17
Improved a little	62
Not improved	22

Table 6. Impact on suppliers

Relationships	80% no change
Face-to-face contact	92% no change
More or fewer (suppliers)	87% no change

Table 7. Barriers to implementation

BARRIER	PERCENT
Time	24
People	27
Cost	20
Fear	7
Risk averse key people	7

Perhaps surprisingly, it is the organisation's own strategy to implement e-procurement rather than being customer driven. The results of improvements in customer relationships are given in Table 5.

Clearly, some improvement in relationships had occurred but by no means could they be described as overwhelmingly positive. This is perhaps reflected in that 33% of organisations considered business had increased on average by 10% as a result of being able to trade electronically, with only 16% considering that broader supply market opportunities had been identified. Only 10% experienced less face-to-face contact with customers. It is interesting that very little change in supplier relationships were observed; see, for example, Table 6.

Similarly, 95% of organisations had not experienced any legal or IPR (industrial property rights) problems as a result of e-procurement activity. The most significant impact in terms of suppliers, is 30% of organisations claim cost savings averaging 7%. In terms of general changes to trading, pricing and so forth, 90% claim no change in their pricing policy, 90% claim no change in their product portfolio, and 90% claim there are no changes in employee working hours or locations. Some 62% of companies stated that skills updating had not been necessary and 52% had not changed either their business processes or organisational structures. Barriers to implementation of e-procurement are given in Table 7.

Time was identified in terms of gaining the necessary knowledge, developing Web sites, and updating Web sites. The people constraints were finding someone to develop e-procurement, finding someone to drive it forward, and a lack of internal expertise in terms of knowledge, computer skills, and design capacity. Problem people were seen as finance and IT managers, with most staff seen as generally sceptical about e-procurement. In terms of fear, misuse of e-procurement, data corruption, and computer viruses were the main elements identified. Costs were identified as prohibitive for wiring renewal, building facilities, and new computers. Allied to these costs, companies felt financing implementation (finding the finance), difficulties in quantifying benefits, and a reluctance of their customers to utilise e-procurement were all significant barriers.

Managerial Implications of E-Procurement

The research suggested several paths could be explored for organisations to exploit the competitive advantage possible through effective deployment of e-procurement. Sustainability of such competitive advantage is less clear. The recipe for competitive advantage of rareness, value-added, and organisational structure identified elsewhere is problematic. It does appear that a proactive customer would help suppliers embody e-procurement. A team of e-procurement specialists from larger customers to support suppliers may be helpful; indeed, arguably this could be seen as ongoing supplier development rather than a one-time venture. It is clear there are real difficulties in formulating e-procurement strategy in any organisation. I have tried to reflect those difficulties in Figure 52.

Anecdotally, the general attitude toward e-procurement is one of positive curiosity. Clearly, there is a long way to go from such curiosity to achieving reality of effective e-procurement. The issues that were of highest importance (i.e., leadership, strategy, marketing, waste reduction, and financial management) were very positive. Those issues of lowest importance to the firms are surprising. E-procurement (ranked 12 out of 17, where 1 is of highest importance), research and development, supplier development, and staff development are areas in which competitive advantage can be improved and are areas normally associated with innovation.

Overall, the research does indicate some progressive approaches and awareness of those factors critical to a company's success. The research does, however, highlight the elements of innovation as having low priority. In this case, the innovation might be the introduction of purchasing professionalism in organisations

Figure 52. Factors affecting e-procurement strategy

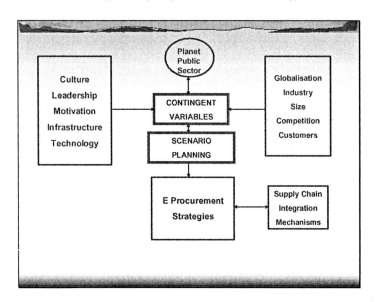

and possibly in larger purchasers. Moreover, any organisation must manage itself; it may be that customers may be trying to managing suppliers rather than managing the interface. There is some case research to show that good e-procurement can impact significantly on the profitability of the organisation — in both public and private sectors. It appears that organisations do not recognise this and see no disadvantage in their own lack of purchasing capability. Given their contribution to the GDP and employment, as was noted previously, and the opportunities for economic development both locally and nationally, it would appear that developing purchasing expertise in organisations might be considered a key factor in industrial policy making. It is truly difficult to evaluate software and claimed solutions — although not impossible.

One of the best evaluatory tools has been produced by the Clarus Corporation (2001). In essence, they suggest that the critical factors are supplier profile, core functionality, collaboration with trading partners, and integration of the system/software. For me the key is core functionality. Does the system do what you need it to do? Indeed, have you carried out an internal needs analysis to determine what you need it to do? Fundamentally, I am sure you will agree! First we need an e-procurement strategy.

The human factors that affect e-procurement strategy are those of culture, leadership, motivation, infrastructure of the organisation, and deployment of technology. The contextual variables are of globalisation, industry, market size, nature of competition, and customer needs. Public-sector factors are seen in terms of government restrictions on trade, local legislation, or disaster regulations (e.g., foot and mouth epidemic). The need for a flexible strategy is axiomatic.

Let us look at the 12 points to consider when implementing e-procurement (Williams, 2001). First, process. Conduct a study to identify any areas of the procurement process that can be improved. Is it too timely or too costly? Use benchmarking and comparative studies based on historical cost and supplier behaviour. Create your own supplier ratings based on a matrix of what is important to you: for example, price, speed of delivery, method of transit, quality of product, payment terms, payment method, customer care, or after-sales support. Where are the inefficiencies really?

Price efficiency is solely focused on driving the purchasing price as low as possible. This is the key driver for the smaller organisation that may not be able to increase the buying power that is enjoyed by the larger company. Savings of a few percent on raw materials, or other high-value spend, can have an immediate impact. A saving of 10% on procurement costs can be equal to a 12% increase in sales. Although the traditional supplier base may become uneasy as their margins are strained, e-procurement will open up channels to many new buyers.

Process efficiencies are more complex and harder to quantify. The aim here is to lower the cost of the transaction, but not just through price. The large, relatively price-efficient firms will be most attracted to this area as they strive to shave a few percent more off the cost of transaction and will be more rigorously measured on the results they achieve. In streamlining the process, it may become apparent that the business unit will become much more dependent on IT, technology, and other areas of the business for support.

What are your objectives? Are you looking to cut the purchase price or for better returns across an entire process or area? In either case, it is very important to determine which products are suitable for e-procurement. It may be those that have long cycle times, complex attributes and specifications, are prone to price change and price manipulation, or simply expensive compared to your peer group. Resources are a difficult problem. Obvious really, but surprising how many organisations forget to do this!

A steering is needed group, and aside from the initiator, it is also important to gain support from the financial, technology, and IT departments. Set up a steering group with a reporting structure and establish an e-procurement strategy that reflects your ambitions. Meet regularly to monitor your progress and allocate responsibilities with timelines. As part of the strategy, you should set a target return on investment that covers not only any capital, such as the cost of technology, but also any internal resources and time allocated. A project manager should be appointed to drive the initiative and champion the cause internally—they should also look outside the organisation to gather knowledge and information about e-procurement practices and peer-group activity.

What about technology? Providers of e-procurement solutions should not focus solely on technology. To be successful, they must have an implicit understanding of the supply chain and existing methodologies employed within large companies. Depending on your strategy and goals, it may be important for you to consider several of the following attributes: speed of implementation; price and payment structure; external hosting/hardware infrastructure (ASP); ability to integrate with existing technologies, such as ERP; future development plan; existing customer installations; and stability/financial standing.

What else? Larger organisations will probably have established IT infrastructures, strong in-house expertise, or access to consulting firms for implementation. Others will be more dependent on the solution provider not only for implementation but also for a customer service capability in running and monitoring e-procurement events and training the supplier base. They should also be able to draw on their previous customer experience to advise on the best transaction structure and methodology to determine the best results.

When you have a system, try it out! It is important to "test drive" any new application. The best way to do this is for the provider to host a pilot programme of e-procurement events with real suppliers and nonessential products. This is definitely worthwhile, as it identifies required features and functionality as well as highlighting any potential problems. Also, it allows the suppliers to get used to dealing with you online. A pilot event can be set up and run in 7 to 14 days from initiation to delivery. A well-run pilot event is likely to yield a ROI in its own right before you have implemented a full solution across your organisation.

And, oh yes, the users. Not only must the system be easy and functional to use for those who are using it, but it must also work well for the supplier base; if it is clumsy or difficult to operate, you will not get the best out of them. Seek their input and make them feel part of the decision-making process to get their "buy-in."

Careful, too, of flexibility needs. Choose a provider whose applications are built on a scalable architecture that can be rolled out on a large scale, if necessary. Also, if you intend to implement a common solution across a number of countries, does the provider have the resources to support your local initiatives in those regions? Look at their development plan and ensure that it is compatible with your own future e-procurement strategy and with likely future requirements.

And finally, remember that you need a strategy before you start, and it helps if the procurement function is part of the organisations strategic planning process. A subjective view of e-procurement is that it is mostly hype and, consequently, companies have yet to fully utilise the concept. Similarly, companies may simply be risk-averse, with a greater understanding of costs than benefits. It could, of course, be simply a matter of timing — such as the general economic situation and the impact of 11 September 2001 and subsequent terrorist attacks worldwide. It is more likely, based on this research, that if organisations wish to maximise e-procurement, they need to revisit their business processes and overall business strategy. They need to decide if perhaps e-procurement is merely a tool to improve operational efficiency or if e-procurement is a method of developing competitive advantage.

Viewpoint

The Danger of Tantric Purchasing: Too Many Mystical and Magical Writings

We appear to be saturated with *spiritual* beliefs that e-business is the solution to purchasing problems. These solutions, where they provide an effective solution, are unlikely to lead to sustainable competitive advantage, because they can normally be replicated by competitors. This needs to be balanced against a failure to be "first," leading to an unrecoverable loss of market share. Waiting for the "bugs" to be ironed out of e-business solutions is an attractive proposition. The continued hype and very little substance about e-business will also increase the attractiveness of the wait-and-see proposition. However, e-business puts purchasing firmly at the top of the business agenda. E-business is clearly seen as a desirable method of trading by various people and organisations. If it is successful, it should open up markets. To compete in a wider marketplace, organisations need to be price and quality attractive. With profit margins already squeezed, this will be problematic. The dichotomy of even tighter margins or not competing in the widened market place is interesting.

There appears to be national government strategies for e-business. Primarily, they have six strands. These are to establish a brand in e-commerce both domestically and internationally; transform existing business; foster e-commerce creation and growth; expand the e-commerce pool of talent; provide leadership in international e-commerce policy and development; and government on line should be priority. There is evidence of government on line e-business.

Where are the nonhype case studies to allow decision making by organisations? By case studies I mean costed business cases with simple ROIs. There is a great deal of hype about survivability. There are cases of disenchantment with e-business (and their service providers) who maybe have gone down the e-business route on gut feeling rather than solid business case. Seems to me that more research is needed before the national strategy will work outside the publishing, music, and food sectors. Anecdotally, Thomas Watson — chairman of IBM — is believed to have said in 1943, "I think there is a world market for about five computers." He turned out to be slightly wrong. It is unlikely a similar mistake will be made with e-business. E-business does represent an opportunity to engage huge numbers of organisations but rather a limited number that tend to be engaged in pilot schemes. Notwithstanding a view that e-business is essential, it is not the real end game. It is a vehicle to address the business processes wherein it is highly likely the real problems lay. It is a bit of a cliché, but in the current business climate, the ability to achieve and maintain competitive advantage is important to any organisation operating in any market. E-business is the effective design and management of the supply chain process (with or without the "e"), which is the key factor in achieving such an advantage (Jenner, 2001).

References and Bibliography

References

Alderman, N., & Thomson, A. (1998). *Supply chain management in capital goods manufacturing industries: Summary of the key issues* (pp. 2-7). BPRC, University of Newcastle.

Arbin, K. (2002). E-procurement maturity in industry. *Proceedings of 12th IPSERA Conference* (pp. 21-32). University of Twente, The Netherlands.

Axelsson, B., & Larsson, J. (2002). Developing purchasing and supply management skills in SMEs: An innovative concept for transfer and development of urgently needed knowledge. *Proceedings of 11th IPSERA Conference* (pp. 42-53). University of Twente, The Netherlands.

Barney, J. (1991). Firm resources and sustainable competitive advantage. *Journal of Management, 17*(1), 99-120.

Bibby, S. (2003). *Supply chain management and regional development in Europe*. Virtual environment for Innovation Management (VERITE). Wales, UK: University of Cardiff.

Biomni. (2001). *E-procurement implementation: Building a business case*. Retrieved from www.biomni.com

Blackhurst, J., Wu, T., & O'Grady, P. (2005). PCDM: A decision support modelling for supply chains. *Journal of Operations Management, 23*(3/4), 325-343.

Boulding, K. E. (1956). General system theory: The skeleton of science. *Management Science, 2*, 197-208.

Buvik, A. (2001). The industrial purchasing research framework: A comparison of theoretical perspectives from micro economics, marketing and organisational science. *Journal of Business and Industrial Marketing, 16*(6), 439-451.

Caldwell, N., Harland, C., Powell, P., Woerndl, M., & Zheng, J. (2002). The role of e-business in large firm supply chain interactions with manufacturing SMEs. *Proceedings of the 12th IPSERA Conference* (pp. 123-133). University of Twente, The Netherlands.

Carr, A., Leong, G. K., & Sheu. (2000). A study of purchasing practices in Taiwan. *International Journal of Operations and Production Management, 20*(12), 1427-1446.

Cavinato, J. L. (1992). A total cost/value model for supply chain competitiveness. *Journal of Business Logistics, 13*(2), 285-301.

Cavinato, J. L. (2001). Business change: It's not just purchasing & supply. *Purchasing Today, 12*(12), 38-42.

CBI. (2000, July). *SME trends report*. London.

Christopher, M., & Gattorna, J. (2005). Supply chain cost management and value based pricing. *Industrial Marketing Management, 34*(2), 115-121.

CIPS. (1997). *Supply chain management: Technical services guide*. Easton, UK: Chartered Institute of Purchasing & Supply.

CIPS. (2001). *E-business report 2001*. Boston, UK: Earlsgate Press.

CIPS. (2003). *Ethical business practices in purchasing and supply*. Retrieved from www.cips.org

Clarus Corporation. (2001). *Evaluating electronic procurement solutions*. Retrieved from www.claruscorp.com

Compton, K., & Jessop, D. (1995). *Dictionary of purchasing & supply*. Easton, UK: CIPS.

Croom, S. (2001). Restructuring supply chains through information channel innovation. *International Journal of Operations & Production Management, 21*(4), 504-515.

Crosby, P. (1979). *Quality is free*. London: McGraw Hill.

Cross, R., & Leonard, P. (1994). Benchmarking a strategic and tactical perspective. In B. G. Dale (Ed.), *Managing quality* (2nd ed.). Prentice Hall.

Cullen, P. A., Martin, J., & Simpson, H. (2002). Managing security and trust for e-tender. *Proceedings of 12th IPSERA Conference,* University of Twente, The Netherlands.

Curkovic, S., Vickery, K., & Droge, C. (2000). An empirical analysis of the competitive dimensions of quality performance in the automotive supply industry. *International Journal of Operations and Production Management, 20*(3), 386-403.

Davies, H., & Ellis, P. (2000). Porters competitive advantage of nations: Time for the final judgement. *Journal of Management Studies, 37*(8), 1189-1213.

De Boer, L., Harink, J., & Hejboer, G. (2002). A conceptual model for assessing the impact of electronic procurement. *European Journal of Purchasing & Supply Management, 8*(1), 25-33.

Dekker, H. (2003). Value chain analysis in interfirm relationships. *Management Accounting Research, 14*(1), 1-23.

Deming, W. E. (1988). *Quality, productivity and competitive position* (MIT study, pp. 29-30). Cambridge, MA.

Dobler, D. W. (1990). *Purchasing and materials management text and cases* (5th ed.). New York: McGraw Hill.

Dooley, K. (1995). Purchasing and supply: An opportunity for OR? *OR Insight, 8*(3), 21-25.

Earnst & Young. (2000). *Survey of value chain strategy* (pp. 21-27). New York.

Elliott-Shircore, T., & Steele, P. (1985, December). Procurement planning overview. *Purchasing and Supply Management,* 23-26.

Ellram, L. (1990, Fall). Supplier selection in strategic partnerships. *Journal of Purchasing and Material Management,* 8-14.

Emiliani, M. (2000). Business to business online auctions: Key issues for purchasing process improvement. *Supply Chain Management, 5*(4), 176-186.

Emiliani, M., & Stec, D. (2002). Realising savings from online reverse auctions. *Supply Chain Management An International Journal, 7*(1), 12-23.

Essig, M., & Arnold, U. (2001, Autumn). Electronic procurement in supply chain management: An information economics based analysis of electronic markets. *Journal of Supply Chain Management,* 43-49.

Fawcett, S., & Magnan, G. (2002). The rhetoric & reality of supply chain integration. *IJPDLM, 32*(5), 339-361.

Ferrin, B., Landeros, R., & Reck, R. (2001). Integrated supply matrix management. *International Journal of Physical Distribution & Logistics, 31*(7/8), 520-536.

Fraser, J., Fraser, N., & McDonald, F. (1999). Welcome to 'e' world. *Logistics Solutions, 1*(2), 18-21.

Freigenbaum, A. (1983). *Total quality control.* New York: McGraw Hill.

Fung, P. (1999). Managing purchasing in a supply chain context: Evolution and resolution. *Logistics Information Management, 12*(5), 362-366.

Gardiner, J. (2001). UK businesses ignoring online B2B. Retrieved from www.silicon.com/global

GATT. (1992). Trade and the Environment Uruguay Round. World Trade Organisation, Geneva.

Goa, T., Sirgy, M. J., & Bird, M. M. (2005). Redesigning buyer decision making in organisational purchasing. *Journal of Business Research, 58*(4), 397-405.

Golicic, S., Davis, D., McCarthy, M., & Mentzno, J. (2002). The impact of e-commerce on supply chain relationships. *International Journal of Physical Distribution & Logistics Management, 32*(10), 851-871.

Gowen, C., & Tallon, W. (2003). Enhancing supply chain practices through human resource management. *Journal of Management Development, 22*(1), 32-44.

Gunasekaren, A., Forker, L., & Kobu, B. (2000). Improving operations performance in a small company. *International Journal of Operations & Production Management, 20*(3), 316-336.

Gunasekaren, A., & Ngai, E. (2003). Successful management of a small logistics company. *International Journal of Physical Distribution & Logistics Management, 33*(9), 825-842.

Harink, J., & Van Rooijen, G. (2002). Framework for the application of e-procurement framework at Dutch Railways. *Proceedings of 12th IPSERA Conference* (pp. 253-261), University of Twente, The Netherlands.

Harland, C., Lamming, R., & Cousins, P. (1999). Developing the concept of supply strategy. *International Journal of Operations and Production Management, 19*(7), 650-673.

Haynes, P., & Helms, M. (1991). An ethical framework for purchasing decisions. *Management Decision, 29*(1), 11-18.

Heller, R. (1999, April). Profit goes to the swift and lithe. *Management Today,* 32.

Hendry, J. (1995). Culture, community and networks: The hidden cost of outsourcing. *European Management Journal, 13*(2), 193-200.

Holweg, M., & Miemczyk, J. (2002). Logistics in the 3 day car age. *International Journal of Physical Distribution & Logistics Management, 32*(10), 829-850.

International Standards Organisation. (2000). *Quality management systems ISO 9000*. Geneva.

International Standards Organisation. (2003). *Freight containers*. 17712:2003. Geneva.

Jabjiniate, B., & Gilbert, G. (2004, January). RFID warrants a strategic approach. *Business Intelligence Journal,* 20-21.

Janda, S., & Seshadri, S. (2001). The influence of purchasing strategies on performance. *Journal of Business and Industrial Marketing, 16*(4), 294-308.

Jennar, I., & Johnson, T. (2002). Is current best practice supply chain management relevant for SMEs? *Proceedings of 12th IPSERA Conference* (pp. 342-354), University of Twente, The Netherlands.

Jenner, I. (2001, October). Best practice management in an SME environment. *Focus,* 38-45.

Juran, J. (1974). *Quality control handbook*. New York: McGraw Hill.

Kacheria, N. (2003). *Supply chain management: Responsiveness, reality and relationships* (pp. 1-32). Paper presented at a seminar of the Ninma Institute of Technology, Ahmedabad, India.

Kauffman, R. (2002). Supply management: What's in a name? *Journal of Supply Chain Management, 38*(4), 46-50.

Ketshen, D., & Guinipero, L. (2004). The intersection of strategic management and supply chain management. *Industrial Marketing Management, 33*(1), 51-56.

Kinder, T. (2002). Emerging e-commerce business models: An analysis of case studies from West Lothian, Scotland. *European Journal of Innovation Management, 5*(3), 130-151.

Knudsen, D. (2002). Uncovering the strategic domain of e-procurement. *Proceedings of 12th IPSERA Conference* (pp. 397-406). University of Twente, The Netherlands.

Kraljic, P. (1993, September-October). Purchasing must become supply management. *Harvard Business Review,* 111.

Lamming, R. (1993). *Beyond partnership: Strategies for innovation and lean supply*. Hemel Hempstead: Prentice Hall.

Larson, P., & Halldorsann, A. (2002, Fall). What is SCM and when is it? *The Journal of Supply Chain Management, 38*(4), 36-42.

Lee, H. L. (2004, October). The triple A supply chain. *Harvard Business Review, 82*(10), 102-112.

Leonard, A., & Spring, M. (2002). E-procurement must become supply management. *Proceedings of 12th IPSERA Conference* (pp. 456-470), University of Twente, The Netherlands.

Lummus, R., & Vokurka, R. (1999). Defining supply chain management: A historical perspective and practical guidelines. *Industrial Management & Data Systems, 99*(1), 11-17.

Lysons, K., & Farrington, B. (2005). *Purchasing and supply chain management* (7th ed.). Harlow: FT Prentice Hall.

Macbeth, D., Ferguson, N., Neil, G., & Baxter, L. (1989, November). Not purchasing but supply chain management. *Purchasing and Supply Management*, 30-32.

Mahoney, K., & Baker, D. (2002). Elton Mayo and Carl Rogers: A tale of two techniques. *Journal of Vocational Behavior, 60*(3), 437-450.

McAdam, R., & McCormack, D. (2001). Integrating business processes for global alignment and supply chain management. *Business Process Management Journal, 7*(2), 113-130.

McIvor, R., Humphreys, P., & McAleer, E. (1997). The evolution of purchasing. *Strategic Change, 6*(3), 165-179.

Min, H., & Galle, W. (2001). Electronic commerce based purchasing: A survey on the perceptual differences between large and small organisations. *International Journal of Logistics, 4*(1), 79-95.

Min, H., & Galle, P. (2003). E-purchasing profiles of adopters and non-adopters. *International Marketing Management, 32*(3), 227-233.

Mollenkopt, D., & Dapiran, P. (2005). World class logistics in Australia and New Zealand. *International Journal of Physical Distribution & Logistics Management, 35*(1), 63-74.

Mullane, J., Peters, M., & Bullington, K. (2001), Entrepreneurial firms as suppliers in business to business e-commerce. *Management Decision, 39*(5), 388-393.

Murphy, E. (1996, February 15). Electronic systems alter the buying process. *Purchasing, 15,* 29-30.

Myer, R. (1989). Suppliers - Manage your customers. *Harvard Business Review, 89*(6), 160-168.

New, S. J. (1997). The scope of supply chain management research. *Supply Chain Management, 2*(1), 15-22.

Oakes, I., & Lee, G. (1999). Between a rock and a hard place: Some dilemmas for small component suppliers. *International Journal of Quality and Reliability Management, 16*(3), 252-262.

Osmonbekov, T., Bello, D., & Gilliland, D. (2002). Adoption of electronic commerce tools in business procurement: Enhanced buying centre structure and processes. *Journal of Business and Industrial Marketing, 17*(2/3), 151-166.

Parfett, M. (1998). *What is EDI?* Electronic Commerce Innovation Centre, University of Cardiff.

Perrings, C., & Ansuategi, A. (2000). Sustainability, growth and development. *Journal of Economic Studies, 27*(1), 19-54.

Poirer, C., & Bauer, M. (2002). E-supply chain: Using the Internet to revolutionise business. *International Journal of Quality and Reliability Management, 19*(4), 485-486.

Porter, M. (1987, May/June). From competitive advantage to corporate strategy. *Harvard Business Review*, 43-59.

Porter, M. (1998). The microeconomic foundations of economic development. *The Global Competitiveness Report*, World Economic Forum.

Porter, M. (2001). Strategy and the Internet. *Harvard Business Review, 79*(3), 62-78.

Porter, M., & Ketels, C. (2003). *Moving forward to the next stage.* DTI Economics Paper no. 3.

Porter, M. E. (1979, March-April). How competitive forces shape strategy. *Harvard Business Review*, 137-145.

Quayle, M. (2002a) The competitiveness of Wales. *Journal of Global Competitiveness, 10*(2), 1-20.

Quayle, M. (2002b). Purchasing in small firms. *European Journal of Purchasing & Supply Management, 8*(3), 151-159.

Quayle, M. (2002c). E-commerce: The challenge for UK SMEs in the 21st century. *International Journal of Operations & Production Management, 22*(10), 1148-1161.

Reynolds, J. (2000). E-commerce a critical review. *International Journal of Retail and Distribution Management, 28*(10), 417-444.

Ringwald, K., & Brookes, A. (1999). Big buyers – small suppliers: A study of local supply chain opportunities. *Proceedings of 8th IPSERA Conference*, Dublin.

Ritchie, B., Brindley, C., & Peet, S. (1999). E-business, IS development and risk management for SME's operating in a global market. *Cyprus International Journal of Management, 4*(1), 4-18.

Rugman, A. (2001). The myth of global strategy. *International Marketing Review, 18*(6), 583-588.

Saunders, M. (1994). *Strategic purchasing and supply chain management.* London: Pitman.

Schonberger, R. J. (1986). *World class manufacturing: The lessons of simplicity applied.* London: Free Press.

Slone, R. E. (2004, October). Leading a supply chain turnaround. *Harvard Business Review, 82*(10), 114-121.

Snijders, C., Tazelaar, F., & Batenburg, R. (2002). Electronic decision support for procurement management. *Proceedings of 12th IPSERA Conference* (pp. 687-695), University of Twente, The Netherlands.

Spekman, R., Kamuaff, J., & Salmond, D. (1994). At last purchasing is becoming strategic. *Long Range Planning, 27*(2), 76-84.

Sriram, V., & Bannerjee, S. (1994). EDI does its adoption change purchasing policies and procedures. *International Journal of Purchasing and Materials Management, 30*(1), 31-40.

St. Pierre, J., Parks, C., & Waxman, R. (1999). Electronic commerce of component information workshop. *Journal of Research of the National Institute of Standards and Technology, 104*(3), 291-297.

Stocklin Logistics Switzerland. (2003). UK office Stevenage. Retrieved from www.stocklin.co.uk

Sum, C., Teo, C., & Ng, K. (2001). Strategic logistics management in Singapore. *International Journal of Operations & Production Management, 21*(9), 1239-1260.

Sunil, V. (2002). *The new framework: Marketing strategy and sustainable competitive advantage* (Working paper 2002-07-01, pp. 1-12). Institute of Management Phmedabad.

Sweeney, E. (2002). Supply chain management in Ireland – The future. *Logistics Solutions, 3*(3), 14-15.

Tan, K., Lymans, S., & Wisner, J. (2002). Supply chain management: A strategic perspective. *International Journal of Operations and Production Management, 22*(6), 614-631.

Taninecz, G. (2000, May 15). *Forging the chain.* Industry Week and Ernst & Young. Retrieved from www.findarticles.com

Tanner, J. F. (1998). User's role in the purchase: Their influence, satisfaction and desire to participate in the next purchase. *Journal of Business & Industrial Marketing, 12*(6), 479-491.

Telgen, J. (1998). Revolution through electronic purchasing. *Proceedings of the 7th Annual IPSERA Conference* (pp. 499-504), London.

Tikkanen, H. (1998). The network approach in analysing international marketing and purchasing operations: A case study of European SME's focal net 1992-95. *Journal of Business and Industrial Marketing, 13*(2), 1-19.

van Hooft, F. P. C., & Stegwee, R. (2001). E-business strategy: How to benefit from hype. *Logistics Information Management, 14*(1/2), 44-54.

van Weele, A. J., & Rozemeijer, F. A. (1996). Revolution in purchasing. *European Journal of Purchasing and Supply Management, 2*(4), 153-160.

Wagner, B., Fillis, I., & Johansson, U. (2002). E-commerce adoption and e-supply strategy in the Scottish smaller firm. *Proceedings of 12th IPSERA Conference* (pp. 721-733), University of Twente, The Netherlands.

Weber, M., & Kantamneni, S. (2002). POS and EDI in retailing: An examination of benefits and barriers. *Supply Chain Management, 7*(5), 311-317.

Wilcox, T. (1999). Net not seen as critical. *Supply Management, 4*(24), 13.

Winser, J., & Tan, K. C. (2000). Supply chain management and its impact on purchasing. *Journal of Supply Chain Management, 36*(4), 33-42.

Wood, G. (1995). Ethics at the purchasing and sales interface. *International Marketing Review, 12*(4), 7-19.

Wrennall, W. (2000). Demystifying the supplier – Customer interface. *Work Study, 49*(1), 18-23.

Wymbs, C. (2000). How e-commerce is transforming and internationalising service industries. *Journal of Services Marketing, 14*(6), 463-477.

Yeo, K., & Ning, J. (2002). Integrating supply chain and critical chain concepts in engineer – Procur-construct projects. *International Journal of Project Management, 20*(1), 253-262.

Bibliography

Ammer, D. (1974). *Materials management* (3rd ed.). Homewood, IL: Irwin.

Atlas, M. (1998, July). New trends in Internet commerce. *Journal of Internet Purchasing.*

Attwood, R. (1998, July 30). E-com coming. *Supply Management,* 37-39.

Audit Commission. (1984). *Reducing the cost of local government purchases.* London: HMSO.

Bailey, P. (1983). *Purchasing systems and records.* Aldershot, UK: Gower.

Bailey, P. (1991). *Purchasing and supply management* (5th ed.). London: Prentice Hall.

Bailey, P., & Farmer, D. (1985). *Purchasing principles and management*. London: Pitman.

Bain, J. S. (1959). *Industrial organisation*. New York: Wiley.

Bauer, P. T., & Yamey, B. S. (1968). *Markets, market control and market reform*. London: Weidenfeld & Nicholson.

Black, G. (1996, October 15). Critical information. *Financial Times*.

Bolton, J. F. (1972). *Small firms*. Cmnd 4811. London: HMSO.

Branwell Report. (1964). *The placing and management of contracts for building and civil engineering works*. London: HMSO.

BS5750/ISO 9000. (1987). *A positive contribution to better business*. London: BSI.

Buckner, H. (1967). *How British industry buys*. London: Hutchinson.

CIPS. (1990a). *Electronic data interchange*. Easton, UK.

CIPS. (1990b). *Just in time: The purchasing viewpoint*. Easton, UK.

Clothier, K. (1998, March). The role of systems integrators in electronic commerce. *Journal of Internet Purchasing*.

Croell, R. C. (1977). Measuring purchasing effectiveness. *Journal of Purchasing and Materials Management, 13*(1), 3-4.

Cyert, R. M., & March, J. G. (1963). *A behavioural theory of the firm*. Englewood Cliffs, NJ: Prentice Hall.

Dickie, H. F. (1951, July). ABC analysis shoots for dollars not pennies. *Factory Management and Maintenance*.

Doran, D. (2001). Rethinking the supply chain: An automotive perspective. *Proceedings of the 10th International Annual IPSERA Conference*, University of Twente, Enschede, The Netherlands.

Economist Intelligence Unit. (1986, April). *Retail business, 338*. London.

Edwards, R. S., & Townsend, H. (1985). *Business enterprise, its growth and organisation*. London: Macmillan.

Farmer, D. H. (1972). Source decision-making in the multi-national company. *Journal of Purchasing, 8*(1), 5-18.

Fearon, H. E. (1961). *Purchasing research in American business*. Unpublished doctoral dissertation, Michigan State University.

Fraering, M., & Prasad, S. (1999). International sourcing and logistics: An integrated model. *Logistics Information Management, 12*(6), 451-459.

Gattorna, J. (1990). *The Gower handbook of logistics and distribution* (4th ed.). Aldershot, UK: Gower.

Gubi, E., Arlbjorn, J., & Johansen, J. (2003). Doctoral dissertations in logistics and supply chain management. *International Journal of Physical Distribution & Logistics Management, 33*(10), 854-885.

Heinritz, S. F., & Farrell, P. V. (1981). *Purchasing: Principles and applications.* Englewood Cliffs, NJ: Prentice Hall.

Hoffman, M. (1998, March). The future of interbusiness commerce. *Journal of Internet Purchasing.*

Jeffcoate, J., Chappell, C., & Feindt, S. (2002). Best practice in SME adoption of e-commerce. *Benchmarking: An International Journal, 9*(2), 123-132.

Johnson, G., & Scholes, K. (1992). *Exploring corporate strategy text and cases.* London: Prentice Hall.

Kavanegh, J. (1998, March 6). The logistics chain: Electronic data interchange fresh enthusiasm. *Financial Times.*

Kostishack, J. D., & South, J. C. (1973). The composition of industrial buyer performance. *Journal of Purchasing, 9*(3), 50-63.

Kotabe, M., & Murphy, J. (2004). Global sourcing strategy and sustainable competitive advantage. *Industrial Marketing Management, 33*(1), 7-14.

Kotler, P., & Balachandrian, V. (1975, August). Strategic remarketing, the preferred response to shortages and inflation. *Sloan Management Review.*

Kotler, P., & Levy, S. J. (1973, January). Buying is marketing too. *Journal of Marketing.*

Lauer, S. (1967). Westinghouse plant X. In Bailey & Farmer (Eds.), *Purchasing problems.* London: POA.

Lee, L., & Dobler, D. (1977). *Purchasing and materials management.* New York: McGraw-Hill.

Leenders, M. R. (1965). *Improving purchasing effectiveness through supplier development.* Cambridge, MA: Harvard University Press.

Lejeune, M., & Yakova, N. (2005). On checking the 4C's in supply chain management. *Journal of Operations Management, 23*(1), 81-100.

Lewis, C. D. (1970). *Scientific inventory control.* London: Butterworth.

Little, D., & Barclay, I. (1986, January). Materials management: The technologist's role in controlling materials costs. *Purchasing and Supply Management.*

Meopham, B. (1985). *ICE conditions of contract - A commercial manual.* London: Waterlow.

Moos, S. (1971). *Research report 13*. Committee of Enquiry on Small Firms. London: HMSO.

Muhlenmann, A., Oakland, J., & Lockyer, K. (1992). *Production and operations management*. London: Pitman.

Nam, C. C. (1998, July). Increase your profit margin through electronic procurement. *Journal of Internet Purchasing*.

New, S. J. (1994). Supply chains: Some doubts. *Proceedings of the IPSERA Conference* (pp. 345-362), Cardiff.

Newing, R. (1996, February 10). Software moves to meet supply chain needs. *Financial Times*.

Newman, R. G. (1985, Summer). Validation of contract compliance under systems contracting. *Journal of Purchasing and Materials Management*.

Parfett, M. (1998). *High level EDI overview*. Electronic Commerce Innovation Centre, University of Cardiff.

Parfett, M. (1998). *The Internet*. Electronic Commerce Innovation Centre, University of Cardiff.

Parfett, M. (1998). *An introduction to electronic commerce*. Electronic Commerce Innovation Centre, University of Cardiff.

Porter, M. (1990). *The competitive advantage of nations*. Free Press.

Porter, M. (1996). What is strategy? *Harvard Business Review*.

Porter, M. (1998). Clusters and the new competitive agenda for companies and governments. *On Competition*. Harvard Business School Press.

Quayle, M. (1991, April). Prime contractorship. *Purchasing and Supply Management*.

Quayle, M. (1992, February). Developing industrial purchasing policy. *Purchasing and Supply Management*.

Quayle, M. (1996). Supply chain management and the factors affecting sourcing decisions. *Proceedings of the Chartered Institute of Marketing Eastern Region Conference Focus on Customers, Getting Them and Keeping Them,* Imperial War Museum.

Quayle, M. (1997). Purchasing in U.K. and Switzerland: An empirical study of sourcing decisions. *Proceedings of an International Purchasing and Supply Education Research Association (IPSERA) Workshop Purchasing Decisions,* University of Twente, Enschede, The Netherlands.

Quayle, M. (1997). The supply chain: Organisation impact of factors affecting sourcing decisions. *Proceedings of International Research Symposium Effective Organisations*, University of Bournemouth, Bournemouth.

Quayle, M. (1998). The impact of strategic procurement in the U.K. government sector. *Proceedings of Seventh International Purchasing & Supply Education and Research Association (IPSERA) Conference*, London.

Quayle, M. (1998). Industrial procurement: Factors affecting sourcing decisions. *European Journal of Purchasing & Supply Management, 4*(4), 199-205.

Quayle, M. (1998). Supplier development for high technology small firms in UK *Proceedings of the 6th Annual High Technology Small Firms Conference,* University of Twente, Enschede, The Netherlands.

Quayle, M. (2003). E-business in a turbulent world: Usage in European SME's. *International Journal of Electronic Business, 1*(1), 41-52.

Rees, G. (1969). *St. Michael, a history of Marks and Spencer*. London: Weidenfeld & Nicholson.

Roberts, J. S. (2001). Great expectations: E-procurement and work processes. *Purchasing Today, 12*(10), 24-30.

Roberts, J. S. (2001). Navigating the ethics of e-commerce. *Purchasing Today, 12*(12), 28-37.

Rook, A. (1972). *Transfer pricing*. London: British Institute of Management.

Rowe, D., & Alexander, I. (1968). *Selling industrial products*. London: Hutchinson.

Sheng, M. (2002, December). The impacts of Internet based technologies on procurement strategy. *Proceedings of the 2nd International Conference Electronic Business*, Taipei, Taiwan.

Sohal, A., & D'Netto, B. (2004). Incumbent perception of the logistics profession. *International Journal of Logistics Systems and Management, 1*(1), 5-25.

Strauss, G. (1962, September 7). Tactics of lateral relationships: The purchasing agent. *Administrative Science Quarterly*.

Van Donk, D., & Vandervaart, T. (2004). Business conditions, shared resources and integrative practices in the supply chain. *Journal of Purchasing & Supply Management, 10*(3), 107-116.

Webster, F. E., & Wind, Y. (1972). *Organisational buying behaviour*. Englewood Cliffs, NJ: Prentice Hall.

Welford, R., & Prescott, K. (1992). *European business: An issue-based approach*. London: Pitman.

Williams, F. (1997, March 21). EDI data exchange spreads its wings. *Financial Times*.

Womack, J. P., Jones, D. R., & Roos, D. (1991). *The machine that changed the world*. New York: Harper Perennial.

About the Author

Dr. Michael Quayle (mquayle@glam.ac.uk) is the Robert Bosch professor (chair) in purchasing & supply chain management at the University of Glamorgan, UK. The university's business school is the largest in Wales and the 14th largest (out of circa 120) in the United Kingdom. Before entering academia, he gained significant procurement and project management experience in the European electronics and defence industries. An adviser to the UK HM Office of Government Commerce (OGC), the Welsh Assembly Government (WAG), he is a registered purchasing and supply management specialist with and senior consultant to the United Nations (UNCTAD) International Trade Centre (ITC) and has published extensively in the fields of management development, leadership, supply chain management, purchasing, materials management, and logistics. He is also the UK Chartered Institute of Purchasing & Supply (CIPS) ambassador to Wales. Dr. Quayle is a fellow of the UK Chartered Institute of Purchasing and Supply, chartered fellow of the UK Institute of Logistics & Transport, member of the UK Institute of Management, and member of the UK Chartered Institute of Personnel and Development. He has a doctoral degree in procurement from the University of Lancaster, UK, a master's degree (MLitt) in industrial relations from the University of Glasgow, UK, and a first degree (BSc) in business management from the University of Maryland, United States.

* * *

Sir Roger Jones, OBE is the founder and former owner of Penn Pharmaceuticals Ltd. UK, one of the world's leading pharmaceutical development companies. He is the former governor of the BBC and chairman of the BBC Broadcasting Council for Wales as we;; as the past chairman of the Institute of Directors Wales and Chairman of the Welsh Industrial Trust. He is the former chairman of Children in Need and the former chairman of the Council of Welsh Training and Enterprise Councils. Currently he is the chairman of the Welsh Development Agency.

Copyright © 2006, Idea Group Inc. Copying or distributing in print or electronic forms without written permission of Idea Group Inc. is prohibited.

Index

A

aircraft support group 143
appraisal costs 95
audit 121
automotive industry 58
average price 192

B

batch quantity 184
benchmarking 13, 69
bottlenecks 112
budget 23
budgetary control 312
bullwhip effect 112
business strategies 5
buying decisions 21
buying links 7

C

CAD/CAM 227
case study, procurement business strategy 73
cash generation 87
centralisation 62
centralised purchasing 54
centralised storage 237
change 133
change, political nature of 135
change, recipe for 134
change, strategic 134
change, supply chain and 135
classical management 130
collaboration 14
competence 19
competitive advantage 1, 10
competitiveness 13
containers 276
contracting 2
corporate plan 23
corporate planning 21
corporate social responsibility 10
cost price 190
costs, initial 140
costs, recurring 140
customer service 108
cyclical provisioning 169

D

decentralisation 63
degrees, master's and doctoral 17
demand 170
diploma 17

distance learning 17
distribution 17, 303
distribution planning 304
distributive organisations 56

E

e-business 320
e-commerce 13
e-procurement 320, 325
economic development 11
economic order quantity 184
EDI (electronic data interchange) 320
education 1, 16
effectiveness 11
efficient consumer response 89
electrical stackers 251
electronic data interchange (EDI) 320
ethical purchasing 21, 47
exponential smoothing 168
external failure costs 94

F

failure costs, external 94
failure costs, internal 94
failure modes, effects and criticality analysis (FMECA) 147
FIFO (first-in-first-out) 190
finance 26
financial management 13
first-degree 17
first-in-first-out (FIFO) 190
five-fold grading scheme 127
fleet management 266
flexible strategies 41
fluctuations 182
FMECA (failure modes, effects and criticality analysis) 147
FMS 227
forecast error 168

G

gap analysis 32
global marketplace 13
globalisation 5
goods movement theory 245

H

handling equipment 245, 248
hubwagon 252
human relations 131
human resource management 18

I

identification and coding of materials 198
ILS (integrated logistic support) 138
in service date (ISD) 141
industrial trucks 249
information strategy planning (ISP) 150
information technology (IT) 18, 320
initial costs 140
innovation 14
integrated logistic support (ILS) 138
interlock strategy 113, 117
internal failure costs 94
International Standards Organisation (ISO) 276
Internet 105
intracompany trading 51
inventory control 161
inventory control system 174
inventory management 108
ISD (in service date) 141
ISO (International Standards Organisation) 276
ISO 4000 89
ISO 9000 89
ISP (information strategy planning) 150
IT (information technology) 320

J

JIT (just-in-time) 161, 227
job descriptions 120
job enlargement 132
job enrichment 132
just-in-time (JIT) 161, 227

K

Kanban 227

L

LANs (local area networks)) 321
last-in-first-out (LIFO) 190
LCN (logistic control number) 146
LCNR (low cost, nonreturnable) pallets 279
leadership 13, 18
lean supply 221
level of repair analysis (LORA) 148
life cycles 15
LIFO (last-in-first-out) 190
local area networks (LANs) 321
logistic control number (LCN) 146
logistic support 143
logistic support analysis (LSA) 145, 146
logistic support date (LSD) 141
logistics 17
LORA (level of repair analysis) 148
low cost, nonreturnable (LCNR) pallets 279
LSA (logistic support analysis) 145, 146
LSD (logistic support date) 141

M

make or buy 43
management, classical 130
management, neoclassical 130
managerial implications 336
manufacturing 5
manufacturing resource planning (MRPII) 226
market price 193
marketing 13, 23, 25
materials management 4, 18, 71, 108
materials requirements planning (MRP) 224
modelling 18
MRP (materials requirements planning) 224
MRPII (manufacturing resource planning) 226
multiple sourcing 41
multiproduct operations 66
multisite operations 66

N

National Institute of Industrial Psychology 127
negotiating links 57

neoclassical management 130
networking 85

O

obsolescence 182, 197
open access stores 242
operating manuals 124
outsourcing 1, 4
Own Fleet 290

P

packaging 190, 278
palletisation 276, 278
Pareto analysis 162
partnerships 13
performance 105
physical distribution 303
planning and marketing strategy 107
planning, strategic 176
point of sale (POS) 172
policy 50
popularity storage 242
POS (point of sale) 172
prevention costs 95
price, market 193
price analysis 195
price, average 192
price, cost 190
price, selling 193
price, standard 191
pricing 189
pricing, methods 190
procurement 1, 2, 3
procurement agencies 21, 48
production 23, 25
production planning 107
programmes and budgets group 143, 144
progressing or expediting 56
provisioning 161
provisioning, cyclical 169
provisioning, methods 166
public sector 68
purchasing 1, 3, 21, 23, 50, 107
purchasing and supply 26
purchasing resources 22
purchasing strategies 38

Q

quality control 274
quality management 89

R

rail freight 295
rate of issue 181
reciprocal trade 51
recurring costs 140
resource-based view 10
road haulage 287
road vehicle design 282

S

security 275
selling price 193
single sourcing 41, 222
small- and medium-sized enterprises (SMEs) 326
SMEs (small- and medium-sized enterprises) 326
socioeconomic factors 31
sourcing form 64
sourcing, multiple 41
sourcing, single 41
SOW (statement of work) 145
staff 17
staffing 120
stakeholder 10
standard price 191
statement of work (SOW) 145
stockyards 230, 233
storage and materials handling 108
stores buildings 230
stores management 228
stores, open access 242
stores, types 235
stores, work-in-progress 242
strategic planning 29, 176
strategic purchasing management 20
strategy 12
structure 53
supplier change 3
supplier control group 143, 144
supply 1
supply chain 7
supply chain management 4, 104
supply chain mix 107
supply chain, scope 109
supply management 4
support costs 139
sustainability 10
sustainable supply chain 9
sustainable supply chain management 1
SWOT 32

T

tantric purchasing 340
technical support 108
technology 13
time to market 13
total quality management (TQM) system 100
TQM (total quality management) system 100
transport 108, 264
transport, planning and management 18
trust 13

U

unit of issue 181
unitisation 276, 277

V

value chain 2
value-added network service providers (VANs) 323
VANs (value-added network service providers) 323
vehicle replacement 267
vehicle scheduling 269
virtual purchasing organisation 3
vision statements 136
vocational qualifications 17

W

Wales 10
warehouses and stores 108
warehousing 2
warehousing operations 18

waste 11
waste reduction 13
work-in-progress stores 242

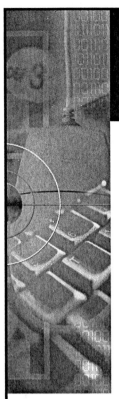

Single Journal Articles and Case Studies Are Now Right at Your Fingertips!

Purchase any single journal article or teaching case for only $18.00!

Idea Group Publishing offers an extensive collection of research articles and teaching cases that are available for electronic purchase by visiting www.idea-group.com/articles. You will find over 980 journal articles and over 275 case studies from over 20 journals available for only $18.00. The website also offers a new capability of searching journal articles and case studies by category. To take advantage of this new feature, please use the link above to search within these available categories:

- Business Process Reengineering
- Distance Learning
- Emerging and Innovative Technologies
- Healthcare
- Information Resource Management
- IS/IT Planning
- IT Management
- Organization Politics and Culture
- Systems Planning
- Telecommunication and Networking
- Client Server Technology
- Data and Database Management
- E-commerce
- End User Computing
- Human Side of IT
- Internet-Based Technologies
- IT Education
- Knowledge Management
- Software Engineering Tools
- Decision Support Systems
- Virtual Offices
- Strategic Information Systems Design, Implementation

You can now view the table of contents for each journal so it is easier to locate and purchase one specific article from the journal of your choice.

Case studies are also available through XanEdu, to start building your perfect coursepack, please visit www.xanedu.com.

For more information, contact cust@idea-group.com or 717-533-8845 ext. 10.

www.idea-group.com

IDEA GROUP INC.